WOMEN IN WORLD HISTORY

Volume 2

Readings from 1500 to the Present

Sources and Studies in World History

Kevin Reilly, Series Editor

WOMEN IN WORLD HISTORY

Volume 2

Readings from 1500 to the Present

Sarah Shaver Hughes
Brady Hughes

M.E. Sharpe
Armonk, New York
London, England

Cover photograph: Tina Modotti. Woman with Flag. 1928.
Palladium print by Richard Benson, 1982. 9¾ × 7¹¹/₁₆ in. (24.8 x 19.1 cm.)
The Museum of Modern Art, New York. Courtesy of Isabel Carbajal Bolandi.
Copy Print © 1997 The Museum of Modern Art, New York.

Library of Congress Cataloging-in-Publication Data

Hughes, Sarah S.
Women in world history / Sarah Shaver Hughes and Brady Hughes.
v. cm. — (Sources and studies in world history)
Includes bibliographical references.
Contents: v. 1. Readings from prehistory to 1500.
v. 2. Readings from 1500 to the present.
ISBN 1-56324-310-5. — ISBN 1-56324-311-3 (pbk.) (v. 1)
ISBN 1-56324-312-1. — ISBN 1-56324-313-X (pbk.) (v. 2)
1. Women—History. I. Hughes, Brady, 1933–
II. Title. III. Series.
HQ1121.H93 1995
305.4'09—dc 20   94–23644
CIP

Printed in the United States of America

The paper used in this publication meets the minimum requirements of the
American National Standard for Information Sciences—
Permanence of Paper for Printed Library Materials,
ANSI Z 39.48-1984.

BM (c) 10 9 8 7 6 5 4 3 2
BM (p) 10 9

CONTENTS

FOREWORD

Neither world history nor women's history was widely taught a generation ago. Proponents of women's history had to fight the widespread assumption that conventional histories of "man" or "mankind" were universal, that they spoke for the lives of women as well as men. A major problem with such histories was that the preponderance of sources used were written by men. Despite the insistence that "man" stood for women as well as men, students were often left with the distinct impression that history was made by men.

In the last twenty years, scholars of women's history have shown that there were many more important women, more sources written by women, and more sources about women than had previously been assumed. A first stage of scholarship in women's history called for the inclusion of women writers, artists, thinkers, rulers, and public figures.

The recovery of important women, largely from elite families, was a valuable correction. But histories that only added women were still centered on what came to be seen as men's topics: war, diplomacy, statecraft, and industry.

Increasingly, historians became conscious of the degree to which past societies had been divided along sexual lines, expecting different work and preparing different lives for men and women. In this second stage of scholarship, it became obvious that the historical experiences of men and women were different. There was no way that the lives of men could represent those of women. The prior historical division of men's and women's lives had defined the male role as public and political, concerned with city, state, war, and foreign relations. History had been written largely by and for men as a way of understanding and celebrating those male activities.

The second stage of scholarship in women's history has challenged this idea of history. A generation of studies has taught us to see the ways in which men and women are socially and culturally conditioned to certain kinds of behavior. This is why scholars speak now about "gender," the social and cultural behavior that may build upon or ignore biological sexual identity. To see gender in history is to see the ways in which men and women are trained in different (and similar) activities, to explore those diverse realms, and to understand the dynamic of gender interaction. In plain words, this means not just adding a queen for a day but studying kinship as well as kingship, the family as well as the state, domestic relations as well as foreign relations. Activities in which women have played more important roles than men—childrearing, planting, clothing production, local marketing, health care, education—and those, like art and religion, in which women's role has been as great as men's, are as important a part of the human past as the largely male-dominated "outside" activities of traditional history books.

Thus, the new historians of women have opened up vast realms of human activity that were largely ignored in past histories because men did not deem them important. And since men's records of the past are more numerous than women's, they have shown us how to read between the lines of those documents, to find new sources in myths, oral traditions, art and artifact—in short, to develop new methods of investigation and analysis.

It is remarkable that scholars of women's history and allied scholars of what has come to be known as the "new social history" (the study of everyday life, average and marginal people, daydreams, diets, dreads, diseases, hopes, and haircuts) have opened up the past at the same time that world history as a field of study has become established. The field of history has exploded both within and beyond traditional boundaries.

There is no turning back. Just as we cannot ignore the daily lives and inner experiences of women, we cannot ignore the peoples of Asia, Africa, and the Americas. We must know all of ourselves and all of our world.

Sarah and Brady Hughes have set themselves an enormous task. To "gender world history and globalize women's history" is a tall order. But it is a necessary one, and one for which they are especially well qualified. They both have been teaching women's history and world history throughout the recent decades of explosive innovation. They have been leaders in the effort to make world history genuinely inclusive while expanding our knowledge of women in the world. In this book they show us how easy it is to do both at the same time.

Kevin Reilly

PREFACE

This volume of readings (and its companion volume on the period before 1500) was prepared to meet dual needs: to gender world history and to globalize women's history. Many world history texts are misnamed, for too often they are histories of the activities of the world's men. The authors seem to be unaware that their portrayal of the historical male emphasizes the aggressive, power-driven, and sadistic aspects of his character. Stirring in a dollop of women's history only contrasts with narratives focused on how powerful empires dominate weaker neighbors. Accurate history demands more than the inclusion of fragments of women's history as a gesture toward equity to half of humankind. The social interactions of women and men in the household are a fundamental dynamic of any society, an explanatory factor crucial to understanding other relationships of power between clans, classes, political factions, religions, or nations. Until scholars develop an adequate base of knowledge about gender relationships, our understanding of the structure underlying any society's political, economic, or intellectual history will remain flawed. This book attempts only to suggest how considering the lives of women reveals the complex personal basis of social hierarchies and the family-oriented politics of premodern and modern societies.

Synthesis of women's history generally has been debated within the narrow confines of the Mediterranean region and Western Europe as preludes to the American experience. Somewhat tardily, historians in the past fifteen years began considering contemporary women's activities in a global framework but were slower to examine earlier centuries. As they recently have published monographs on numerous topics and translated documents from many of the world's languages, new possibilities emerge. Viewing women's modern history of the centuries since 1500 through a wider lens that also encompasses societies of Asia, Africa, and the Americas reveals a far more complex panorama. Patriarchy did not triumph in the same ways everywhere, and women were not always denied public, political, or economic roles. Instead of female status in Western civilizations being regarded as the measure of women's possibilities, it is evident that the expansion of European empires into the Americas, Asia, and Africa frequently undermined conquered women's prior rights and social power. Scholars can now prove that the clash of cultures on imperial frontiers was often mediated by gender. And even in the nineteenth century, when North American and European women pioneered in building feminist movements demanding education and civil rights, their counterparts on other continents raised similar voices soon afterward. Their stories, particularly of the past two hundred years, form a substantial new literature. This volume is only an appetizer, though one that opens up a very promising banquet.

Women in World History, Volume 2—Readings from 1500 to the Present, is organized on a regional basis, with readings within each chapter placed in chronological sequence. Themes emphasize female agency in the state, religion, the arts, economy, and family, as well as oppressive ideologies, laws, and customs. As we attempted to shape a narrative that would be useful to students in world or women's history courses, some hard choices and compromises were necessary. The societies of Southeast Asia, the Pacific islands, and Eastern Europe are omitted: a difficult decision because the relevant literature is large and significant. Religion in this volume appears most often in an oppressive guise, but we hope students realize that religious belief could also motivate and empower women. Individual readings barely suggest the vast treasure of women's novels, poetry, diaries, and letters or the immense scholarly literature on suffrage movements, colonialism, economic development, and the welfare state.

We are indebted to the numerous scholars who have been translating important texts for two centuries and to those who have recently reexamined the past, seeking the overlooked and ignored history of

our ancestors. We have special debts to Kevin Reilly, editor of M.E.
Sharpe's Sources and Studies in World History series, and to Signe
Kelker and Diane Kalathas of the interlibrary loan department of
Shippensburg University.

Sarah S. Hughes
Brady Hughes

ABOUT THE EDITORS

Sarah Shaver Hughes and **Brady Hughes** have taught world history and women's history for many years. Brady Hughes retired in 1990 from the faculty of Hampton University, Virginia; Sarah Hughes teaches at Shippensburg University, Pennsylvania. Sarah Hughes received her doctorate from the College of William and Mary in 1975; Brady Hughes received his from the University of Wisconsin, Madison, in 1969.

INTRODUCTION
Gendering World History, Globalizing Women's History

In 1835, the American abolitionist Lydia Maria Child published a *History and Condition of Women in Various Ages and Nations.* Lydia Maria Child was a compelling and popular author, despite her radical views advocating inter-racial marriage, the equality of all religions, and empowerment of women, while condemning racism, slavery, and war. Her *History and Condition of Women in Various Ages and Nations* began in volume I with Asia and Africa, while volume II surveyed Europe, the Americas, and the South Sea Islands. Child's volumes reflected a need women had long felt, and expressed in their writings in earlier centuries, to understand their place in the world in the broadest historical context. Their popularity in the nineteenth century is proved by the continuous reprinting of five editions, which kept the *History and Condition of Women* before its public for more than twenty years.

In the 160 years since Child wrote, history has been professionalized, too often marginalizing efforts to comprehend the global history of women. In the past 20 years, that has begun to change. Understanding the comparative dimension of women's past—answering questions about why women as a group have been excluded so systematically from the public power that commands so much respect in history—is a project undertaken by thousands of scholars, often under the auspices of international agencies, in the years since the United Nations Decade for Women, 1975–1985. Some of that scholarship is now appearing in print, but still there is no

1

satisfactory general history of all women available in English.

Nor is this volume a comprehensive history of the world's women in the modern era; its readings suggest the richness of women's history beyond North America and Europe and of world history beyond the impersonal, implicitly male story of cities, economies, wars, and empire. The readings are structured within regional chapters to correspond with modern history's geographic/national structure. Selections reveal critical facets of women's lives in particular places and periods. But important themes that cross boundaries of culture and time also appear. So a reader may compare the impact of colonialism, industrialism, nationalism, and revolutions upon women in different regions and times. Recurring global themes analyze the political power of women as queens and prime ministers; women's fundamental contributions to the production of goods and services necessary to sustain society and to develop economies; marriage practices, motherhood, and widowhood; and religious and social beliefs that proscribed some women as beyond respectability. A few samples of literature written by women also appear. In these pages, there are some famous women, such as Nur Jahan of Mughal India, Queen Njinga of Ndongo and Matamba, Maria Theresa of Austria, George Sand of France, Huda Shaarwi of Egypt, and Indira Gandhi of India, along with many less well known or anonymous ones.

Women's Empowerment

One of the most striking changes of the modern world is mass participation by women in politics. In 1500, monarchies were found everywhere. Only women within the palace had much influence, and they were more likely to wield power on behalf of their sons or brothers than their gender. Family-based power continues to be significant in the late twentieth century, when in South and Southeast Asia, as well as in Latin America, women are chosen as national leaders as representatives of their patrician clans. Sometimes politics has motivated queens, presidents, or prime ministers to endow schools for girls or appoint commissions to evaluate women's status; as often, they have, like Margaret Thatcher and Violeta Chamorro, seen their duty in dismantling public programs that served women. Of what importance is it, then, to know that women have at times in the past exercised great power in states of

Asia, Africa, Europe, and the Americas? Is it to learn that women can govern as well as men or wage wars as disastrous for their subjects? Or that kinship and class have outweighed sisterhood?

Women clearly lost power as monarchies were replaced by modern republics and democracies. Although exceptionally powerful queens ruled in England, Russia, and Austria in the eighteenth century of the American and French Revolutions, their abilities suggested no precedent for enfranchising women along with men.

Europeans and Americans were in the forefront of the woman suffrage movement. Women's equal right to civil and personal liberties was articulated publicly in Europe during the French Revolution. But after Napoleon's defeat in 1815, European governments were quite open in their opposition to women's participation in politics.

In the United States, abolitionist women, denied the public right to protest slavery, enunciated their own need for civil liberties. Revolutionary European women echoed these demands during the nineteenth century as male suffrage became universal. Socialist women secured commitment of their parties to political equality, an accomplishment whose importance became evident in the twentieth century as socialist revolutions spread beyond Europe to Asia, Africa, and Latin America. While socialism was still in its infancy in Europe, middle-class women absorbed feminist ideals of education, personal autonomy, and political rights in China, India, Egypt, Argentina, and Mexico. Women of New Zealand and Australia were the first in the world to vote in national elections. Political equality was finally won, usually after long campaigns, in Finland, Norway, Iceland, the Soviet Union, England, the United States, Poland, Sweden, the Netherlands, and Germany by 1920. By 1950, most women in independent countries could vote and hold office; after 1960, when the former colonial nations of Africa and Asia achieved independence, their new constitutions usually included woman suffrage.

The rise of religious fundamentalism since 1970 poses a threat to women's electoral power. More serious than that potential retreat from equality is the question of why electoral politics has brought women so little power. In no major state of the world do women exercise political clout through holding seats in legislatures, judicial posts, or executive offices in proportion to their population.

Colonialism

For women of the Americas, European conquest after 1492 was disastrous. Though gender divided indigenous societies in various ways, not all of which were advantageous to women, they lost property rights, social authority, and personal liberty when Europeans entered their lands. Epidemic diseases, Christianity, persecution for witchcraft, European misogyny, enslavement, endemic war, and rape accompanied the mostly male conquerors. European concepts of personal property in land and patrilineal inheritance deprived women of their fields. It should not be surprising that numerous Native American women who resisted colonial rule can be found to offset those famous women like Pocahontas and La Malinche (called Marina by Hernán Cortés) who assisted Europeans.

Colonial market demand brought millions of African women across the Atlantic Ocean to American slavery. That they became progenitors of a significant proportion of the population of the Western Hemisphere testifies to their courage and the importance of motherhood in African cultures.

Europeans claimed as colonies much of Asia and nearly all of Africa during the nineteenth century. By 1914, a few European governments and the United States controlled most of the world. In tropical areas, colonial powers sought to develop natural resources, either agricultural or mineral, for sale in global markets. Indigenous women, as well as men, lost coastal farmland to colonists backed by distant governments. Another common effect was migration of African and Asian men to the plantations, mines, or urban areas for work, leaving the women behind to raise food for themselves and their children. A variation of this pattern occurred when, as slaves were emancipated, indentured short-term workers were sought among the men of China, India, the Philippines, Jamaica, and West Africa.

Women lost many legal and personal rights when colonial administrators backed powerful local male elites or ignored women's social roles because they differed from Western ones. Women from European or American colonizing powers participated in exploiting colonized women as domestic workers or plantation labor. Even when Western women built schools and hospitals or were Christian missionaries, their patronizing racism divided them from the women with whom they worked.

Most nations achieved independence from direct colonial rule between 1945 and 1975. In most regions, a heritage of dependency on military weapons, trade, or markets for export of natural resources lingers. For women of the former colonies, the heritage is even more complex. Patriarchal customs and laws were enhanced by colonial rulers in many nations of Africa and Asia. Traditional divisions of agricultural resources and labor were disturbed, as were divisions of responsibility within the family. Men often now control contemporary cash crops for export, leaving their wives to grow food for the entire family but expecting the women to pay their share of children's school expenses. Before 1985, these women's roles in the economy, though essential, were invisible to technicians who distributed loans and foreign aid for economic development.

Work and Family

In the 1990s, increasing numbers of women consider work as a career and expect their career decisions to be given equal weight within the family with those of men. Women's share of the adult paid labor force has risen sharply throughout the world in the twentieth century. In 1990, in most parts of the world, women did more than 40 percent of all paid labor; only in Islamic western Asia and North Africa was women's share (at 25 and 21 percent, respectively) less than one-third. Throughout much of the world, women work more hours for pay (at less pay per hour) each week than men do; even fully employed women spend more hours weekly on housework and child care than men. Although the leading economic sectors employing women today vary considerably by world regions, outside of sub-Saharan Africa and southern Asia, where agriculture remains women's largest employer, women are everywhere more likely to work providing services than in manufacturing or transport industries. Despite the inequities remaining between men and women in 1990, it is the rapid pace of change on every continent since 1950 in women's employment outside the home that is most remarkable. The contrast is even greater when comparison is made to the preindustrial world.

Five hundred years ago, the family was considered a corporation, and normally an agricultural corporation. Women's and men's work was gendered in traditional ways between home and fields, without much individual variation within regions. As industrialization spread in the nineteenth century across Western Europe, then into other countries around the world, women gained new opportunities. Industrial work that was once done in the home by the whole family moved to factories. The textile and food-processing industries were notable for hiring women, especially young, single ones, because they could be paid less than men. The growing urban centers attracted more women, who became domestic servants of the increasing middle class. Few women planned careers because most still hoped to work outside their homes only before marriage, though many had to continue to earn (often by poorly paid homework) to supplement their husbands' wages.

Continuing economic development in the twentieth century led to a proliferation of occupations, most reserved for men, but some offering clerical, retail, or professional opportunities to women. However, when many women entered a field—as happened at various times and places in teaching, clerical jobs, retail sales, and banking— both prestige and pay dropped sharply.

Despite persistent inequities, working for pay revolutionized women's lives. Educating girls became an asset. Young women defied parents to escape arranged marriages and traditional restrictions on their behavior. Divorce rates escalated as women chose independence in preference to unhappy marriages. Fertility declined sharply as women exercised options other than motherhood. In developed regions of the world, by 1995, total births per woman were below the population-replacement level of 1.9. Only in southern Asia and sub-Saharan Africa did women continue to have more than five infants each.[*]

International Organizations

Early in the nineteenth century, some European and American women attended male-organized antislavery conferences. By the end of

---

[*]All statistics and analysis are based on chapter 5 in the United Nations publication *The World's Women, 1995: Trends and Statistics,* rev. ed. (New York: United Nations, 1995).

the century, they were organizing their own international meetings to plot concerted action to get the vote and other legal rights, to end the international transportation of women for prostitution, to encourage temperance, and to banish war.

Women's organizations supported the League of Nations, organized in 1919, to promote world peace. Its covenant encouraged its members to work for fair and humane working conditions for men, women, and children and discouraged the trafficking in women and children. The League began collecting data on women's conditions in different countries preparatory to drawing up international agreements to improve the status of women, but World War II forced the termination of the project.

The Charter of the United Nations, organized in 1945 as a successor to the League, reaffirmed equal rights for men and women. The Universal Declaration of Human Rights of 1948 stated more specifically women's claims to equality in citizenship, nationality, and marriage. Without means to enforce these rights in any country, the United Nations acted mainly by organizing task forces to collect and publicize data, then formulating new standards for the world community. Essential to publicizing and lobbying governments to implement these standards have been the nongovernmental organizations (NGOs), or private groups of women and men. From forty-two NGOs accredited to the founding United Nations conference, their numbers have multiplied until the thousands of women attending NGO forums at United Nations conferences since 1985 far exceed the official delegates from member states.

In the early 1960s, prodded by the United Nations Commission on the Status of Women and by national commissions, governments began adopting laws to protect women's rights. In 1975, the first major U.N. conference on women was held in Mexico City to inaugurate the International Women's Year. Its success in mobilizing women had a significant impact in Latin America. The next year marked the beginning of the United Nations Decade for Women. One outcome was the United Nations' adoption in 1979 of the Convention on the Elimination of All Forms of Discrimination against Women (CEDAW). This comprehensive international bill of rights for women took more than thirty years to draft but was ratified by the requisite 20 nations by 1981. The Decade for Women ended in 1985 with a *Forum* in Nairobi, Kenya, attended by an estimated 16,000 women from 150 countries. After Nairobi, record numbers of women from NGOs participated in drafting plans of action at other U.N. conferences and in preparing for the 1995 conference in Beijing, China.

Although the issues of greatest concern have changed over the fifty years since the United Nations was founded, several points stand out in historical importance. First, there has been an exceptional public commitment by United Nations member states from most of the world to international standards defining women's right to equality. Second, there has been much discussion, if not international agreement, about issues of birth control as they affect women and of population control as it affects nations. Third, the international community changed its attitude about women's contributions to economic development of nations. Women—who were once invisible to the World Bank, the International Monetary Fund, and engineers and agronomists of many nations—have recently become regarded as essential to development, and it has been widely recognized that no factor is more important than female education in achieving economic growth and control of population size. Perhaps most significant has been the adoption of new standards condemning gender-based violence and affirming women's human rights.

Gender-Based Violence and Women's Human Rights

Violence against women is not new: it has a long history. In this volume, there is documented the gender-based public violence of the European witchcraze in the sixteenth and seventeenth centuries; the Chinese Qing dynasty laws excusing rape by its soldiers; the female infanticide, harassment of widows, and/or *sati* found in India, China, and Cameroon; the worldwide trade in and enslavement of women as workers and concubines; and female genital mutilation still practiced in several parts of the world.

One outcome of the second wave of feminism in the 1970s was public action by women to remove issues of rape, sexual harassment, and domestic violence from the realm of women's private and personal shame. Instead, small groups of women formed shelters for battered women and rape crisis centers, then lobbied for public protection for victims and criminal prosecution of violent men. As this movement spread from North America to Mexico and Brazil (facilitated by the 1975 United Nations conference in Mexico City), to India, to South Africa, and to Europe, women's NGOs initiated a campaign that culminated at the 1993 U.N. World Conference on Human Rights in Vienna, Austria, in a new Declaration on the Elimination of Violence against Women, adopted by the forty-eighth U.N. General Assembly that year. By spelling out clearly what is condemned, this document denies the validity of ancient laws exempting the family from state intervention, does not excuse religious or traditional customs, and declares rape or other violence against women to be a war crime. It is on this basis that it is now possible for international war crimes tribunals to issue indictments for rapes committed by soldiers during wars.

Suggested Further Readings

Basic comparative data on contemporary women are available in *The World's Women, 1995: Trends and Statistics* (New York: United Nations, 1995). This second edition of a volume originally issued in 1991 contains information, by country, on household and family composition, population, migration, the environment, health, education, work, politics, and the media. More comprehensive statistics are available on the companion CD-ROM, *Women's Indicators and Statistical Database (Wistat), Version 3.* Another United Nations publication is a compilation of all documents adopted by that body pertaining to women: *The United Nations and the Advancement of Women, 1945–1995* (New York: United Nations, 1995). The text of the 1979 Convention on the Elimination of All Forms of Discrimination against Women (CEDAW) is included, as are documents from the United Nations Decade for Women. Hilkka Pietila and Jeanne Vickers analyze the history of U.N. actions in *Making Women Matter: The Role of the United Nations,* rev. ed. (London: Zed Books, 1994). Essays in *The Politics of Women's Education: Perspectives from Asia, Africa, and Latin America,* edited by Jill Ker Conway and Susan C. Bourque (Ann Arbor: University of Michigan Press, 1995), focus on the connection between women's education and national economic development. Women's emergence as a political force in modern states is considered by numerous authors in Barbara J. Nelson and Najma Chowdhury, eds., *Women and Politics Worldwide* (New Haven, CT: Yale University Press, 1994), the result of a nine-year project organized at the 1985 U.N. Conference on Women in Nairobi, with excellent summary essays and comparative data on forty-three countries; in Francine D'Amico and Peter R. Beckman, eds., *Women in World Politics: An Introduction* (Westport, CT: Bergin and Garvey, 1995); and in Jill M. Bystydzienski, ed., *Women Transforming Politics: Worldwide Strategies for Empowerment* (Bloomington: Indiana University Press, 1992).

PART 1
1500–1800

–1–

CHINA AND JAPAN
The Neo-Confucian Regimes of the Qing Monarchy and the Tokugawa Shogunate

Japanese washerwomen in an eighteenth-century print by Kitagawa Utamaro.
(The Metropolitan Museum of Art, H.O. Havemeyer Collection.)

In the modern era, the male neo-Confucian ideal of the woman who devoted her life to pleasing and obeying men was enshrined in ideologies and laws of East Asian states. The social stability achieved by the governments of the Manchurian Qing dynasty in China and the Tokugawa dynasty of shoguns in Japan was, in both cases, predicated upon diminishment of women's status to gain support of men. In China, as the Ming dynasty's power waned, the Manchurians of the northern borderland conquered territory and won allies even within the Forbidden Palace. Once they replaced the Ming emperors, Qing rulers sought to make minimal changes beyond putting their loyal followers in important government offices and stationing troops in selected urban centers. Their goal was to govern with support of the Chinese scholars and officials, a strategy that maintained the Qing monarchy for nearly 250 years, from 1644 to 1912. In Japan, Ieyasu Tokugawa's assumption of the reins of government as shogun in 1603 ended the civil wars that had been recurrent since the fourteenth century. Japanese feudalism also ended as the aristocracy's privileges and power yielded to that of the centralized Tokugawa state.

Neo-Confucian dogma became the explicit justification of the new seventeenth-century rulers in China and Japan, who regulated ranking of social classes as they glorified the gender inequality implicit in the patriarchal family. For men, hereditary stratification was undermined by wealth and education, particularly in China, where the examination system offered entry to the elite on the basis of merit. For women, there were fewer opportunities. Little research has been done on what changes the growth of commerce, with concurrent population mobility and urbanization, offered Chinese women in new occupations or status within merchant or artisan families. In Japan, by the eighteenth century, urban women shared key managerial responsibilities in such families. Chinese women, whose property rights were more restricted by the state and custom, might benefit from upward mobility through marriage or concubinage, for their society sanctioned men's relationships with women of lower social status. For most women of both China and Japan, marriage was the critical career choice, and giving birth to a son was necessary to confirm social worth.

1.1 Qing Rape Laws, 1646

One of the first instances of Qing neo-Confucian policy was redefining forcible rape. As their armies advanced into China,

Qing soldiers raped many Chinese women—a consequence of defeat desperately feared by victims of all ages in a society that valued feminine chastity above life itself. Jonathan Spence translated a story about Mongol soldiers (a significant force among the Manchurian bannermen) who tried to rape "Chang's Wife." The story, written in the 1670s by P'u Sung-ling, was set in northeastern China a generation after the Qing conquest.

In the year 1674, when the Three Feudatories had risen in rebellion, the expeditionary troops being sent south were bivouacked with their horses in the area of Yen; not a dog or chicken was left, the hearths were empty, women and girls all suffered their outrages.

At this season there had been heavy rains, and the fields were covered in water, like lakes; the people had nowhere to hide, so they climbed over the walls and went into the fields of standing kaoliang. Knowing this, the troops stripped off their clothes and rode naked on their horses after them, tracking them down in the water and raping them. Few escaped.

Only the wife of a certain Chang did not lie low but stayed quite openly in her own home. At night, with her husband, she dug a deep pit in her kitchen and filled it with dried reeds; she screened over the top and laid matting upon it so that it looked like a bed. And then she went on with her cooking by the stove.

When the troops came to the village she went out of the door of the house, as if offering herself. Two Mongol soldiers seized her and prepared to rape her, but she said to them, "How can I do such a thing in the presence of others?" One of them chuckled, jabbered to the other, and went away. The woman went into the house with the other and pointed at the bed, to get him to climb up first. The screening broke, and the soldier tumbled in. The woman took the matting and again placed it on the screen over the hole; then she stood by it, to lure the other when he came. He returned after a short while and heard the shouting from within the pit, though he couldn't tell where it was; the woman beckoned to him with her hand and her smile, saying, "Over here." The soldier climbed onto the matting and also fell in. The woman threw more brushwood on top of them and set the whole pile on fire. The flames blazed up, and the house itself caught fire. The woman called out for help. When the fire was extinguished, there was a strong smell of roasted flesh; people asked her what it was, and the woman replied, "I had two pigs, and feared they would be taken from me by the troops. So I hid them in that pit."

From *The Death of Woman Wang* by Jonathan D. Spence (New York: Viking Penguin, 1979), 103–4. Copyright © 1978 by Jonathan D. Spence. Used by permission of Viking Penguin, a division of Penguin Books USA Inc.

P'u Sung-ling reflects Chinese men's disregard of female identity in allowing his heroine no name of her own. Qing officials had made prosecution for rape nearly impossible when they revised the legal code soon after the dynasty assumed power. Although the core of laws from the previous Ming dynasty was retained, modifications show how the Manchus sought the support of Chinese male scholars. Vivien Ng explains:

In 1646 the Qing dynasty issued its first Qing Code. In the section on "Sexual Violations," the Qing retained all eight of the Ming statutes on sex crimes; however, it added a modifier to the statute on forcible rape. In one stroke, the Qing government made it very difficult for women to prove that they were rape victims. For the crime of rape to be irrefutably established, the victim must provide evidence that she had struggled against her assailant *throughout* the entire ordeal. Such evidence must include: (1) witnesses, either eyewitnesses or people who had heard the victim's cry for help; (2) bruises and lacerations on her body; and (3) torn clothing. Moreover, when initially violence had been used, but subsequently the woman had submitted "voluntarily" to the act, the case was not considered rape, but one of "illicit intercourse by mutual consent," in which case the woman would be subject to punishment [80 blows with a heavy bamboo if not married, 90 blows if married]. Additionally, the modifier stipulated that, "when a man, having witnessed an illicit affair, proceeded to force himself on the woman, the incident could not be regarded as rape, because the woman was already a fornicator." In such a case, the episode would be considered one of "illicit sexual intercourse in which both parties intrigued to meet away from the woman's house," in which case the punishment for both parties could be 100 blows with a heavy bamboo. . . .

What motivated the Qing government to introduce such a stringent definition of rape, one that was so obviously prejudiced against the rape victim? It has been suggested that, because rape was often difficult to prove and consequently was frequently the subject of false accusation, solid evidence was required to substantiate the complaint. Thus, the stringent definition. . . .

This explanation at first sight appears too convenient, presuming that many rape charges were indeed false accusations, a presumption that, incidentally, is still held today in this country by opponents of rape law reforms. In fact, the Qing government did try actively to discourage people from bringing false charges against others. There is ample evidence to suggest that one of the early concerns of the new dynasty was the large number of lawsuits, both legitimate complaints as well as false accusations, that were being brought before district magistrates. Top government officials considered this to be an undesirable development, because in their opinion litigation was a sign of social disharmony. . . . Several times during the first year of the Shunzhi reign, people living in newly pacified areas were exhorted to desist from unnecessary litigation. In fact, such urgings seemed to have become a necessary part of postpacification proclamations. . . . It is probable, therefore, that the stringent definition of rape was part of the *general* effort to discourage litigious tendencies among the populace. . . .

Pacification required both subjugation of enemy forces and restoration of order and peace of mind. . . . Lingering doubts about the Manchu conquerors had to be dispelled by whatever means available. Thus, the introduction of the stringent definition of rape in 1646 was probably part of the effort to discourage the Chinese from bringing rape charges against Manchu soldiers, because such accusations would only damage the pacification process.

Pacification of China also meant winning the cooperation of the literati. Toward this end, the Manchus presented themselves as restorers and guardians of Cheng-Zhu Neo-Confucianism, which had been the state ideology of the Ming and which emphasized, among other things, obedience to authority, loyalty to superiors, and chastity for women. . . . Intensification of state support for the cult of chastity was part of the Qing efforts to sponsor their own Confucian renewal, in order to convert conservative Chinese scholars to the side of the Qing government. Herein lies another explanation for the stringent definition of rape, and one that I believe is the most likely.

At first glance, there seems to be a paradox. If indeed chastity were such a paramount virtue, why did the Qing government make it more difficult to establish rape? It would seem more logical for the government to enact laws that promised swift and severe punishment for any man who forced himself upon a woman, whether violently or not. Is it possible that the main thrust of the new rape law was actually to ensure that women in Qing China would forcefully defend their chastity, even if it meant giving up their lives?

Such an interpretation, of course, would make the Qing rape law both misogynic and sadistic, but so was the cult of chastity. "It is a small matter to starve to death, but a serious matter to lose one's virtue" was only one of many aphorisms used to indoctrinate young women in Qing China. Often, a woman who found herself disgraced was impelled to commit suicide in order to redeem her good name and that of her family. Women were expected to be chaste even after being widowed, and widow remarriage was fiercely opposed by Neo-Confucian moralists.

Vivien W. Ng, "Ideology and Sexuality: Rape Laws in Qing China," *Journal of Asian Studies* 46 (February 1987): 57–60. Reprinted with permission of the Association for Asian Studies, Inc. References omitted.

1.2 Qing Laws Encouraged Widows' Chastity

Qing China is generally considered "a straitlaced, sexually repressed society" (Ng 1987, 57). Certainly, the state's effort to prevent widows' remarriage fits into that pattern. Strong pressure on a widow to remarry could come from her husband's relatives and neighbors who wanted her husband's property. Jonathan Spence cites the relevant clause from the Qing Code to illustrate how greed could lead to distortion of the law:

"If a widow remarries, her husband's property, as well as the dowry that she originally brought with her, shall become the property of her former husband's family." The clause, originally intended to encourage a widow to stay true to her dead husband's memory, had an obvious negative effect if—far from encouraging her in her sentiments of loyalty—the husband's relatives pushed the widow to remarry against her will. They would not just be divesting themselves of the costs of her upkeep and of child care, but be gaining substantial profits as well.

This clause of the [Qing] *Legal Code* helps to explain the pressures that were placed on woman P'eng in T'an-ch'eng [county of Shantung province] during the spring and early summer of 1670. She fulfilled part of her obligations immediately by enrolling her son, Lien, in the village school; it was only a small school, and the teacher was a part-time one who had to supplement his income by working in his own fields, but this was an important first stage if Lien was to gain literati status and honor his father. But almost from the first her husband's relatives, instead of supporting her, began to harass her. The main villains were her son's second cousins, the three brothers Ch'en Kuo-lin, Ch'en Kuo-hsiang, and Ch'en Kuo-lien. The youngest of them took her ox and refused to return it; this was a serious act, since the ox was not only an essential animal for families with fields to plow but was also treasured evidence of a family's status, well looked after and tethered before the doorway to the house (when not at work) for all to see. After taking the ox, Ch'en Kuo-lien extorted three taels from woman P'eng. The middle brother, Ch'en Kuo-hsiang, moved uninvited into her house and tried to drive her out. The clan head, Ch'en San-fu, did not intervene to help her. . . . But if they were trying to force her to move away from the area or to find another husband so as to protect herself and her son, they failed completely. Woman P'eng vowed she would not leave her home, and had an angry confrontation with the cousin Ch'en Kuo-hsiang, who swore, "I'll make sure that no scrap of anything is left to you."

From *The Death of Woman Wang* by Jonathan D. Spence (New York: Viking Penguin, 1979), 72–73. Copyright © 1978 by Jonathan D. Spence. Used by permission of Viking Penguin, a division of Penguin Books USA Inc.

Eventually, Ch'en Kuo-hsiang killed the widow P'eng's son Lien in an unsuccessful plot to seize her property legally. She managed to keep her house and land but did not regain the ox.

Spence derives from the county archives actual stories of other widows in the same county. Woman An, widowed after only a half year of marriage, managed to hang herself despite efforts of those around her to prevent it. Woman Wu was driven to return to her clan with her one-month-old baby. She was fortunate that her natal family would accept her. Many a widow knew that the family property had already been divided among her brothers, who would gain complete possession on the death of her parents—so there was nothing left to support her.

Widows were in a dangerous position: they could seldom return to their natal families, and their husbands' families were often willing to take extreme measures to force them to give up their inherited property. Furthermore, they were often as young as Woman An and Woman Wu, mentioned earlier. Mindful of this, Qing officials mounted a campaign to center public morality on women's chastity, especially the chastity of widows. Counties were instructed to keep and publicize the names of exceptional women. Their stories became part of the rhetoric that the local literati used to encourage county pride. The central government authenticated chaste widows and authorized their families to erect memorial arches honoring their names in family temples. Susan Mann explores the widow's position:

The still-fecund widow in the Chinese family became an instant source of ambiguity and anxiety. Without a "free bench" or some other assurance of property to support herself in her old age, she remained dependent upon her dead husband's family, but her presence in the household was bound to produce sexual attraction and tension. With her physical charms and reproductive powers still at their peak, she could bring a handsome price on the remarriage market—but the norms of Qing society forbade widow remarriage. Somehow the sexual and reproductive powers of a young widow had to be contained and protected within the structures of her dead husband's family. She could not become involved sexually with other males in the family; she could not bear children; and she could not control property. However, she could serve: rear heirs (including adopted ones), produce food and clothing, and care for her aging in-laws.

Susan Mann, "Widows in the Kinship, Class, and Community Structures of Qing Dynasty China," *Journal of Asian Studies* 46 (February 1987): 44–45. Reprinted with permission of the Association for Asian Studies, Inc. Notes omitted.

Mann continues her analysis by describing the situation of young widows in poor families, who decide that staying with their husbands' families was their best chance for a satisfying life. Mann explains that the type of family where this might occur is called a "stem family" by specialists.

A family comprising three generations, with the middle generation . . . consisting of only [the young widow]. . . . If the senior couple in the family were old or infirm when their son died, the young widow would temporarily become the virtual household head. Among the gentry, such households were not the norm. The ideal Confucian family, as everyone knows, consisted of many married sons and their wives and children, living with their parents under one roof. A *stem phase* in the Chinese family system was merely that: a cyclic interval between the marriage of an eldest son and his brothers.

On the other hand, among poorer families the stem phase tended to become a permanent condition. Poor families had difficulty rearing more than one son to adulthood; even in cases where two or more sons survived, a family of modest means might have resources to bring in only one bride. Finally, in poor families sons tended to marry late, increasing the likelihood that, if a son died while his own children were still young, the grandparents would already be well advanced in years. It is significant, therefore, that a dominant theme in chaste widow biographies is the emotional and material strain on stem families caused by the death of the sole surviving male heir. The apparent preponderance of stem families in chaste widow biographies may, of course, be precisely a measure of the success of government moral education campaigns that reached out to the lower classes. . . .

In general the picture drawn by biographers of chaste widows sketches a household in the throes of a survival crisis. An only son, perhaps married late, has died soon after producing an heir—sometimes during his wife's pregnancy. His parents are past their productive working years. The children, if sons, must be educated; if daughters, married. . . .

And in most cases, the triumphant end to the chaste widow's tale tells us that the young woman dutifully served her parents-in-law and instructed her children, until the former were properly buried and the latter properly married. Often, her sons go on to success in their examinations, or at least to a respectable livelihood.

What does this profile suggest? First of all, that we are most likely to find chaste widows in households where the deceased husband had no surviving brothers to support his parents in old age, and where the widow in question had offspring to raise. In those families who were most vulnerable to the death of a male heir, the parents' emotional commitment to the young woman on whom their present survival and their future existence depended is easy to understand. So is the fear, transparent in these biographies, that the young widow might—in a fit of despair—kill herself.

What of the young widow herself? [If she stayed with her husband's family,] her parents-in-law might weep with gratitude, her son shed tears in her memory. But she was the one who had to act. Suicide in itself was an honorable, if frightening, alternative, particularly for the widow who feared that her husband's relatives might force her to remarry. Remarriage was not only undesirable in the discourse of Confucian moralism; the widow who entered another patriline found herself in a position still more marginal and vulnerable than the one she first encountered as a bride. [But] the young widow in a stem family did not face the threat of a forced remarriage into another family. No brothers-in-law coveted her heir's claim on the patrimony; no brideprice could tempt her parents-in-law to relinquish her services. For such a woman, suicide did indeed offer an escape from long years of hardship and privation in the service of her dead husband's family. Inducing her to stay alive, on the other hand, was society's reward—delayed in coming, but as tangible as any she could expect: the reward of being remembered by a successful son, enshrined on the ancestral altars of his household for generations to come.

Susan Mann, "Widows in the Kinship, Class, and Community Structures of Qing Dynasty China," *Journal of Asian Studies* 46 (February 1987): 45–47. Reprinted with permission of the Association for Asian Studies, Inc. Note omitted.

Widows who sought alternatives to family dependency had fewer options than their counterparts in other world cultures. Chinese law denied daughters legacies from their natal families that Islamic law required, their dowry rights were negligible in comparison to those of Hindu women, while their limited claims to inherited property as widows left little scope for the independence exercised by European women in similar circumstances. Without capital or even a respectable home, widows might become servants—even sell themselves into bondage—or laborers in cottage textile production or prostitutes.

Within the growing number of wealthy urban families, Chinese women's cultural and economic influence increased. Literate women became a sign of family affluence as education spread in the eighteenth century. Though female scholars could never gain appointment to government posts or control of family businesses, a few were able to use their skills to help support their families.

1.3 Chinese Women Artists

Though Chinese women of the period 1500–1800 lived within social restrictions that were among the most severe in the world, some surmounted gender limitations to achieve memorable distinction as painters. They, like aristocratic women writers in Heian Japan, used conventions of privileged femininity to advantage. As accomplished artists, their work was admired by contemporaries.

A few women artists worked before the Song dynasty (960–1279), which was the first dynasty with a sizable number of women painters. However, it is in the Ming (1368–1644) and Qing (1644–1912) dynasties that women's art can be identified today as a distinct, significant body of work. By then, serious Chinese paintings often included a written poem or short essay. An artist had to be literate, familiar with the writing brush, and knowledgeable in art history. Women painters belonged to scholar-official (gentry) families or were courtesans, nuns, or members of artisan families. Some were members of imperial families. However, most were members of gentry families or courtesans who served gentlemen of this class. Marsha Weidner explains:

The women of the gentry and courtesans were counterparts to the male scholars whose art theories and practices eventually came to dominate Chinese painting in the Ming (1368–1644) and Qing (1644–1912) dynasties.

These scholars—members of the literary intelligentsia who served in China's government, or at least prepared for official careers—painted as amateurs and regarded their own work as superior to that of professional artists. They maintained that meaningful art was created only by refined, learned individuals who took up the brush for personal reasons or for the pleasure of their friends and that the quality of this art depended upon the character of the artist. . . . Their success was measured not in sales or commissions, but by the reputations they established among their peers.

Marsha Weidner, "Women in the History of Chinese Painting," in *Views from the Jade Terrace: Chinese Women Artists, 1300–1912,* edited by Marsha Weidner, Ellen Johnston Laing, et al. (Indianapolis: Indianapolis Museum of Art, 1988), 13.

The male scholars practiced their art in their private libraries and residential gardens as a leisure activity, while not slighting their official duties. Women artists adopted the same practices. Fortunately, they could paint without stepping outside of their homes, since women in gentry families were not expected to leave their homes to paint or study with teachers.

Women in the gentry families who became skilled painters usually had the support and assistance of male family members. Accounts of their lives emphasize that they and their husbands shared an interest in art that formed a romantic bond between them. Often, the wife–artist was a secondary wife or a concubine.

Not all were dependent on being taught by their male family members. Some learned from the females in their family who were artists. If a girl expressed an interest but no one in her immediate family was an artist, her parents might find a teacher from some of her more distant relatives. Chen Shu's (1660–1721) life was a good example of an artist in a gentry family. Her son wrote her biography.

As a child she learned to read by asking the boys of her clan to pass along what they learned in school. Her strict mother initially frowned on such unfeminine conduct and forbade her to take time away from her needlework to practice with the brush. Undeterred, Chen Shu one day made a copy of a famous painting hanging on the wall of her father's study. For this she was beaten, but a god intervened by appearing to her mother in a dream and saying: "I have given your daughter a brush. Some day she will be famous. How can you forbid it?" This tale served to underscore the idea that Chen Shu was destined for great achievement and perhaps was used to explain her devotion to pursuits regarded by some as unnecessary, even undesirable, for women.

Chen Shu married into the Qian family . . . becoming the second wife of Qian Lunguang (1655–1718). Qian did not distinguish himself as an official, but he did earn a modest reputation as a calligrapher and poet. Shared artistic interests were a part of the couple's relationship, and Qian occasionally added poetic inscriptions to Chen's paintings. . . .

The Qian family associated with some of the leading scholars of the area and took pleasure in entertaining guests, evidently in a manner beyond the family's means. To defray the costs of these gatherings, Chen Shu pawned her clothing and sold her jewelry and paintings. . . .

The shape of Chen Shu's artistic career was determined by her primary roles as wife and mother. From the 1680s through the first decade of the seventeenth century, much of her time was devoted to caring for her four children . . . , parents-in-law, and mother. . . . Chen Shu undoubtedly continued to paint during these busy years, but her last three decades seem to have been her most productive; her surviving dated paintings were executed between 1700 and 1735.

In 1721 Qian Chenqun, her eldest son, became a Metropolitan Graduate (*jinshi*) and received an appointment to the Hanlin Academy. . . . When her son asked the [imperial] court's permission to visit her in 1735, she nobly insisted that he stay at his post and . . . set out to join him in the capital. . . . She was then seventy-five years old. . . . Late in the spring of the following year she died in Beijing. . . .

In the course of his successful career under the Qianlong emperor (r. 1735–95), Qian Chenqun frequently presented paintings by his mother to the throne. The emperor received Chen Shu's works with pleasure and wrote on many of them with his characteristic lack of restraint.

Marsha Weidner, Ellen Johnston Laing, et al., eds., *Views from the Jade Terrace: Chinese Women Artists, 1300–1912* (Indianapolis: Indianapolis Museum of Art, 1988), 117–18. Note omitted.

Her son's biography lists several of Chen Shu's pupils who later achieved fame.

Occasionally, imperial women were artistic. One of the most interesting was Empress Dowager Cixi (1835–1908). She was one of the strongest rulers of China and also an excellent painter. She gave "her" paintings to people whose support she needed. There were too many paintings needed for the time she could devote to her art, so she employed as many as eighteen painters to produce them in her style. She put her seal on these. Some paintings she did herself, writing special phrases on them. Gifts of those were particularly treasured.

1.4 Rural Japanese Women during the Tokugawa Period, 1600–1868

In Japan, the Tokugawa aristocracy sought to replace the remnants of a matrilocal system with a universal patriarchy. Because of this, the Tokugawa period is usually thought of as one in which women were docile and dominated by men. Feminine research in Japan recently has developed a more varied picture of changing gender relationships. For example, the Tokugawa elite was never able to control the practices of the peasants, whose women continued to preserve some freedoms. To gain a perspective on what had been the norm before the Tokugawa period, note the summary by Hitomi Tonomura:

> In the first century and a half (592–770) of Japan's imperial rule, . . . emperorship was accorded to women as frequently as it was to men, until the imperial seat, along with all bureaucratic posts, became gendered male. The Sun Goddess, a female deity, was chosen to be the ancestral deity of the imperial lineage. Marriage practice was more matrilocal than patrilocal. Aristocratic and warrior-class women were significant heirs of property and even adopted children in order to pass down their property. The practice of *yobai* (night crawling) and sex-centered village festivals sanctioned promiscuity for both women and men, although men usually proposed the liaison and women accepted or rejected it. . . . But, by 1500—to take an arbitrary year—women were no longer emperors, occupied no formal governmental positions, rarely held property, and were increasingly considered biologically polluted, while marriage had become patrilocal and descent patrilineal.[*]

---

[*]Hitomi Tonomura, "Black Hair and Red Trousers: Gendering the Flesh in Medieval Japan," *American Historical Review* 99 (1994): 131. Notes omitted.

By 1600, the country was just recovering from a period in which the emperor's government was helpless to control the widespread warfare between regional warlords. The restoration of the central government and repression of the warlords was accomplished by an alliance of three warlords, in which leadership eventually fell to the Tokugawas. The leader of the Tokugawas had the title of shogun and ruled from Edo (present-day Tokyo). As part of their campaign to create peace and stability, they decreed that the population would be divided into four castes. In descending order of importance, the four were: samurai (warriors), peasants, artisans, and merchants. Legally, males had to follow the occupation of their caste and could not marry outside it.

Another Tokugawa innovation was to encourage all households to follow the *ei* form, a variation of the patriarchy that was found in China and other civilizations. Influenced by neo-Confucianism, *ei* usually had a male as head of household and one child, usually one of his male children, succeeding to his position. Women were responsible for the home and the productive labor done there. Wives were to obey their husbands, brides their mothers-in-law, and widows their sons.

Adoption of *ei* was extensive among the top caste, the samurai households. In the lower three castes, especially in the peasant households, women found considerable freedom, as Anne Walthall illustrates:

Parents appear to have made few distinctions between boys and girls in infancy. . . . Gender distinctions became more apparent in naming customs, gift giving, and ritual observances as infants grew into young children. . . . Although boys may have received more attention at the major milestones of their early childhood, the upbringing of both sexes in their early years, as far as we can tell, was otherwise fairly equal. . . . Although the evidence is inconclusive, it appears that the first five years of any child's life were made as pleasant as family circumstances permitted. When the child showed sufficient maturity, he or she was assigned age- and gender-appropriate tasks and treated more strictly. . . .

Girls everywhere were expected to be obedient and gentle, discreet in speech, clean and tidy, and industrious in women's tasks. Their education in practical skills was acquired in needle shops (*ohariya*) and girls' rooms (*musume yado*), which paralleled young men's associations and like them were established village by village. Attendance was compulsory . . . from age fourteen to marriage, and in some regions a girl was not considered a respectable, marriageable adult until she had been a member for several years. During the day she would help with the work at home, but at night she would go to the *musume yado,* where she would learn handicrafts, talk with other girls and older women who supervised work and play, and perhaps sleep. . . . Needle shops, which were open only during the winter, likewise concentrated on the skills required for everyday life. . . .

In the villages near Edo, wealthy peasant entrepreneurs bent on acquiring the best and most expensive education available for their daughters had them become servants in the homes of daimyō [local nobility] and *hatamoto* (high-ranking retainers in the shōgun). Here, at no small cost to their families, they learned feminine deportment: good posture and graceful movement, elegant and deferential language, appropriate dress and bodily care, and techniques of managing a household. . . .

For the daughters of wealthy peasants who lived too far from samurai households and the educational opportunities they offered, costly pilgrimages functioned more or less as finishing schools. The pilgrimage both strengthened faith and provided an occasion for sightseeing and observation; it was a learning experience that took young women outside their home communities and forced them to interact with strangers. Taken usually a year or so before marriage, the pilgrimage made it possible for teen-agers to travel with their friends and female relations largely apart from male society, except for one companion-escort. . . .

The poor usually could not afford to lavish resources on daughters, however. When girls from ordinary peasant and tenant farm families began to leave their homes and villages in the latter half of the Tokugawa period, they went to work as indentured servants (*hōkōnin*). . . .

Sending a young unmarried girl out to work for the sake of the rest of the family could have dire consequences. Parents worried that their daughter might be mistreated or sold into prostitution. Worse yet, once freed from her parents' supervision she might run away to the city, causing them embarrassment and financial hardship. Many girls left their families at the age of twelve to serve strangers, receiving as payment two changes of clothing and yearly salaries remitted to their fathers. . . . Children even younger could often find work as nursemaids.

Factors such as the spread of indentured servitude (which took girls out of the village), the growing emphasis on education, and the opportunity to go on pilgrimages conceivably influenced sexual practices preceding marriage, the choice of marriage partner, and the age of marriage, perhaps reducing the community's ability to control its women through the old custom of *yobai* (night visits). . . .

Official samurai teachings frowned on premarital sexual promiscuity. The "Instructions for Women" sent to peasant villages by the lord of Matsumoto in 1793 announced that "after a girl is ten, she should not mix with boys. After she is twelve or thirteen, she should not come near men. It is best to be modest and discreet." Yet evidence gathered by folklorists and historians, while sketchy and not altogether in agreement, suggests that peasants generally ignored these precepts.

Several historians believe that premarital sex among village girls and boys was common. . . . Meiji ethnographer Yanagita Kunio further argued that the young men's associations of each village, and not the parents, actually controlled the selection of marriage partners by means of night visits. The boys would spend evenings with members of the girls' groups, working, singing, and chatting before pairing off and sleeping together. They would then tell their parents whom they had chosen as a marriage partner.

Evidence from other areas, however, suggests that sexual relations were permitted only after the couple became engaged. . . . In other areas, both boys and girls were criticized only if they had sex with more than one partner. . . .

Under ordinary circumstances, marriage marked the major metamorphosis in a woman's life. . . . Detailed studies of marriage patterns show that rich married rich, poor married poor, sometimes kin married kin, and families with sidelines that contributed significantly to the household economy found brides skilled in business management. Marriage thus tended to reinforce economic divisions and social distinctions. This fact may have been advantageous to Japanese women, who, although typically entering their husband's family as strangers and needing to be trained in the ways of their new home, may not have been as intimidated and unprepared to assume new household responsibilities as Chinese women, who tended to marry into families of higher status than their own and to be overawed by the power and wealth of their in-laws. . . .

Harmony was usually the bride's responsibility and meant that she had to refrain from quarreling with the members of her new household, do the work expected of her position, and conform to family customs. Yet according to the precepts written for peasants by samurai intellectuals and the peasants themselves, the basis for harmony lay in the connubial relations of the couple itself. "The married couple is the foundation of morality. A couple is basically lustful, and if they get along, they produce a righteous harmony, but if they do not, everything falls apart." Thus affection and social necessity went hand in hand, and herein lay the possibility of intimate space for the married couple apart from the family. The author of *Nōyaku kikō* (Observations of agricultural practices) suggests as much in his account of an overnight stay at a farmhouse in the Kiso valley. The newlyweds in his host family went to bed early and, separated from the others by only a screen, began noisy lovemaking. "Outrageous," exclaimed the guest, whereupon the old woman of the family got angry. "Harmony between the husband and wife is the basis of prosperity for the descendants. Rather than not have this auspicious intimacy, I permit their coupling day and night. People who laugh at their passion are themselves outrageous. Get out!" . . . The mediating factor here was lust, a passion validated in the practice of premarital night visits and evidently given greater latitude within the Japanese peasantry than the military aristocracy. . . .

In addition to preserving family harmony, married women also bore a responsibility comparable to their husband's for the family economic survival. Unlike samurai women whose sideline industries, if any, were always subordinate to and separate from their husband's official duties, in peasant families women and men worked closely together. Generally the women did the tedious and time-consuming work, whereas men did the work that was heavy and dangerous. Agricultural development in the eighteenth century required peasant women to add handicrafts and field work to their domestic chores. . . . Although women worked alongside men in the fields, they were not paid equal wages. . . . Even when women did the same work as men, however, their pay was less, possibly because the supervisors were male. Household work, including cottage industries that produced a cash income, was always valued less than a man's work. . . .

Committed to the prosperity of her family and her descendants, a farm woman expected no less than to work long, hard hours. But in the culture of marriage, a woman was more than a beast of burden; she was the helpmate of her husband. The precepts handed down from the ruling class may have emphasized a wife's subordination to her husband and his family, but among the peasantry women held a more equitable position, one that even enabled them to talk back to their husbands, as did Tomi from Sagamihara in 1846. Her husband came home one night to find her absent, and when she appeared and he asked her what she had been doing, she replied, "None of your business." They then started shouting so loudly the neighbors interfered.

Anne Walthall, "The Life Cycle of Farm Women in Tokugawa Japan," in *Recreating Japanese Women, 1600–1945,* edited by Gail Lee Bernstein (Berkeley: University of California Press, 1991), 44–58. Copyright © 1991 The Regents of the University of California. Used by permission of the University of California Press. Notes omitted.

Suggested Further Readings

Readings on Chinese Women: Susan Mann discusses marriage in the context of social class in "Grooming a Daughter for Marriage: Brides and Wives in the Mid-Ch'ing Period," from *Marriage and Inequality in Chinese Society,* edited by Rubie S. Watson and Patricia Buckley Ebrey (Berkeley: University of California Press, 1991). Mann also reviews literature addressed to increasing numbers of educated women in eighteenth-century China. Joanna F. Handlin assesses similar literature of a period two centuries earlier in "Lu K'un's New Audience: The Influence of Women's Literacy on Sixteenth-Century Thought," in *Women in Chinese Society,* edited by Margery Wolf and Roxane Witke (Stanford, CA: Stanford University Press, 1975). Dorothy Ko addresses the subject more broadly in *Teachers of the Inner Chambers: Women and Culture in Seventeenth-Century China* (Stanford: Stanford University Press, 1994). Changes in widows' options are the subject of Ann Waltner's "Widows and Remarriage in Ming and

Early Qing China," in *Women in China: Current Directions in Historical Scholarship,* edited by Richard W. Guisso and Stanley Johannesen (Youngstown, NY: Philo Press, 1981). Also see Mark Elvin, "Female Virtue and the State in China," *Past and Present* 104: 111–52, and Evelyn S. Rawski, "Ch'ing Imperial Marriage and Problems of Rulership," in *Marriage and Inequality in Chinese Society,* edited by Watson and Ebrey. Dorothy Ko deconstructs connections between the Chinese state and women in "The Shifting Meanings of the Body as Attire: Footbinding in Seventeenth-Century China," *Journal of Women's History* 8 (winter 1997): 8–27. Ann Waltner and Pi-ching Hsu introduce English readers to "Lingering Fragrance: The Poetry of Tu Yaose and Shen Tiansun," *Journal of Women's History* 8 (winter 1997): 28–53.

Readings on Japanese Women: For a general survey, see Haruko Wakita's "Marriage and Property in Premodern Japan from the Perspective of Women's History," *Journal of Japanese Studies* 10 (1984): 77–97. Louise Allison Cort investigates the social significance of clothing in "Whose Sleeves . . . ? Gender, Class, and Meaning in Japanese Dress of the Seventeenth Century," in *Dress and Gender: Making and Meaning,* edited by Ruth Barnes and Joanne B. Eicher (Providence: Berg Publishers, 1992). Anne Walthall assesses peasant women's roles in rice riots and other challenges to the Tokugawa class system in "Devoted Wives/Unruly Women: Invisible Presence in the History of Japanese Social Protest," *Signs* 20 (autumn 1994): 106–36. The articles in *Recreating Japanese Women, 1600–1945,* edited by Gail Lee Bernstein (Berkeley: University of California Press, 1991), are very valuable. Included are analyses of women who married out of their natal families and of women who chose not to marry out: teachers, a poet–painter, and a sake (rice wine) brewer. Neo-Confucian texts that prescribe women's inferiority are reviewed in chapter 5 of Marjorie Wall Bingham and Susan Hill Gross, *Women in Japan* (St. Louis Park, MN: Glenhurst Publications, 1987). Patricia Fister has examined the condition of *Japanese Women Artists, 1600–1900* (Lawrence, KS: Spenser Museum of Art, 1988).

–2–
THE MIDDLE EAST
Women of the
Ottoman Empire

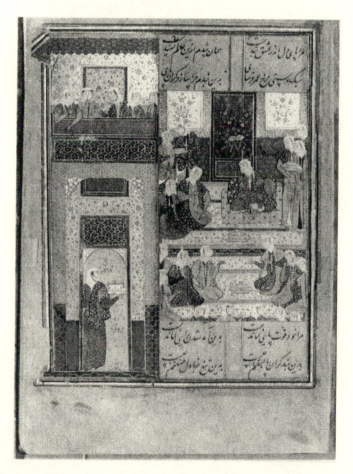

Zulaikha with her handmaidens in the Palace. (From *Jami: Yusuf and Zulaikha*, Iran, Shiraz, sixteenth century. The Metropolitan Museum of Art, Gift of Alexander Smith Cochran.)

Two empires dominated the Islamic Middle East in the sixteenth and seventeenth centuries: the Turkish-ruled lands of the Ottoman monarchs—stretching from eastern Europe across ancient Anatolia (now called Turkey), Syria, Iraq, Arabia, and North Africa—and the Persian kingdom (now called Iran), ruled by the Safavid dynasty. Both the Ottoman and Safavid dynasties originated among Turkic peoples of Central Asia, whose centuries of expansion into southwestern Asia were accompanied by conversion to Islam. The Ottoman sultans were militant defenders of Sunni Islam, whereas the Safavid shahs established Shi'ism as Iran's religion. The transition from pastoral nomadic life to urban-centered sedentary empires also affected mores of gender. Central Asian women's relative autonomy, open socialization with men, and political influence disappeared as the millennia-long traditions of misogyny, seclusion, veiling, and slave concubinage of the eastern Mediterranean proved dominant.

In a regional historical tradition that predated Islam, a state's decline was attributed to the destructive influence of women in public affairs. Chroniclers of the Ottoman and Safavid Empires, and the modern scholars who uncritically accept their verdicts, equated female political influence with the corruption and weakness of male rulers. This chapter focuses on Turkey under the Ottoman dynasty during an era usually denigrated as "the sultanate of women." Although scholars such as Leslie P. Peirce offer nuanced explanations of women's real roles in the Ottoman court and society, too often the decline of the dynasty is still attributed to the harem—even though Ottoman men remained in power for more than 250 years longer.

2.1 Paths to Power at the Ottoman Court

Ottoman rule depended on an army and a civil bureaucracy of male slaves, who were paralleled by a harem of women slaves. The dynasty built upon an ancient Middle Eastern practice of royal concubinage. Among the Muslim dynasties, the Abbasid caliphs had begun the practice of allowing sons of slaves, as well as of their wives, to succeed them as monarchs. This was possible because Islamic law did not deny legitimacy to children of slave women, nor did it necessarily enslave them. A slave woman's sons and daughters had the status of their father rather than of their mother. A male slave's children remained in slavery; a free man's children were born free with rights to inherit his property. A slave woman did not gain her freedom by bearing a child with her male owner, although she could not afterward be sold and was freed when the owner died. Early in the fifteenth century, the Ottoman sultans revolutionized the traditional policy of permitting monarchs both polygynous marriage and concubinage by refusing to marry and by having all their children only with slave women. Furthermore, the dynasty developed a peculiar policy of serial concubinage. As soon as a concubine gave birth to a son, she was banished from the sultan's bed. Henceforth, her status was entirely dependent on her being the mother of a prince rather than the lover of the king. If her son succeeded his father as sultan, she attained her freedom and the position of queen mother. If her son was not the successor, she retired as a free woman to a quiet life in a provincial town. All women in the sultan's personal entourage were still slaves, had been slaves, or were the daughters of slaves. Women's paths to power in Turkey rose only from the depths of slavery.

The reasons for the Ottoman refusal to recognize women of noble families in their own or rival monarchies as worthy of marriage bonds are complex. The policy left the dynasty without alliances customarily forged through marriage, but also independent. It avoided competition from feudal families with claims to rule based on landholdings and collateral descent from a royal ancestor. The Ottoman Empire was a patrilineal government with only males allowed to succeed to the throne. But not only men exercised power in Istanbul's palaces. Officials' careers depended on the power and influence of their patrons, who were often secluded women in the Sultan's harem, as Leslie Peirce explains:

For roughly one hundred years, from the mid-sixteenth to the mid-seventeenth centuries, women of the Ottoman royal family exercised so much influence on the political life of the empire that this period is often referred to, in both scholarly and popular writing, as "the sultanate of women." High-ranking dynastic women, especially the mother of the reigning sultan and his leading concubines, were considerably more active than their predecessors in the direct exercise of political power—in creating and manipulating domestic political factions, in negotiating with ambassadors of foreign powers, and in acting as regents to their sons. In addition, this period is notable for the important role acquired by dynastic women, the queen mother in particular, in the symbolics of sovereignty—the ceremonial demonstrations of imperial legitimacy and patronage of artistic production. . . .

The persistence of the [traditional] view that the exercise of public power by women is illegitimate derives largely from two areas of misunderstanding of traditional Ottoman society. The first is a misunderstanding of the nature and function of the harem institution. In stark contrast to the historically persistent Western image of a group of concubines existing solely for the sexual convenience of their master, the harem of a household of means included women related to the male head of household and to each other in an often complex set of relationships, many of which did not include a sexual component. The harem of a prosperous household would include the wife or wives of the male head of the household and perhaps one or more slave concubines, children of the family, perhaps the widowed mother or unmarried or divorced sisters of the head of the household, and female slaves, who might be the personal property of the women or men of the family.

The imperial harem was similar but more extensive and its structure more highly articulated. The mother of the reigning sultan was the head of the harem. The queen mother exercised authority over both family members . . . and the administrative/service hierarchy of the harem. . . . High-ranking administrative officers of the harem— all of them women—received large stipends. . . . These women oversaw not only the large number of servants who performed housekeeping tasks of the harem but, more important, the training of select young harem women who would wait on the sultan or his mother. . . .

A harem is by definition a sanctuary or a sacred precinct and by implication a space in which certain individuals or certain modes of behavior are forbidden. Mecca and Medina, the two holiest cities of Islam, are commonly referred to as "the two noble harems" and in Ottoman usage the interior of a mosque is known as its harem. Because Islamic law limits open contact between the sexes to a specified degree of kinship, the private quarters of a house and by extension the female members of the household are its harem. . . .

A second misunderstanding of the nature of Ottoman society is the erroneous assumption that the seclusion of women precluded their exercising any influence beyond the walls of the harem. . . . Women of superior status in this female society, the matriarchal elders, had considerable authority not only over other women but also over younger males in the family, for the harem was also the setting for the private life of men. Furthermore, female networks sustained through formal visiting rituals provided women with information and sources of power useful to their male relatives.

Leslie P. Peirce, "Beyond Harem Walls: Ottoman Royal Women and the Exercise of Power," in *Gendered Domains: Rethinking Public and Private in Women's History*, edited by Dorothy O. Helly and Susan M. Reverby (Ithaca, NY: Cornell University Press, 1992), 40–44. Copyright © 1992 by Cornell University. Used by permission of the publisher, Cornell University Press. Notes and Turkish words omitted.

The power and influence of harem women increased in the sixteenth century when Sultan Suleiman I (r. 1520–66) centralized the Ottoman government in Istanbul. Previously, power had been decentralized as the sultan sent out his grown sons, with each prince accompanied by his slave mother, to gain experience as governors of provinces. These departures were orchestrated with great ceremony as evidences of the power of the sultan. The sultan's daughters, princesses, were married to other provincial governors, in part to encourage their husbands' loyalty and to maintain a conduit of reliable information back to the sultan. The mothers and sons gathered support for the inevitable battle of succession. All princes were eligible to succeed their father on the throne, and civil war usually broke out when the sultan died. The losers were executed or blinded, as were their sons. Some princely governors, not willing to wait for their father's death, might try to overthrow the sultan while he was alive. Suleiman's grandfather had been such a victim of his son, Selim I.

The sixteenth century witnessed a reversal of this policy of dynastic decentralization, as the royal family was gradually centralized in the capital and lodged in the harem quarters of the sultan's palace. This process began with two innovations introduced by Suleiman. . . . He married his sisters, daughters, and granddaughters to top-ranking statesmen, whenever possible to his grand viziers. Since the duties of such statesmen required them to remain in proximity to the sultan, their wives lived in the capital rather than in the provinces. Suleiman also abandoned the practice of serial concubinage; . . . this practice appears to have been aimed at ensuring that the mother of a prince would have no more than one son so that no prince would be disadvantaged in the contest for succession. Suleiman raised one of his concubines, Hurrem, to an extraordinarily privileged position: he had five sons and a daughter by her, contracted a legal marriage to her, and established in his palace a permanent residence for her where she remained when her sons were dispatched to the provinces.

Leslie P. Peirce, "Beyond Harem Walls: Ottoman Royal Women and the Exercise of Power," in *Gendered Domains: Rethinking Public and Private in Women's History*, edited by Dorothy O. Helly and Susan M. Reverby (Ithaca, NY: Cornell University Press, 1992), 46. Copyright © 1992 by Cornell University. Used by permission of the publisher, Cornell University Press. Notes and Turkish words omitted; "Suleyman" changed to "Suleiman."

Before her marriage, Hurrem had to compete with other concubines for the sultan's support. Concubines gained access to the sultan by seniority in the harem, but Hurrem was impatient. Ambassador Bernardo Navagero of Venice reveals an incident in her struggle to be first among the concubines.

This sultan has two highly cherished women; one a Circassian, the mother of Mustafa the firstborn, the other, whom in violation of the custom of his ancestors he has married and considers as wife, a Russian, so loved by his majesty that there has never been in the Ottoman house a woman who enjoyed greater authority. It is said that she is agreeable and modest, and that she knows the nature of the sultan very well. The way in which she entered into the favor of the sultan I understand to have been the following. The Circassian, naturally proud and beautiful, and who already had a son, Mustafa, understood that [Hurrem] had pleased the sultan, wherefore she insulted her, and as she was doing so she scratched her all over her face and mussed up her clothing, saying, "Traitor, sold meat, you want to compete with me?" It happened that a few days later the sultan had this Russian summoned for his pleasure. She did not let this opportunity pass, and angrily told the eunuch agha who had come to fetch her that she was not worthy to come into the presence of the sultan because, being sold meat and with her face so spoiled and some of her hair pulled out, she recognized that she would offend the majesty of such a sultan by coming before him. These words were related to the sultan and induced in him an even greater desire to have her come to him, and he commanded again that she come. He wanted to understand why she would not come and why she sent him such a message. The woman related to him what had happened with Mustafa's mother, accompanying her words with tears and showing the sultan her face, which still bore the scratches, and how her hair had been pulled out. The angry sultan sent for the Circassian and asked her if what the other woman said was true. She responded that it was, that she had done less to her than she deserved. She believed that all women should yield to her and recognize her as mistress since she had been in the service of his majesty first. These words inflamed the sultan even more, for the reason that he no longer wanted her, and all his love was given to this other.

Quoted in *The Imperial Harem: Women and Sovereignty in the Ottoman Empire* by Leslie P. Peirce (New York: Oxford University Press, 1993), 59–60. Copyright © 1993 by Leslie P. Peirce. Used by permission of Oxford University Press. Notes omitted.

Hurrem's achievement in breaking the pattern of serial concubinage was remarkable. The first royal Ottoman concubine to be freed and married, she was also the first wife of a sultan in nearly a century. The marriage of Hurrem and Suleiman I so broke with custom that it aroused public antagonism, even charges that she must have bewitched the sultan with magic charms. Outlasting the furor, the marriage was based on affection, companionship, and respect. Suleiman I took no further wives and had no other children with concubines in the thirty-seven years from Hurrem's first pregnancy until her death. Known as Hurrem Sultan, she was a queen who exercised exceptional personal power.

Like all of the Ottoman royal concubines, Hurrem was neither of Turkish ancestry nor born a Muslim. Sometimes described as Russian, sometimes as Polish, sometimes as Ukrainian, Hurrem was born in Christian Central Europe, probably to ethnic Ruthenians of the Carpathian Mountains when they were ruled by Poland. This region lay just beyond the northern boundary of Turkish conquests in territory that must have been disrupted by years of invasion. Hurrem (known to Europeans as Roxelana) was reputedly captured by Tatar raiders in the town of Lvov. According to a Venetian ambassador, she was not beautiful when she captured Suleiman's heart. What intellectual and emotional qualities must such a young woman have had to survive capture, enslavement, sale, forced conversion to Islam, education in new languages, and competition in the harem? Concubines had no fathers, uncles, or brothers to promote their interests, nor mothers, aunts, or sisters to teach them. Ambitious slave women who rose to power in the Ottoman harem overcame personal adversity to create themselves as individuals whose achievement was their own. Such women could be as brutal as the sultans. Hurrem participated in a palace plot with her son-in-law, the grand vizier, that led to Suleiman's executing his eldest son, Mustafa, and leaving her own sons as the only heirs to the empire. How Hurrem could connive in the conspiracy is explained by Leslie Peirce.

The last support in the edifice of dynastic decentralization—the princely governorate—was dismantled by Suleiman's son and grandson. With the demise of their political role, princes became faceless individuals, strictly confined to the palace, where they were kept in a perpetual state of preadulthood, denied the right to marry or to father children by concubines. . . .

Women of considerable status and political influence now pursued their careers and promoted those of their sons in close proximity to one another. . . . Women began to fill the vital role of publicly demonstrating the dynasty's legitimacy and magnificence, a role left empty by the departure of princes from the stage of royal politics. Where once princes' weddings were ceremonial occasions, the marriages of princesses were now lavishly celebrated. The sultan's mother, featured in numerous royal progresses in the capital and in surrounding provinces, became the most celebrated public figure after her son. . . .

[Suleiman's] creation and exploitation of family-based networks [was] . . . a political strategy. This strategy was useful in building a personal base for the sultan's authority and creating a political force

to oppose increasingly entrenched interests, for example the Janis-
sary corps [slave army], that might resist the sovereign.

Despite their often considerable influence, women of the imperial
harem were inescapably confined to the palace. They left the royal
residence only under the tight surveillance of the black eunuch
guards of the harem. . . . It was essential that harem women develop
links with individuals or groups in the outside world. There was no
lack of parties eager to cooperate, for as the harem came to enjoy a
greater share of imperial authority, not only did its residents seek
outside channels through which they might accomplish their political
goals, but outsiders were anxious to form ties with potential patrons
within the palace.

Like the sultans during this period, harem women built much of
their networking on family-based relationships. It is crucial to recognize that the family was not limited to blood relationships but included the entire household, the vast majority of which, in the case of
the dynastic family, was composed of slaves. Like other Muslim
states before them, the Ottomans based their authority on a military
slave elite, which was recruited from outside the empire, converted
to Islam and carefully trained, and instilled with loyalty to the dynasty. From the second half of the fifteenth century on, this slave
elite came to dominate the ruling class, taking over administrative
positions from the native Turkish elite. . . . What has gone unnoticed
is the remarkable parallel between the growing influence of male and
female slaves in the ruling class: the dynasty began to rely exclusively on slave concubines for its reproduction at the same time that
the highest offices of the state began to be awarded to male slaves.
By the reign of Suleiman, . . . the only free Muslim women in the
imperial harem were the sultan's sisters, daughters, aunts, and
mother (originally a slave concubine, the latter, by virtue of having
borne a child to her master, was freed according to Islamic law upon
his death). Toward the end of the sixteenth century, the male
"harem" in the imperial palace—the third courtyard, where select
young slaves were trained for the offices that would eventually be
granted them—began slowly to be penetrated by native Muslims, but
the female harem appears to have maintained its exclusively slave
nature.

For the members of the dynastic family, the harem served as residence. For female slave members of the sultan's household, it might best be described as a training institution, where the education given to young women had as its goal not only the provision of concubines for the sultan but also the provision of wives for men near the top of military/administrative hierarchies. . . . Just as the third-courtyard school prepared men through personal service to the sultan within his palace or service to the dynasty outside the palace, the harem prepared women through personal service to the sultan and his mother to take up their roles in the outer world. Manumitted and frequently married to graduates of the palace school, these women, together with their husbands, would form households modeled on that of the palace. For both men and women, the palace system of training had as one of its fundamental goals the inculcation of loyalty to the ruling house. But because women as well as men sustained the ties that bound the empire's elite, the focus of the latter's loyalty was not only the sultan himself but the women of his family as well.

Within the imperial harem, the sultan's mother and favorite concubine or concubines were best positioned to build for themselves and/or for their sons factional support bridging the palace and the outer world. . . . It was a meritorious act for a Muslim, male or female, to educate and manumit a slave. The manumission of a slave also worked practically to the benefit of the former owner, who enjoyed the loyalty of the former slave in a clientage relationship. The seventeenth-century historian Mustafa Naima praised the generosity of the queen mother . . . who appears to have taken pains to cultivate close ties of patronage with her freed slaves:

> She would free her slave women after two or three years of service, and would arrange marriages with retired officers of the court or suitable persons from outside, giving the women dowries and jewels and several purses of money according to their talents and station, and ensuring that their husbands had suitable positions. She looked after these former slaves by giving them an annual stipend, and on the religious festivals and holy days she would give them purses of money.

Manumitted slaves might act as agents for their former mistresses, just as princess daughters, when married, could help their mothers, who remained within the imperial compound. Both princess daughters and manumitted slaves might be counted on to influence their husbands to act as advocates; for this reason, harem women strove to exert as much control as possible over the choice of husbands for their daughters or slaves. . . .

Probably the most important links with centers of power outside the palace were forged by harem women through the marriages of their daughters, the princesses of the dynasty, to leading statesmen. To become a royal son-in-law was a mark of high honor, conferred generally on the highest-ranking government officers or on promising younger officers. These weddings were lavishly celebrated state occasions, . . . to demonstrate imperial magnificence and munificence. . . .

The dynasty had always used the marriages of princesses for political ends; what stands out in this period is the frequency with which they occurred. By the seventeenth century, serial marriages of princesses were common. The most extreme example of this practice was two daughters of Kösem Sultan and Ahmed I, Ayshe and Fatma, who were married six and seven times respectively; Ayshe was approximately fifty and Fatma sixty-one at their final betrothals. Serial marriage was possible because princesses might first be married at the age of two or three; by the time a princess reached puberty she could be in her third or fourth marriage because her husbands encountered many risks in high office, including death in battle or execution.

Leslie P. Peirce, "Beyond Harem Walls: Ottoman Royal Women and the Exercise of Power," in *Gendered Domains: Rethinking Public and Private in Women's History,* edited by Dorothy O. Helly and Susan M. Reverby (Ithaca, NY: Cornell University Press, 1992), 47–53. Copyright © 1992 by Cornell University. Used by permission of the publisher, Cornell University Press. Notes and Turkish words omitted; "Suleyman" changed to "Suleiman."

Harem women undertook responsible roles in governing on the sultan's behalf. Hurrem, whose limited capacity to write in Turkish forced her to rely on scribes early in her marriage, became a fluent author and perceptive observer of Istanbul politics. Suleiman trusted her personal reports during his years of military campaigning and after her death relied on those of their daughter, Mihrimah. Royal women also corresponded with foreign courts.

Diplomatic contacts with Hurrem's native Poland were frequent during Suleiman's reign. Poland sent more embassies to the sultan—eighteen in all—than did any other power. Largely because of Hurrem's influence, Sigismund I, king of Poland, was able to maintain peace with the Ottomans. Hurrem enjoyed a private correspondence with his son, Sigismund II, who became king in 1548. Upon his accession she wrote personally to congratulate him. Later, responding to a letter from Sigismund, she wrote that she had transmitted to the sultan his assurances of friendship and that, in his pleasure over this news, Suleiman had responded, "the old king and I were like two brothers, and if it pleases God the Merciful, this king and I will be like son and father."

From *The Imperial Harem: Women and Sovereignty in the Ottoman Empire* by Leslie P. Peirce (New York: Oxford University Press, 1993), 221. Copyright © 1993 by Leslie P. Peirce. Used by permission of Oxford University Press, Inc. "Suleyman" changed to "Suleiman"; note omitted.

Queen mothers favored a familial tone—especially when writing mother-to-mother to European royalty, such as Catherine de Médicis, the French queen mother and regent for Henry III. Widespread recognition in Europe of the Christian origins of most Ottoman harem slaves enhanced royal women's status in writing to the Venetian Doge or Queen Elizabeth I of England. Elizabeth, who was hoping for the sultan's aid in fighting the Spanish Hapsburgs, was reassured by Safiye Sultan, mother of Mehmed III:

I have received your letter . . . God-willing, I will take action in accordance with what you have written. Be of good heart in this respect. I constantly admonish my son, the Padishah, to act according to the treaty. I do not neglect to speak to him in this manner. God-willing, may you not suffer grief in this respect. May you too always be firm in friendship. God-willing, may [our friendship] never die.

Quoted in *The Imperial Harem: Women and Sovereignty in the Ottoman Empire* by Leslie P. Peirce (New York: Oxford University Press, 1993), 228. Copyright © 1993 by Leslie P. Peirce. Used by permission of Oxford University Press, Inc.

2.2 Muslim Women's Rights in
Seventeenth-Century Turkish Courts

Women of the sultan's harem had respect, power, and wealth, but did the women outside the palace also enjoy these advantages? Scholarly research has begun to consider the majority of women of the vast Ottoman Empire. The diversity of their circumstances—as free or slave women; as Muslims, Christians, or Jews (each subject to the laws of their own religious authorities); as Albanians, Greeks, Turks, Syrians, Kurds, Armenians, or Egyptians; as peasants or urbanites—suggests the variety of feminine lives within this Middle Eastern state. Did their lives change as much as those of court women in the sixteenth and seventeenth centuries? How much did the wealth flowing into Ottoman lands profit women?

Documentary sources include the writings of Turkish Muslim leaders who both prescribed proper behavior and criticized women's neglect of their advice. Their sixteenth- and seventeenth-century censures are reminiscent of those Ibn al-Hajj directed at women of Cairo in the fourteenth century. Records of how the *shar'ia,* or Islamic law, was interpreted in Ottoman courts also reveal some of the situations of ordinary free women. Ronald Jennings examined court records from the Turkish city of Kayseri from 1600 to 1625. The cases pertained to problems of settlement of estates, guardianship of children, control of property, domestic abuse, marriage, and divorce. Women had easy access to the Kayseri court for protection of their rights, within the constraints of Islamic law, and won their suits as often as men did. Legally, women enjoyed the full use of their property, whether acquired before or after marriage. If a woman's property was sold without her consent, the court immediately returned it to her.

Çinar bint [daughter of] Bagadasar of Talas village sets forth a claim in the presence of Sefer veled [son of] Firoz: He struck me, pulled my hair saying, 'I'll make use of you,' and again struck me. I demand that he be punished according to the sharia. Sinan veled Kavan and Sunbul veled Yunus confirm that Sefer knocked Çinar to the ground, pulled her hair, and struck her, and they rescued her from him. . . .

Gul Ana bint Mehmed: Ali bn [son of] Sinan cut off the tail and ears of my horse and the tails of my two oxen. Confirmed by two witnesses. . . .

Gul Ana bint Ugurlu of Bektaş mahalle [village] sets forth a claim in the presence of Isa bn Mehmed: My husband Kutluşeh v. Iskender sold one of my vineyards without my permission. I want it. Kutluşeh admits having given Gul Ana the vineyard as *mehr* [dowry] and then having sold it unlawfully for 17 *guruş*. Mehmed asks that Kutluşeh and Gul Ana take oaths that she was not consulted in the sale, and they do. Then the vineyard is ordered restored to Gul Ana. . . .

Mehmed bn Yakub sets forth a claim in the presence of his mother Yasemin bint Abdullah: My mother has taken possession of a guesthouse (*tabhane*) at Debbaglar mahalle [village] that I inherited from my late father. Yasemin says Mehmed's father, her husband Yakub, sold her the *tabhane* for 3000 *akçe*, which was paid in full. Two witnesses confirm her.

Ronald C. Jennings, "Women in Early 17th Century Ottoman Judicial Records— The Sharia Court of Anatolian Kayseri," *Journal of the Economic and Social History of the Orient* 18 (1975): 62–63, 68. Note and some Turkish words omitted.

When an estate was settled, the shares of relatives were determined by rules of the *shar'ia*. The closer the relationship, the larger the share. In general, a female relative received one-half the share of a male who had the same degree of relationship to the deceased. Thus, a daughter's share would be one-half that of a son. The court was very careful to force relatives to give female relatives their share.

Guardianship of dependent children may have been given to the father's family in earlier legal practice, but in Kayseri, a mother usually served as the children's guardian if she survived her husband.

Melek, Sofya, and Sultan benat Kara Beg of Talas set forth a claim in the presence of . . . Haci Huseyn bn Mehmed: Haci Huseyn has in his possession two shares of the seven shares of a field, a garden, and two vineyards that we inherited from our late father. Haci Huseyn

claims he bought the fields from their brother Mihail five years earlier, but he has no witnesses and so is restrained. The property is
ordered to the sisters. . . .

When Tamam, the mother of Devlet, the orphan of the late (name
illegible) of Talas village, re-married, the right of raising the child
went to his mother's mother. . . .

Ronald C. Jennings, "Women in Early 17th Century Ottoman Judicial Records—
The Sharia Court of Anatolian Kayseri," *Journal of the Economic and Social History of the Orient* 18 (1975): 62, 74, 75. Note and some Turkish words omitted.

A Muslim woman was required to obey her husband and to
accept his marriage to other wives and/or his sexual relationships
with concubines in their household. But her husband was a man
of her own choice, for she could not be sold by her parents or
forced to marry against her will. In Turkish courts, an adult woman
was not required to have the consent of her father to marry—as
were women in much of Christian Europe in this period. Girls who
were still minors could be bound into a marriage by fathers or
guardians, but they remained in their parents' homes until of age,
without consummating the marriage; as an adult, the bride had the
right to decline to consummate such a marriage, and its annulment
left her free to marry another man. Disputes over parental attempts
to limit women's spousal choices often came before the court:

Nazili bint Murad: I did not give permission to be married to Bahşi v.
Kaplan. I have no witness. I will go marry Vartan. . . .

Haci Bola bint Huseyn, of age, . . . of Salurci Dere village . . . sets
forth a claim saying: On 28 I Cumadi 1034 my father Huseyn married me . . . to Spahi Mehmed Beg. When I heard this, I refused to
accept it. I want that marriage cancelled . . . and I want to marry this
Ibrahim Çelebi bn Keyvan. I did not give my consent to be married
to Mehmed. . . . [Evidence] is presented that if she is of age, her
father cannot marry her against her wishes. . . . The marriage is an-
nulled and permission is given for her to marry Ibrahim Çelebi. . . .

Halil bn Yakub: I gave my daughter Cemile in marriage to Abdul-
Gaffar bn Hasan. They did not live together.

Cemile: They said they had married me to Abdul-Gaffar. When he came, I screamed and when I tried to flee, he beat me and used force. We stayed together two months. This is denied by Abdul-Gaffar. My uncle was vekil [agent for contracting marriage] for me. Cemile says: I was married by force. . . .

[Later], Cemile bint Haci Halil: I have been Abdul-Gaffar bn Hasan's wife for five months. Two months ago I fled from him. . . .

Cemile bint Haci Halil was entrusted to Yusuf for safe keeping. When she would not go to Abdul-Gaffar of her own free will, it was recorded that two conditions were made: that she would not be taken away from here and that she would not be struck contrary to the sharia [because she had not obeyed her husband].

Ronald C. Jennings, "Women in Early 17th Century Ottoman Judicial Records— The Sharia Court of Anatolian Kayseri," *Journal of the Economic and Social History of the Orient* 18 (1975): 77, 78. Note and some Turkish words omitted.

Under Islamic law, the wife was at a disadvantage if she wanted a divorce, since only men could request a divorce. In practice, a dissatisfied wife might "buy" her divorce from her husband. Jennings explains:

Divorce, like marriage, was normally performed outside the court. . . . However, the special kind of divorce called *hul'* is a divorce granted by a husband at the request of his wife. Unlike conventional divorce which is unilateral on the part of the husband, *hul'* has an element of reciprocity and common participation on the part of the two partners. When a man consented to this kind of divorce, the woman usually agreed to give up her claim to her *mehr-i mueccel, 'iddet* [dowry] . . . in short she was required to make some kind of sacrifice (sometimes, in fact, only token, but other times very considerable) to deserve the favor she was being allowed. . . .

Should a man not agree to grant *hul'* to his wife, she still might flee to her father or a brother who would receive her. The woman or her family might make claims against the husband for beating her, for not supporting her, for deserting her. . . .

The *hul'* divorce offered her relief only if her husband consented. A woman might take her property and go live with her parents or other relatives, or even set up a household of her own and be assured that her husband would not be allowed to bother her, but divorce was something that only he could grant. . . .

Of course, the Koran [Quran] makes explicit that "Men are in charge of women, because God hath made the one of them to excel the other"; so good women are obedient. Wives may even be beaten, though only for rebelliousness, and after warnings and banishment to separate beds has failed (Koran 4:34). However, the court supported any woman who had been beaten contrary to the sharia or in an unlawful place. The wife must not be struck on the head or face, for example, and her husband must not beat her in rage.

Ronald C. Jennings, "Women in Early 17th Century Ottoman Judicial Records—The Sharia Court of Anatolian Kayseri," *Journal of the Economic and Social History of the Orient* 18 (1975): 82, 84, 87, 91. Note and some Turkish words omitted.

Suggested Further Readings

Much of the history of Middle Eastern women between 1500 and 1800 is unexplored. Nikki R. Keddie provides a succinct overview in "Introduction: Deciphering Middle Eastern Women's History," in Keddie and Beth Baron, eds., *Women in Middle Eastern History* (New Haven, CT: Yale University Press, 1991), 1–22. Leila Ahmed discusses the period in chapter 6, "Medieval Islam," of *Women and Gender in Islam: Roots of a Modern Debate* (New Haven, CT: Yale University Press, 1992), 102–24. Ahmed's book also touches upon the lives of Christian and Jewish women. Much of her evidence is drawn from Ottoman records. Other studies from that dynasty's domains include Ian C. Dengler, "Turkish Women in the Ottoman Empire: The Classical Age," in *Women in the Muslim World,* edited by Lois Beck and Nikki Keddie (Cambridge, MA: Harvard University Press, 1978), 229–44; Abraham Marcus, "Men, Women and Property: Dealers in Real Estate in Eighteenth-Century Aleppo, [Syria,]" *Journal of the Economic and Social History of the Orient* 26, part 2 (1983): 136–63; Mervat Hatem, "The Politics of Sexuality and Gender in Segregated Patriarchal Systems: The Case of Eighteenth- and Nineteenth-Century Egypt," *Feminist Studies* 12 (1986): 250–74;

Judith E. Tucker, "Marriage and Family in Nablus, [Palestine], 1720–1856: Towards a History of Arab Muslim Marriage," *Journal of Family History* 13 (1988): 165–79; and "Ties That Bound: Women and Family in Eighteenth- and Nineteenth-Century Nablus," in Keddie and Baron, *Women in Middle Eastern History*, 233–53. Some reasons for the dearth of modern scholarship about Persian women of the Safavid dynasty are offered by Hammed Shahidian in "Islam, Politics, and the Problems of Writing Women's History in Iran," *Journal of Women's History* 7 (summer 1995): 113–44.

–3–

INDIA
Women of the Mughal Empire

Princess Nur Jahan and attendants.
(India, Mughal School, eighteenth century. The Metropolitan Museum of Art.)

Central Asian Turkic invaders established Islam permanently in North India in the thirteenth century. Babur's invasion from Afghanistan in 1525–26 launched a new Muslim dynasty, known as the Mughals. When Babur's descendants defeated the Hindu rulers of southern kingdoms, Islam penetrated far across the subcontinent. The Mughal Empire's legendary wealth derived from rule of much of contemporary Afghanistan, Pakistan, Bangladesh, and India from the midsixteenth until the early eighteenth century. Islam under this powerful state became India's second religion, dominant at the court and influential in law and culture. India's supreme architectural glory, the Taj Mahal, was built by Shah Jahan in the seventeenth century as a shrine at his wife's tomb.

What did Mughal rule mean for women? In the north, in Punjab and Bengal, Islamic beliefs and law penetrated into agricultural villages both through conversion of peasants and through Mughal land grants that allowed Muslims to clear forests and construct irrigation systems, thus extending farming as their new villages intruded on new frontiers. Rural villagers further south remained overwhelmingly Hindu, with daily lives more influenced by caste rules than Mughal decrees. Regardless of religion, customs of female seclusion influenced elites, so that its Indian form, *purdah,* expanded among higher-caste Hindus as well as Muslims. For the nonelite majority of Hindu and tribal women, slavery was a graver threat than *purdah.*

Indian slavery expanded after 1500 beyond the debt bondage and rural serfdom common among Hindus. Islamic law permitted enslavement of non-Muslims as a means of bringing them into the community of believers. Mughal administrations raided forest tribal peoples for slaves, took thousands of prisoners as they invaded the south, and subjected those who defaulted on taxes to slavery. Revenues were often remitted to Agra or Delhi across long distances in the form of slaves to be auctioned in the capital or Gujurat. Men were sought for the army as well as for labor; women were sought for agricultural labor, domestic work, and concubinage. Whereas Hindu debt bondage had reduced whole families or their children into a serfdom that could become permanent slavery, they served local elites in their home villages. Under the Mughals, individuals were sold by desperate families or seized as prisoners to be auctioned alone in distant realms. Famines that were endemic to Mughal civil strife of the seventeenth century meant that large numbers of Indian women entered slavery and lost what protection their families had given them. Among poor Hindus, however, families had offered women little protection for centuries.

3.1 Hindu Bhakti Poets

When women's voices speak through poetry, some tell of hard struggles to survive by their own poorly paid labor. Widows who had no property rights except their dowry of jewelry and saris, abandoned wives and mothers, daughters whose families could provide no dowry were paid little by those who perceived them only as necessary and cheaper workers. Their gender exploitation was characteristic of their culture's caste system.

Hindu India by 1500 was hierarchically ranked in castes, boundaries between groups of families that were justified by both religious belief and custom. Society had four categories, called varnas, or castes: priests and teachers (brahmins); warriors and administrators; merchants, artisans, and farmers; sharecroppers and farm laborers (sudras). The three higher castes owned most of the land, were privileged in religion, and demanded services from the sudras. Each caste was subdivided into many occupational subcastes (*jati*), whose members remained permanently in the subcaste of their parents, practiced endogamous marriage within that group, and avoided eating with outsiders. Below the castes were people whose work and status made their very "touch" dangerous to the spiritual purity of those higher in rank. Midwives, who handled women's polluting blood and afterbirth (which, like all human emissions and materials involved in human or animal deaths, contaminated the person touching them), were among the lowest of the "untouchables." Women's status was entwined in the strictures of caste indirectly. Productive labor was not expected from women of the two highest castes, who were economic dependents of their husbands, but the highest standards of respectability were demanded of them. Women of the two lower varnas, as well as untouchable women, worked in the fields or the family trade. Though these women might assist male family members in their *jati*'s occupation, the trade was identified by the work of the men. In all castes, however, women's responsibilities within the household allotted them tasks crucial to familial ritual purity: drawing water; cooking; caring for infants, children, and the sick. Violation of complex ritual prohibitions governing a woman's domestic duties could cause her to become an outcaste, but her downfall would more likely be the result of events beyond her control: death or bankruptcy of her husband, rape, or conquest of her village.

Just as Buddhism had evolved earlier as an escape from caste obligations, so in the medieval years the mystic spiritualism of the bhakti movement offered an alternative religious experience to Hindu women. Women and men, mostly from the lower castes, who joined the bhakti movement became casteless. Susie Tharu and K. Lalita describe how the bhakti movement empowered women:

With the eighth-century Tamil poet Karraikal Ammaiyar . . . begins a long line of women poet-saints in the medieval bhakti movements. The word *bhakti* means "devotion," and these powerful religious upheavals, which mocked pedantry, rejected ascetic withdrawal, and emphasized the intense, mystic experience of personal devotion, emerged, century after century, first in different regions of southern India . . . in recurring phases from the twelfth to the seventeenth centuries. Later, in the fifteenth and sixteenth centuries, the movement spread north. . . .

The movements arose in different parts of the country apparently independently, and developed various idioms, but they also had several things in common. In each place these artisan groups led what has been called a people's revolt against the domination of the upper castes and the lifeless ritual of vedic Hinduism practiced by the brahmin priests. Washerpeople, leather workers, oil pressers, stonecutters, potters, weavers, silversmiths, artisans, and small tradespeople of all kinds swelled the movements' ranks. And, what is perhaps most significant from our point of view, the path of devotion set up no barriers of caste or sex. The women poets of the bhakti movements did not have to seek the institutionalized spaces religion provided to express themselves, and women's poetry moved from the court and the temple to the open spaces of the field, the workplace, and the common woman's hearth.

The bhakti poets composed in the regional languages, deliberately breaking the literary and religious hold of Sanskrit. They addressed their popular lyrics to the people in the languages the people spoke and could understand. . . .

The devotees, or *bhaktas,* set their poetry in familiar contexts and found their imagery in the everyday lives of working people. As a result, scholars have also argued, they drew their symbolism primarily from nonvedic sources. Their verses cultivate a rough-hewn directness. The devotee cajoles, chides, woos, rages against God, who is a personally chosen husband/lover to the bhakta imaged as wife/lover, and the mystic union is often imagined in sexual terms. In fact status, masculinity, scholarship are seen as *obstacles* to bhakti. Though their poetry often circulated for one or two centuries before it was recorded, the lyrics are easily attributed to individual poets because embedded in the text is the composer's *ankita,* or signature, which is usually the form in which she addresses her lord. Akkamahadevi, for instance, uses the ankita Chennamallikarjuna, which literally means Mallika's beautiful Arjurna. . . .

A surprising number of the bhakti poets were women. Many of them were people who chafed at the strictures of the household and the family. . . . The movement held for them the promise of other things. Biographies of the bhakti saints usually begin with the break—from the family and community—and chart the wanderings of the poet-saints. Yet there is evidence that women had to struggle to find acceptance even within these movements.

Reprinted, by permission, from Susie Tharu and K. Lalita, *Women Writing in India: Volume 1: 600 B.C. to the Early Twentieth Century,* edited by Susie Tharu and K. Lalita (New York: The Feminist Press at The City University of New York, 1991), 56–58. Copyright 1991 by Susie Tharu and K. Lalita.

In Akkamahadevi's twelfth-century poem, she directly addresses Shiva using her ankita, Chennamallikarjuna, whom she imaged as her lover:

Don't despise me as
She who has no one
I'm not one to be afraid,
Whatever you do.
I exist chewing dry leaves,
My life resting on a knife edge
If you must torment me,
Chennamallikarjuna,

My life, my body
I'll offer you, and be cleansed.

Reprinted, by permission, from Akkamahadevi, "Don't Despise Me," translated by Susan Daniel, in *Women Writing in India: Volume 1: 600 B.C. to the Early Twentieth Century*, edited by Susie Tharu and K. Lalita (New York: The Feminist Press at The City University of New York, 1991), 59. Copyright 1991 by Susie Tharu and K. Lalita.

The events reported in Rami's poem about her love for the poet Chandidas (ca. 1440) probably actually happened. A washerwoman, Rami, and a brahmin, Chandidas, could not publicly proclaim their cross-caste love without violating Hindu beliefs. Susie Tharu and K. Lalita describe the tragic circumstances that inspired Rami's poem:

Ramoni, or Rami, was born of low-caste washerfolk. . . . She wandered, destitute, from place to place until she reached Nanur. . . . There Rami found work cleaning the Bashuli Devi temple where the well-known Bengali bhakti poet Chandidas also lived. She worked hard and through her devotion won the respect of the entire village. Soon Rami began composing verses in praise of the deity. . . .

It was not long before the friendship between Rami and Chandidas grew into an intimacy that was noticed and disapproved of by the village. Overtly the complaint was that Chandidas was a brahmin and she of low caste. A relationship between them was improper. . . . Chandidas was exiled from the village and boycotted by his community. Rami lost her job at the temple. . . . [They wandered together.]

The Nawab of Gaur, an important nobleman, invited Chandidas to sing at his palace. His wife, the Begum, was so charmed by Chandidas's poetry that she fell in love with him. Worse still, she made no secret of her feelings. . . . The Nawab was infuriated. He ordered that Chandidas be tortured and put to death even as the Begum watched. Chandidas was tied to the back of an elephant and beaten to death. All through his extended torture, Chandidas kept his gaze fixed on Rami, who was there too. . . .

Reprinted, by permission, from Susie Tharu and K. Lalita, *Women Writing in India: Volume I: 600 B.C. to the Early Twentieth Century*, edited by Susie Tharu and K.

Lalita (New York: The Feminist Press at The City University of New York, 1991),
84–85. Copyright 1991 by Susie Tharu and K. Lalita.

Where have you gone,
my Chandidas, my friend,
Birds thirst without water,
despair without rain.
What have you done,
O heartless lord of Gaur?
Not knowing what it means to love,
you slay my cherished one.
Lord of my heart, my Chandidas,
why did you break
The vows you made
and sing in court?
Now evil men and beasts come swarming round;
heavens turns to hell.
Betrayed by you, I stand in shame;
you've crushed my honor in your hands.
Once, heedless, untouched by Vasuli's threats,
you told the court with pride
You'd leave a brahmin home, you said,
to love a washergirl.
Now, lashed to an elephant's back,
you reach me with your eyes.
Why should the jealous king heed
a washerwoman's cries?
Soul of my soul, how cruelly on your fainting limbs
the heavy whip strikes and falls,
Cleave through my heart, and let me die
with Chandidas, my love.

And then the queen fell on her knees,
"Please stop, my lord," she cried,
"His singing pierced me to the heart.
No more of this, I plead.
Why must you thus destroy
limbs made for love alone?

Free him, I beg of you, my lord,
don't make love your toy.
O godless king, how could you know
what love can mean?"
So spoke the queen, and then, her heart
still fixed on Chandidas, she died.
Rami trembled, hearing her,
and hastened to the place.
She threw herself at those queenly feet
and wept the tears of death.

Reprinted, by permission, from Rami, "Where Have You Gone," translated by Malini Bhattacharya, in *Women Writing in India: Volume I: 600 B.C. to the Early Twentieth Century*, edited by Susie Tharu and K. Lalita (New York: The Feminist Press at The City University of New York, 1991), 85–86. Copyright 1991 by Susie Tharu and K. Lalita.

Many women, like the medieval poet Ratanbai, brought income into the family with their spinning wheels:

My spinning wheel is dear to me, my sister;
My household depends on it.
My husband married me and departed;
He went abroad to earn a living.

After twelve years he returned,
With a copper coin and a half;
He went to bathe in the Ganga,
Dropped the copper coin and a half.

Mother, father, father-in-law, mother-in-law,
One and all rejected us;
The spinning wheel was our savior,
To it we clung.

I paid off all my husband's debts
And over and above
Tying coin after coin in the corner of my sari
I earned a whole rupee.

Reprinted, by permission, from Ratanbai, "My Spinning Wheel Is Dear to Me, My Sister," translated by Nita Ramaiya, in *Women Writing in India: Volume I: 600 B.C.*

to the Early Twentieth Century, edited by Susie Tharu and K. Lalita (New York: The Feminist Press at The City University of New York, 1991), 89–90. Copyright 1991 by Susie Tharu and K. Lalita.

By 1500, the bhakti movements were changing. The poet–saints did not try to reform the caste system or criticize the brahmins. They emphasized their personal devotion to their god. The poet Mirabai (ca. 1498–1565) is an example of this change. Her life and her poetry are still popular in India; indeed, at least ten films have been made depicting her life, and her songs have been made into very influential recordings of Indian religious music. Susie Tharu and K. Lalita explain why her life and her poetry have such wide appeal:

Mirabai belonged to a leading Rajput clan and was married into another powerful royal family. In one poem she speaks about a childhood vision of Krishna, which made such an impact on her that she declared herself his bride and dedicated her life wholly to him. Though she consented to marriage with the crown prince of Mewar, it was a marriage in name only. In her heart she was wedded to Giridhar Naagar [Krishna]. . . .

Central to the accounts of Mirabai's life are the struggles with her husband and his family. Her sisters-in-law, for instance, try to stop her from seeking the company, so improper for a highborn woman, of wandering saints and mendicants. In the most popular legends concerning her, her husband, the Rana, makes two attempts to kill her, but she is miraculously saved both times. . . . It would appear that Mira spent most of her adult life in worship and devotion and in the company of holy men. She soon left Mewar and traveled east to places of pilgrimage associated with the life of Krishna. . . .

Feminist scholars like Neera Desai have pointed to the contradiction between Mira's rebellious life and her poetry, which seems to affirm a woman's traditional place in the family. Her religious imagery, Desai argues, is drawn from the household and all the duties of a wife are celebrated, down to their minutest detail. As lover, Mira images herself as the dasi (or slave) of Giridhar. Unlike other bhaktas, or devotees, she never seems to question the authority of the brahmin, the hierarchies of caste, and the degeneracy of ritual. . . .

[However,] the intensity of Mira's devotion and her courage in resisting every pressure to deviate from her chosen way of life can be a source of strength to women who regard her as an intimate and personal support in their suffering and pain. . . .

Reprinted, by permission, from Susie Tharu and K. Lalita, *Women Writing in India: Volume I: 600 B.C. to the Early Twentieth Century,* edited by Susie Tharu and K. Lalita (New York: The Feminist Press at The City University of New York, 1991), 90–91. Copyright 1991 by Susie Tharu and K. Lalita.

I am true to my Lord.
O my companions, there is nothing to be ashamed of now
Since I have been seen dancing openly.

In the day I have no hunger
At night I am restless and cannot sleep.
Leaving these troubles behind, I go to the other side;
A hidden knowledge has taken hold of me.

My relations surround me like bees.
But Mira is the servant of her beloved Giridhar,
And she cares nothing that people mock her.

Reprinted, by permission, from Mirabai, "I Am True to My Lord," translated by F.E. Keay, in *Women Writing in India: Volume I: 600 B.C. to the Early Twentieth Century,* edited by Susie Tharu and K. Lalita (New York: The Feminist Press at The City University of New York, 1991), 93. Copyright 1991 by Susie Tharu and K. Lalita.

3.2 Family Production of Cotton Cloth

Ratanbai at her spinning wheel speaks proudly of earning her family's bread. India's women hand spinners could also have bragged of their part in creating a textile industry that for a time, before industrialization, seemed to clothe the world. By the sixteenth century, women as spinners and handloom weavers helped to make the cotton cloth that was a commodity important in both India's and the international economy, as S.M. Ikram details:

The manufacture of cotton goods had assumed such extensive proportions that in addition to satisfying her own needs India sent cloth to almost half the world: the east coast of Africa, Arabia, Egypt, Southeast Asia, as well as Europe. The textile industry, well established in Akbar's [Mughal emperor, 1556–1605] day, continued to flourish under his successors, and soon the operations of Dutch and English traders brought India into direct touch with Western markets. This resulted in great demand for Indian cotton goods from Europe, which naturally increased production at home.

S.M. Ikram, *Muslim Civilization in India,* edited by Anslie T. Embree (New York: Columbia University Press, 1964), 224.

Manufacture of cotton cloth in India did not occur in the large, multistoried brick factories that would typify eighteenth- and nineteenth-century European industrialization. Indian male and female weavers worked at home, with the participation of the whole family. Everyone worked when needed as they also did the exhausting daily housework. The family carried out all the steps of production, from separating the seeds from the cotton blossoms to painting designs on the finished textile. All members of the family were in a weaving subcaste, which meant that they ordinarily did no other type of work, except occasional day labor on neighboring farms. Fortunate families owned their looms; less privileged were those who wove on looms owned by the village, by master weavers, or by merchants.

India's weavers produced an incredible variety of cotton textiles. Irfan Habib describes what was available by the middle of the eighteenth century:

The bewildering variety of cotton fabrics mentioned in the contemporary sources—150 names occur in the first ten years of the English . . . [export] records—can be divided into a number of overlapping categories. . . . They were produced as piece-goods or ready-made clothing (which involved a little tailoring); calico, a stout cloth, or muslin (which was thinner); plain (i.e., unbleached), bleached and dyed or patterned, the patterns being produced on the loom with coloured yarns [ikat] but more commonly printed with a wooden block or painted with a pen or stile. Quality was judged by the fineness of the yarn and the number of threads per inch and, in the case of the patterned varieties by the less palpable criteria of artistic excellence. . . .

Besides fabric and items of dress, the range of cotton textile products included the Coromandel sailcloth, cotton carpets, bed-covers, pillow cases, handkerchiefs, mattresses from Sind, embroidered quilts from Bengal, bed-hangings, tents, etc. The last was a very important item used extensively by royalty and the nobility for residential purposes and during campaigns.

Irfan Habib, "Mughal India," *The Cambridge Economic History of India*, vol. I: ca. 1200–1750, edited by Tapan Raychaudhuri and Irfan Habib (New York: Cambridge University Press, 1982), 269–70.

Indian weavers were also famous for their woolens, such as cashmere, and for their silks. Every village in India was basically self-sufficient in providing its own necessities, including cloth. Women of any caste could spin thread for their own use or for sale to weavers. Many must have done so, because spinning is far more labor-intensive and time-consuming than weaving. Members of the weaving subcaste provided everyone in their village with the relatively simple cloth that was easily turned into everyday clothing. In return, the family received a portion of the food that the village farmers produced. Weavers also paid rent to landowners or merchants and taxes in cloth yardage. Any surplus cloth could be sold and that income kept by the weaving family. By the seventeenth century, numerous weaving families had settled in or near cities where a large demand existed for fine cotton, wool, and silk cloth for the Mughal court, for temples, and for export. Even when European merchants assumed control of textile production and export in the later eighteenth century, the skilled work of Indian men, women, and children continued primarily in home production units.

3.3 The Mughal Empress Nur Jahan

Mughal royal women were the key figures in what Leslie P. Peirce, in reference to the Turkish Ottomans, has designated the "politics of procreation." She meant that they gave birth and then educated and directed potential heirs in the competition among the princes to succeed their father. Hence, royal women had a large responsibility for the successful transfer of the family patrimony from an older generation to the younger one. Nur Jahan

(1577–1645), wife of the Mughal Emperor Jahangir (1569–1627), practiced the politics of procreation for fifteen years during her husband's lifetime, thereby earning the admiration of contemporaries and subsequent writers for her political abilities, even as they frequently reproached her husband for allowing a woman so much power.

Succession of a Mughal ruler was, at the beginning of the empire, decided by a war between the emperor–father and a son. As Muslims, the polygamous Mughal emperors had both wives and concubines, all of whose sons were eligible to become emperor. Jahangir led a revolt against his father, Akbar, from 1601 to 1604. When he was defeated, his father forgave Jahangir rather than executing him. The following year, Jahangir became emperor when Akbar died. Almost immediately, his oldest son, Khusrau, revolted against him. When Khusrau failed, Jahangir imprisoned him until his death in 1622. Jahangir's most likely successor was his son Khurram, whose title was Shah Jahan.

Usually, in these struggles, the princes' mothers were important advisers. Occasionally, an underage prince was made ruler; then his mother could be regent until he reached his majority. By the time of his marriage to Nur Jahan in 1611, Jahangir, who was 41, was addicted to opium and alcohol. The combination of his own addictions and his adult sons' ambitions suggested to contemporaries that his reign would be brief. Acutely aware of the danger, Jahangir had already prepared a plan: Nur Jahan would rule on his behalf. Nur Jahan was a thirty-three-year-old widow who had already demonstrated her talent for government. Since he trusted her, Jahangir gradually turned over decision-making powers to her. In effect, she was regent for Jahangir! But unlike most women regents, Nur Jahan was not preserving the succession for her own son. Her plan was to administer the government through a four-person junta that included the heir apparent, Shah Jahan. This meant that he was training to govern under her continual observation.

Nur Jahan could not have exercised the authority she did without a structure that funneled power naturally and immediately to her. The "junta," or the "faction" as Roe [a contemporary English observer] called it, was a skillful outgrowth of the needs and circumstances of the time, comprising at its height Nur Jahan; her father, Itimaduddaula; her brother, Asaf Khan; and her stepson and the eventual heir to the throne as Shah Jahan, Khurram. The power of the junta was substantial and could be carried, as it often was, to extreme excess. "They still strive for an impossible advancement," said Pelsaert [a contemporary observer], "for the world cannot sustain their eminence." Nevertheless, the group managed, by an intricate network of communication and vested interest, to promote their own concerns while at the same time protecting the king from unnecessary responsibility. The junta worked as follows:

> If anyone with a request to make at Court obtains an audience or is allowed to speak, the King hears him indeed, but will give no definite answer of Yes or No, referring him promptly to Asaf Khan, who in the same way will dispose of no important matter without communicating with his sister, the Queen, and who regulates his attitude in such a way that the authority of neither of them may be diminished. Anyone then who obtains a favour must thank them for it, and not the King.

The specific configuration of the junta was, then, extremely important. The group could not have worked without a strategically placed son around whom courtiers could vie for attention, and in whom the hopes for a brilliant succession could be invested. Thus, while the function of the junta was to provide benefits to its members in the present, its rationale was to give caretaker governance to the current emperor in preparation for a glorious succession in years hence. The choice of sons, therefore, was especially significant. Although no real power struggle ever actually took place among them, as Khurram, who had been much loved by Akbar and was his choice to succeed Jahangir, had been the heir apparent in all but name for years, the appearance of a struggle and the constant jealousies were intense.

From *Nur Jahan: Empress of Mughal India* by Ellison Banks Findly (New York: Oxford University Press, 1993), 48. Copyright © 1993 by Oxford University Press, Inc. Used by permission of Oxford University Press, Inc. Notes omitted.

In 1622, Nur Jahan's father, Itimaduddaula, died, and the junta slowly disintegrated. Nur Jahan then became emperor in all but title.

Nur Jahan's growing powers were applied uniformly to benefit an empire that was to experience peace and exceptional prosperity during her reign. Dow [a contemporary English observer] . . . has captured the remarkable nature of what she did:

> Her abilities were uncommon; for she rendered herself absolute, in a government in which women are thought incapable of bearing any part. Their power, it is true, is sometimes exerted in the haram; but, like the virtues of the magnet, it is silent and unperceived. Noor-Jehan stood forth in public; she broke through all restraint and custom, and acquired power by her own address, more than by the weakness of Jehangire.

The channels of authority she had to hand were almost endless. Nur Jahan approved all orders (*farmans*) and grants of appointment that went out under the king's name, ordering her own name, "Nur Jahan, the Queen Begam," to be jointly attached to the imperial signature. She controlled all promotions and demotions that issued from the royal government.

> Her former and present supporters have been well rewarded, so that now most of the men who are near the King owe their promotion to her, and are consequently under . . . obligations to her. . . . Many misunderstandings result, for the King's orders or grants of appointments, etc., are not certainties, being of no value until they have been approved by the Queen.

She put her seal on all grants of land "conferred upon any woman," and took special interest in orphan girls, promoting many of them through generous dowries in marriage. She habitually sat at the balcony of her palace (*jharoka*) receiving petitions from nobles and was a lenient and sympathetic judge to those who sought protection under her. She had coins struck in her name, which bore the twelve signs of the zodiac. She collected duties on goods from merchants who passed through her lands near Sikandra from the eastern provinces and traded with Europeans who brought luxury goods from the continent. She assessed and approved the credentials of all visitors who came to court. She engaged in international diplomacy with high-placed women of other countries. And she routinely erected expensive buildings—rest houses for travelers (*sarais*), gardens, palaces, and tombs—"intending thereby [said Pelsaert] to establish an enduring reputation for herself."

Nur Jahan was careful to encourage the paraphernalia of power around her as well. Dow notes that she was distinguished from the other wives by the title of Shahi or "empress," deriving undoubtedly from the title Shah Begam, given to her either, according to Prasad, in 1613 after the death of the reigning Shah Begam, Salima Sultan Begam, or, according to C. Pant, in 1622. She enjoyed the display of public fanfare and affection for her and did nothing to discourage the easily manipulated popular mythologies; "Nur Jahan Begam used to ride out, with people playing and singing before her, [and] she was received by every one with marks of excessive honour and reverence, even like a goddess." Finally, she gathered wealth to her as a natural perquisite of her position, spending it lavishly on herself and her family, but using it as well to lubricate the gears of the empire.

In the end, her powers grew so vast that she acquired all the rights of sovereignty and government normally due the emperor. She managed "the whole affairs of the realm, and honours of every description were at her disposal," such that she was absolute monarch in all but one thing—that of having the *khutba* read in her name. The *khutba* was an announcement of sovereignty made before the Friday noon prayers in the mosque and after those of the *id,* and its reading would have made her absolute ruler in name as well; it would also have required absolute obedience to her from all subjects. Here, however, its absence was only a religious and political formality as she already wielded all the power there was. Jahangir, still the hereditary holder of the throne, prided himself on having successfully passed over to her not only all the responsibilities of maintaining the empire, but most of its privileges as well, for he was known to brag that having bestowed sovereignty on Nur Jahan, he required nothing else but a *sir* of wine and half a *sir* of meat.

From *Nur Jahan: Empress of Mughal India* by Ellison Banks Findly (New York: Oxford University Press, 1993), 46–47. Copyright © 1993 by Oxford University Press, Inc. Used by permission of Oxford University Press, Inc. Notes omitted.

The traditional view that Muslim women, secluded in a harem (*zenana*), had no contact with the outside world is misleading.

Nur Jahan always wore a veil or sat behind a screen when non-related males were present. Although women could not be seen without a veil, they could accumulate wealth and invest it. Women of the royal harem, such as Nur Jahan and Maryamuzzamani, Emperor Jahangir's mother, were wealthy businesswomen. They received a monthly salary. Akbar had paid women of rank Rs 1,028–1,610 per month, when servants' salaries were Rs 20–50 per month or less. During the reigns of his successors, the amounts paid to royal women increased:

Women of rank seemed to have acquired more control over their wealth as the Mughal period progressed. Not only did they probably have more wealth to begin with—Jahangir, for example, "increased the allowances of all the veiled ladies of my father's harem from 20 percent to 100 percent . . ." upon his accession in 1605—but they had more of their own officers to administer it. Manucci [a contemporary observer] noted that during Shah Jahan's reign each lady of rank had a *nazir* [a eunuch superintendent], who was responsible for looking after her property, land, and income. Nur Jahan had her own *vakils*, who supervised her *jagirs* [revenue-producing landed property] and the construction of buildings on various of her properties, and the emperor's mother, Maryamuzzamani, had numerous agents in and out of the harem appointed to help her oversee her trading activities and to advise her on investments.

From *Nur Jahan: Empress of Mughal India* by Ellison Banks Findly (New York: Oxford University Press, 1993), 96. Copyright © by Oxford University Press, Inc. Used by permission of Oxford University Press. Notes omitted.

Some indication of Maryamuzzamani's wealth can be inferred from the *Rahimi* incident. The *Rahimi* was a large ship that carried goods and pilgrims to Mecca, a voyage for which the Portuguese required the purchase of a pass:

In September of 1613, an exceptionally large and well-known pilgrimage ship called the *Rahimi* belonging to Jahangir's mother, Maryamuzzamani, was captured by the Portuguese at Surat [India] and taken with all her goods and all seven hundred people on board down to Goa [a Portuguese port on the Indian coast]:

The shippe, which arrived at the barre of Suratt the 13th of September, 1613 ... was taken by the Portungales armado of friggotts, notwithstandinge theire passe which they had of the Portungales. This shippe was verye richlye laden, beeinge worth a hundred thowsand pounde; yet not contented with the shippe and goods, but tooke allsoe 700 persons of all sorts with them to Goa. . . .

Jahangir's reaction was one of outrage: "takinge yt soe haynosly that they should doe such a thinge" in blatant disregard of their own rules and, perhaps worse, against the ship of his own mother. . . .

The Portuguese offered to return the *Rahimi* if the Mughal king would "deliver the English that were here into their hands," but Jahangir refused. Thereafter "the wars betwixt the Portingals and the Indians" continued for several years stopping virtually all Portuguese trade in the area; "the Great Mogul's mother was a great adventurer, which caused the Great Mogul to drive the Portingals out of this place."

From *Nur Jahan: Empress of Mughal India* by Ellison Banks Findly (New York: Oxford University Press, 1993), 130–31. Copyright © 1993 by Oxford University Press, Inc. Used by permission of Oxford University Press, Inc. Notes omitted.

Usually, Nur Jahan stayed in the background, manipulating the actions of others. One unusual exception took her into battle. It happened during a short-lived revolt by Mahabat Khan, who had been a boyhood friend of Jahangir. He was a trusted minister and had carried out many assignments for the monarch. But in the summer of 1626, he revolted and captured Jahangir. Nur Jahan helped organize an army to rescue her husband, entering the battle herself mounted on an elephant. When a companion on her elephant was wounded, Nur Jahan emptied four quivers of arrows—she was a famous marksman—into the enemy. The rescue failed, however, and she was also captured. After about three months, Jahangir and Nur Jahan managed to regain control of the government. She never again took such a public role.

Nur Jahan's political power was not so unusual as her critics sometimes suggested. In the thirteenth century, a Turkic Muslim woman, Razia, claimed succession to her father as sultan of Delhi. Razia retained the sultan's title only from 1236 to 1240 before dying while fighting rebellious noblemen. But a contemporary historian appraised her as "a great monarch. She was wise, just and generous, a benefactor to her kingdom, a dispenser of justice, the protector of her subjects and the leader of her armies, she was endowed with all the qualities befitting a king but she was not born of the right sex and so in the estimation of men all these virtues were worthless."[*]

Centuries later, Emperor Babur's daughter, Gulbadan, was an educated and perceptive observer of the Mughal court, a scholar who wrote an official history of the reign of Babur's son, Humayan. Her account offers an insider's understanding of sixteenth-century politics, both within and outside of the harem. Recent studies of South India have also revealed Hindu women rulers of four thirteenth-century medieval kingdoms, as well as a reigning queen of Madurai between 1689 and 1704. Nur Jahan's near contemporaries in noble Rajput zenanas did not achieve formal public office, although many of them played procreation politics, too, as zealously as any of the royal women of the Mughal dynasty.

Suggested Further Readings

Uma Chakravarti and Kum Kum Roy explain how manipulation of women's history in India for political purposes by both the British colonial rulers and their Indian nationalist opponents trivialized perceptions of women who had wielded political power in "Breaking Out of Invisibility: Rewriting the History of Women in Ancient India," in *Retrieving Women's History: Changing Perceptions of the Role of Women in Politics and Society*, edited by S. Jay Kleinberg (New York: Berg Publishers, 1988). Also see essays in Kumkum Sangari and Sudesh Vaid, eds., *Recasting Women: Essays in Indian Colonial History* (New Brunswick, NJ: Rutgers University Press, 1990). Rumer Godden's *Gulbadan: Portrait of a Rose Princess at the Mughal Court* (New York: Viking Press, 1981) is a romantic biography by a novelist. See Gulbadan Begam, *The History of Humayun or Humayun-nama,* translated

---

[*]Minhaj-us-Siraj, *Fabaqat-i-Nasiri* (trans. Elliot and Dawson), in *The History of India As Told by Its Own Historians* (Cambridge, 1931), 332, cited by Uma Chakravarti and Kum Kum Roy, in "Breaking Out of Invisibility: Rewriting the History of Women in Ancient India," in *Retrieving Women's History: Changing Perceptions of the Role of Women in Politics and Society,* edited by S. Jay Kleinberg (New York: Berg Publishers, 1988), 324.

by Annette S. Beveridge (London: Royal Asiatic Society, 1902), for the text of the rare narrative written by a princess of the Mughal court. In Rekha Misra's *Women in Mughal India (1526–1748)* (New Delhi: Munshiram Manoharlal, 1967), the lives of Nur Jahan's predecessors and successors are evaluated. The active political roles of Hindu Rajput women, both before and after the Mughal annexation of Rajasthan, are explored by Varsha Joshi in *Polygamy and Purdah: Women and Society among Rajputs* (Jaipur: Rawat Publications, 1995). This study of the warrior Rajput society from 1200 to 1800, based on local archival sources, provides a broad context for Nur Jahan's assumption of power as well as discussion of the nobility's complex marriage practices, including sati. Mirabai's devotional poems are collected in A.J. Alston, trans., *The Devotional Poems of Mirabai* (Delhi: Motilal Banarsidass, 1980). Richard Maxwell Eaton's *Sufis of Bijapur, 1300–1700: Social Roles of Sufis in Medieval Islam* (Princeton, NJ: Princeton University Press, 1978) describes women mystics of this Islamic religious movement.

–4–
EUROPE
Witches, Workers, and Queens

Dutch women working in a seventeenth-century kitchen. (Hendrick Martensz Sorgh. The Metropolitan Museum of Art. Marquand Collection, Gift of Henry G. Marquand.)

In the period from the sixteenth through the eighteenth centuries, life in Europe was substantially transformed by three revolutions: the Reformation, expansion of a market economy, and centralization of political power in the hands of a monarch. These movements were so powerful that women's lives were altered.

The Reformation redrew the western European map of people's Christianity: before, Catholicism had been universal; afterward, Protestantism dominated northern Europe. A central Protestant idea required each person to assume personal responsibility for salvation. That meant that the largely illiterate population had to be taught to read the Bible in the vernacular. For the first time in centuries, masses of women were educated, which eventually improved their lives. However, authorities—both Catholic and Protestant—attacking witches, mostly women, based their justification on the individual's responsibility for salvation, saying the women had chosen to be followers of the devil. Hatred between the two divisions of Christianity was so intense that three major European wars were fought over religious issues: the French Civil War (1559–89), the Thirty Years' War (1618–48), and the English Civil War (1642–46). Rigid intolerance was normal—so much so that in Anglican England, a highwayman could threaten to kill a woman if she were a Quaker.

At the beginning of the period, urban women were able to own and operate independent businesses. They belonged to guilds of artisans and were skilled workers in the family trade. As transportation improved and demand for exports for world trade grew, economies became more specialized and individual enterprises became larger. Men forced women out of skilled labor— for example, doctors tried to replace midwives. Women owners lasted longest in traditional female industries such as brewing and taverns. Of course, women continued to sell at the stalls in the daily markets and administered the accounts and servants, mostly female, on large farms and estates.

By 1500, centralization of political power was well advanced, especially in Spain, Britain, and France. In the earlier medieval system of small states and cities with weak rulers, aristocratic women had inherited the family estate or succeeded to the throne when there was no male heir. Lineage was more important than gender, and there were notable female monarchs. Before new professionalized bureaucracies froze out the familial power of royal women, there was another era of queens in early modern Europe. Paradoxically, even as political power of nations was concentrated in more powerful monarchs, and philosophers deemed women too emotional to rule, queens claimed crowns to reign in Spain, Austria, Sweden, Russia, Scotland, and England.

The princes of small principalities sometimes became fearful of opposition to their government and initiated local witchcrazes, with showcase executions, to intimidate their citizens. Fearful that they might be denounced as a witch, women avoided trusting anyone, including other women.

4.1 Witchcraze, 1560–1760

Witchcraze is the term historian Anne Llewellyn Barstow coined for the persecution and execution of thousands of European women: and she posits that the witchcraze destroyed women's self-confidence and led them to fear everyone—men and women, husbands and children.

The number of witches accused and killed during the European witch-hunts of the sixteenth through the eighteenth centuries has been reported to have been as high as 10 million and as low as 110,000 accusations and 60,000 deaths. Many records have been lost, and those that have survived are often incomplete and difficult to interpret. Barstow surveyed all the evidence for the period of actual major persecutions (1560–1760), estimating for the missing records, and concludes that 200,000 were accused of witchcraft, with 50 percent of the accused executed. On an average, 80 percent of the accused and 85 percent of those killed were female.[*]

These statistics strongly implicate misogyny and patriarchy as causes of the witchcraze. But these were ancient strands of European culture. What caused misogyny and patriarchy to erupt in violent actions against thousands of women? Social tensions generated by the Protestant and Catholic Reformations played a role, as did the sexual repression that accompanied the intense religiosity of the era. Antagonisms, personal and communal, arising from changes in economies and societies were often central to accusations of witchcraft. Political causes were also part of the

---

[*]Anne Llewellyn Barstow, *Witchcraze: A New History of the European Witch Hunts* (San Francisco: Pandora, 1994), 21–24.

complex brew in which hatred of women and determination to control them thrived.

One political cause was the growth of state power, with ruling elites cynically encouraging witch-hunts to increase their control of their own people, as Anne Barstow illustrates:

Any discussion of sixteenth-century witch persecutions must mention the growing power of the state. . . .

The ducal and royal governments of Europe were becoming more efficient, centralized, and powerful, in other words, more capable of controlling many aspects of more people's lives. Taxation, which fell primarily on the peasantry, increased greatly. Royal agents asserted their influence in parts of Europe never before interfered with. They demanded not only taxes and military levies but also a new ideological conformity: nationalism as we know it first reached rural western Europe in the seventeenth century. Secular courts took over prosecution of sexual crimes, matters formerly reserved for judgment in the more private sphere of church or neighborhood. The state was willing to take on the responsibility and expense of this jurisdiction because these moral judgments helped define what it stood for and allowed for control of the most intimate aspects of the lives of its citizens.

These governments were as intolerant as they were interfering. In an important study, R.I. Moore demonstrated how the European state became an organ of persecution, how, in the eleventh and twelfth centuries, European governments began, for the first time, to identify groups as enemies of the state—heretics, Jews, lepers, homosexuals—and to *create the myths* that would enable rulers to destroy those groups. Observing that there have been two major periods of persecutions in Europe since, the sixteenth and seventeenth centuries (the witchcraze) and the twentieth (the Holocaust), Moore states that intolerance "became part of the character of European society," and that in each case it was the rulers, not the people, who originated and carried out the pogroms. In short, the chief motive behind European racism and bigotry was the drive for political power. Even though none of the victims were powerful enemies, they served as an excuse for governments to use powerful weapons against their own people.

This new system of social control in which centralized governments were willing to prosecute on sexual and religious matters fell heaviest on the lower class, those unable to use the law to protect themselves—too uneducated to learn to use its ways or too poor to afford it. The women who suffered from these handicaps were particularly vulnerable when the state turned its attention to witchcraft.

Excerpts from *Witchcraze: A New History of the European Witch Hunts* by Anne Llewellyn Barstow (San Francisco: Pandora, 1994), 39–40. Copyright © 1994 by Anne Llewellyn Barstow. Reprinted by permission of HarperCollins Publishers, Inc. Notes omitted.

The fate of one poor German family is an example. They were tortured with the strappado, in which victims are hoisted up by a rope, usually with weights attached to their feet, and dropped suddenly, usually dislocating their joints.

Anna Pappenheimer, who was fifty-nine in 1600, was . . . the daughter of a grave digger, an outcast group. . . . Marriage opportunities for outcast women being few, Anna had seized the chance to marry Paulus Pappenheimer, an itinerant privy cleaner, also a member of the underclass. In addition to being suspect as outcasts and as wanderers, the Pappenheimers were Lutherans in a Catholic land, the duchy of Bavaria. . . .

[By] 1600 she had been married thirty-seven years, had borne seven children of whom three sons survived, and had despite constant poverty kept the family together. A respectable woman, one might think.

The Bavarian government thought otherwise. Its young duke, Maximilian, after an intensive Jesuit education, had become concerned about witchcraft in his duchy. . . . Now, worried about unrest among his barons and city oligarchs and a rise in highway robbery and vandalism, he searched for a way to demonstrate his power. Already concerned that witches might have put a curse on him (his wife had not been able to conceive), he called for a witch-hunt. His theological advisors, threatened by the new Protestant movement, were eager to cooperate with him in every way. It was not enough that the Bavarian Council of State was already legislating about almost every aspect of its citizens' lives: "against the marriage of young Catholics into Protestant communities, against the sale of non-Catholic books, against mixed bathing, against dancing in the evening, against extravagant weddings, against fortune-telling and superstition, against vagrancy and highway robbery." Even though Bavaria was filled with ducal spies, still people did not obey these rules. What was needed, the duke decided, was a show trial, a public spectacle that would make it clear to all his subjects, high and low, who was in charge in Bavaria.

When the Pappenheimers . . . were named as witches by a condemned criminal, they were duly arrested and brought to Munich. . . . They were questioned repeatedly but would not admit to sorcery. Tortured with the strappado, however, they began to break. Anna finally confessed to flying on a piece of wood to meet the devil, having sex with her demon lover, murdering children in order to make an ointment from their bodies, making a demonic powder from dead children's hands. . . . After a long, well-publicized trial, the entire Pappenheimer family was convicted of witchcraft.

The execution of the four adult Pappenheimers drew a crowd of thousands from the surrounding countryside. First, they were stripped so that their flesh could be torn off by red-hot pincers. Then Anna's breasts were cut off. The bloody breasts were forced into her mouth and then into the mouths of her two grown sons. . . . This fiendish punishment was . . . used as a particular torment to women. But it was more than physical torture: by rubbing the severed breasts around her sons' lips, the executioner made a hideous parody of her role as mother and nurse, imposing an extreme humiliation on her.

Now a procession formed [including many officials and clergy], over a half a mile long, led by a municipal official carrying a large crucifix . . . . Church bells pealed to celebrate the triumph of Christianity over Satan; the crowd sang hymns; vendors hawked pamphlets describing the sins of the victims.

Meanwhile, Anna's chest cavity bled. As the carts lurched along, the injured prisoners were in agony. Nonetheless, they were forced at one point to get down from the carts and kneel before a cross, to confess their sins. Then they were offered wine to drink. . . .

One can hope that between the wine and loss of blood, the Pappenheimers were losing consciousness. They had not been granted the "privilege" of being strangled before being burned. . . .

The four Pappenheimers were then tied to the stakes, the brushwood pyres were set aflame, and they were burned to death. Their eleven-year-old son was forced to watch the dying agonies of his parents and brothers. We know that Anna was still alive when the flames leapt up around her, for Hansel cried out, "My mother is squirming!" The boy was executed three months later.

Excerpts from *Witchcraze: A New History of the European Witch Hunts* by Anne Llewellyn Barstow (San Francisco: Pandora, 1994), 143–45. Copyright © 1994 by Anne Llewellyn Barstow. Reprinted by permission of HarperCollins Publishers, Inc. Notes omitted.

Who were the thousands of women like Anna tortured and killed with so much pain and humiliation? Generally, they were the poorest of the poor, like Anna, who was a beggar. Most were over fifty, past childbearing, and usually single. They were also independent and outspoken and frequently had a certain authority as healers, midwives, fortune-tellers, or spell-lifters.

They lived during a period of considerable social tensions. Europe had more people than it had resources to support at its level of production. Periods of food scarcity and runaway inflation caused accompanying crises of disease and crime. At such times, people may seek a scapegoat, such as women or a minority, to attack. Attacks on women scapegoats did more than harm those persecuted as witches. Fearful women, driven from the paid economy, retreated to safer domesticity. Again, Anne Barstow explains:

In much of western Europe in the peak years of the craze, any woman might have felt like a hunted animal. When we narrow the focus from the national level to that of village or town, we see the real horror of this period for women. In an attack that ultimately cut across lines of age, class, and income, women found themselves alone. With few exceptions, their families did not speak up for them out of fear and, in some cases, turned against them. . . . They realized there was no way out for them.

Women thus learned to live with a fear far greater even than our current dread of rape and assault. If a woman could be cried out a witch for telling someone's fortune or speaking back to a neighbor, well then, one had better stay to oneself, mind one's business—and obey one's husband. Women learned especially not to trust other women, for what woman might not be called up before the judge and start blabbing?

The sociologist Carole Sheffield maintains, "Sexual terrorism is the system by which males frighten, and by frightening dominate and control females." . . . The chief sixteenth-century device for teaching both sexes about men's ultimate control over women, however, was the public execution of witches. Strangely, little can be found in the trial records or eyewitness accounts about the culmination of the trials: the carrying out of the death sentence is seldom described. . . .

The near silence of the records about this crucial element (crucial certainly for the victim, but also for the crowd) requires us to reconstruct. What did a woman standing in the crowd outside Munich see, think, feel, as she watched Anna Pappenheimer's arms burned with hot tongs, her breasts cut off, her body burned alive?

Excerpts from *Witchcraze: A New History of the European Witch Hunts* by Anne Llewellyn Barstow (San Francisco: Pandora, 1994), 148–49. Copyright © 1994 by Anne Llewellyn Barstow. Reprinted by permission of HarperCollins Publishers, Inc. Notes omitted.

Women were isolated, afraid to protest, afraid to complain, afraid even of other women. Men found them defenseless.

European men looked at and treated their women basically as they did their African slaves and Indian serfs . . . with increasing violence. Viewing women as property, husbands became more authoritarian, a role no less oppressive for being disguised as paternalism. Just as slavery produced the myth of the good master, so patriarchy created the myth of the benevolent ruler of the family.

Excerpts from *Witchcraze: A New History of the European Witch Hunts* by Anne Llewellyn Barstow (San Francisco: Pandora, 1994), 164–65. Copyright © 1994 by Anne Llewellyn Barstow. Reprinted by permission of HarperCollins Publishers, Inc.

4.2 Women's Work

Women's horizons narrowed in Europe between the sixteenth and nineteenth centuries. The worldwide voyages of exploration, trade, and conquest were mainly male ventures. Men traded over distant oceans and continents, and as their companies and partnerships increased in scope and capital, the partnership of husband and wife eroded. The transformation was gradual and uneven before the process of industrialization took hold in the nineteenth century.

Agriculture was the occupation of the vast majority of European families during the early modern period. Farmwork was gender-specific, with women in charge of the house, barn, outbuildings, and gardens. Men were responsible for the fields. Sometimes, women were expected to get the wood for heat and cooking. Families could reorder the tasks according to their situation; for example, because of the prolonged absence of fishermen who spent months catching and drying fish in Canada, their wives also did the field labor of men.

A farm was almost entirely self-sufficient, supplying the wants of its inhabitants. It could not survive without the products supplied by the women, as the first all-male settlers in Virginia declared when they begged for wives. The two sexes were conceived of as mutually dependent.

A 1555 instruction on the duties of an English farm wife details her daily chores: In the morning, she should sweep the house; milk the cows, leaving some for the calves; take up the children; and prepare breakfast, dinner, and supper for husband, children, and servants. Go to the mill to grind corn when needed and bake bread and other pastries. Make butter and cheese from the milk. Feed the swine and poultry and collect the eggs. Plant and harvest the kitchen garden for vegetables and herbs. Harvest the flax and hemp (used for rope). Prepare linen thread and weave sheets, towels, shirts, and smocks. Prepare the wool shorn from the sheep, spin it, and weave clothes, blankets, and coverlets. If she did not have enough wool, she could earn what she needed by spinning thread for weavers. Wash the clothes, make beer, and help in the fields as needed to make hay, cut wheat, drive the dung cart, drive the plow, and load hay and grains. Winnow grains. Go to market to sell butter, cheese, milk, eggs, chickens, pigs, and geese and to buy things necessary for the farm. She was responsible for keeping accurate records of all sales and purchases. Her responsibility included organizing and training the servants, both men and women.

Leaving the farm could be hazardous for women. The long ride from the market on horseback was not free from danger and violence, as Maud, the wife of Thomas Collar of Woolavington, reported to the county justices in 1659. As she was returning from the Bridgewater market on July 7, Adrian Towes of Marke overtook her:

Calling her ugly toad [he] demanded her name; he then knocked her down and demanded her purse, to which, hiding her purse, she replied that she had bestowed all her money in the market. He then said, "I think you are a Quaker," & she denied it, he compelled her to kneel down on her bare knees and swear by the Lord's blood that she was not, which to save her life she did. Another woman came up and rebuked the said Towes, whereupon he struck her down.

Alice Clark, *Working Life of Women in the Seventeenth Century* (1919; reprint, New York: Augustus M. Kelley, 1968), 51.

Women were most numerous in urban crafts that involved women's traditional skills, such as provisioning and beer brewing. In the Middle Ages, women could belong to guilds occasionally as masters. But by the sixteenth century, European women were being excluded from guilds, even as widows inheriting a husband's trade.

Furthermore, as household production gave way to commercial production, women lost jobs. Alice Clark explains how women lost their high status as beer brewers when the English government restricted brewing to large enterprises called common breweries:

It must be remembered that before the introduction of cheap sugar, beer was considered almost equally essential for human existence as bread. Beer was drunk at every meal, and formed part of the ordinary diet of even small children. Large households brewed for their own use, but as many families could not afford the necessary apparatus, brewing was not only practiced as a domestic art, but became the trade of certain women who brewed for their neighbours.

Alice Clark, *Working Life of Women in the Seventeenth Century* (1919; reprint, New York: Augustus M. Kelley, 1968), 223.

———————

In 1532, one county prohibited anyone from brewing and selling beer in the same house. All beer for sale had to come from the common breweries, which did not sell retail. Families were permitted to brew beer for their own consumption. The justification was to simplify the collection of excise taxes and maintain the quality of the beer. The common breweries formed a guild, with apprentices and master brewers. In 1636, counties began compiling lists of licensed common breweries. Although some women's names were on these lists, they were usually a small proportion, such as 8 of 132. Alice Clark assumes those licensed women brewers were mostly widows who were running their deceased husbands' breweries. By the end of the seventeenth century, women had lost their position in the brewery trade. A few women continued to make their living brewing for neighborhood families. Women could sell the beer from the common breweries in stores, but they could not make it.

All over Europe, women were excluded from high-status labor as guilds became male professional associations and corporations or joint-stock companies replaced family production. Some women, against great odds, managed to find riches for their enterprise. Alice Clark describes one exceptional woman's personal story:

Joan Dant was one of the few women "capitalists" whose personal story is known in any detail. Her husband was a working weaver. . . . On his death she became a pedlar, carrying an assortment of mercery, hosiery, and haberdashery on her back from house to house in the vicinity of London. . . . After some years, her expenses being small and her diligence great, she had saved sufficient capital to engage in a more wholesale trade, debts due from her correspondents at Paris and Brussels appearing in her executor's account. In spite of her success in trade Joan Dant continued to live in her old frugal manner, and when she applied to a [Quaker] Friend for assistance in making

her will, he was astonished to find her worth rather more than
£9,000. He advised her to obtain the assistance of other Friends
more experienced in such matters. On their enquiring how she
wished to dispose of her property, she replied, "I got it by the rich
and I mean to leave it to the poor."

Joan Dant died in 1715 at the age of eighty-four.

Alice Clark, *Working Life of Women in the Seventeenth Century* (1919; reprint,
New York: Augustus M. Kelley, 1968), 32–33.

4.3 Many Queens

Sixteenth-century Europe had an unusually large number of ruling queens, including Isabel of Castile (1451–1504), Mary I of
England (1516–58), Elizabeth I of England (1533–1603), and
Mary of Scotland (1515–60). There were fewer in the next two
centuries, although they include outstanding women: Christina of
Sweden (1626–89), Anne of England (1665–1714), Maria Theresa of Austria (1717–80), Elizabeth of Russia (1709–62), and
Catherine II "the Great" of Russia (1729–96). All but Catherine
inherited their crowns. It is unusual in world history to have this
many female rulers in a region in a short period of three hundred
years. Other women ruled as regents for husbands or sons. The
most famous was Catherine de Médicis (1519–89), who was regent for her underage son, the French king Charles IX.

Although Maria Theresa's father, Austria's Emperor Charles VI,
carefully arranged for her succession, he regarded his daughter
as the means to continue the dynasty's lineage rather than as a
ruler. He chose Francis, duke of Lorraine, to be her husband, but
did little to groom Maria Theresa to govern. She was twenty-
three and had been married four years when her father died.
Maria Theresa did not consider yielding her power to her husband; she planned to rule alone. At the beginning of her reign,
she had to fight to keep her crown. Bonnie Anderson and Judith
Zinsser explain that both she and her government were woefully
unprepared for the Prussian invasion of Austrian Silesia:

She had clear title to the lands of her father, Charles VI. Even before
she was born he had prepared for her reign by stipulating the indivisi-

bility of the [Hapsburg] empire in the Pragmatic Sanction presented to Europe's monarchs in 1713. Yet Charles VI had given Maria Theresa no special education or training for her future role. He had merely arranged her marriage. On his death in 1740 his treaty did not prevent Frederick II [the Great] of Prussia from seizing part of the Hapsburg Empire.

Maria Theresa later attributed her trust in "Divine Providence" with giving her the strength and judgment to survive this, her first test as a female ruler. . . . She later described her predicament:

> I found myself in this situation, without money, without credit, without army, without experience or knowledge of my own and finally also without any counsel, because each one of them first wanted to wait and see what things would develop.

She acted quickly to claim the titles Archduchess of Austria and "King" of Hungary. As she explained to Count Kinsky, Chancellor of Bohemia, in 1741, she decided "to stake everything, win or lose, on saving Bohemia," even if it meant "destruction and desolation." She instructed him: "This, then, is the crisis: do not spare the country, only hold it." She noted that he might think her "cruel," but this was of less consequence than appearing the confident, forceful monarch trying to prevent the dissolution of her empire.

Bonnie S. Anderson and Judith P. Zinsser, *A History of Their Own: Women in Europe from Prehistory to the Present,* vol. 2 (New York: Harper & Row, 1988), 58–59. Notes omitted.

In addition to Prussia, Austria was attacked by some of its other neighbors, and no nation would give financial aid. Would the Hapsburg Empire collapse into small independent states? The tide turned when the Hungarians agreed to send troops to Austria. Maria Theresa's speech to them is sometimes credited with convincing them to send the aid. Voltaire's account describes what he thought happened:

The more the ruin of Maria Theresa appeared inevitable, the more courage she revealed; she had departed from Vienna and threw herself into the arms of the Hungarians, treated so severely by her father and ancestors. Having assembled . . . the parliament at Pressburg, she appeared there holding in her arms her young son, barely out of the cradle. Speaking in Latin, a language in which she expressed herself well, she addressed them in words similar to the following: "Abandoned by my friends, persecuted by my enemies, attacked by my closest relatives, I have no other resources than your loyalty, your courage and my steadfastness; I place in your hands the daughter and son of your king who rely on you for their safety." Pulling their swords from their scabbards, all the attending nobles and their friends cried out *"Moriamur pro rege nostro"* (We will die for our king Maria Theresa). They always give the title of king to their queen, and no princess has been more deserving of this title. . . .

Under these circumstances, she excited the zeal of her Hungarians; she inspired England and Holland in her favor, and they gave her financial assistance.

Voltaire, "Precis du siecle de Louis XV," in *Oeuvres completes,* vol. 15 (Paris: Garnier Freres, 1878), 192–93, translated by Karl A. Roider Jr., in *Maria Theresa,* edited by Karl A. Roider Jr. (Englewood Cliffs, NJ: Prentice-Hall, 1973), 92–93. Reprinted with the permission of Simon & Schuster. Copyright © 1973 by Prentice-Hall, Inc.

The speech is a good example of her style in public relations. She played the role of mother—mother of the whole nation.

Maria Theresa realized that Prussia under Frederick was Austria's enemy. Consequently, Austria was at war from 1740 to 1748 and from 1756 to 1763. Frederick had respect for her leadership. He wrote that:

[he] had in the person of the empress-queen an ambitious and vindictive enemy, even more dangerous because she was a woman, obstinate in her opinions and implacable. . . . This superb woman, devoured by ambition, wanted to travel all roads gloriously; she put her finances into an order unknown to her ancestors and not only utilized reforms to make up for the revenues lost when she ceded lands to the king of Prussia and king of Sardinia, but actually increased her overall income. Count Haugwitz became controller-general of finances, and under his administration income rose to 36

million gulden. . . . Her father, Emperor Charles VI, who had even possessed the kingdom of Naples, Serbia, and Silesia, never received that much. . . .

In preceding wars [1740–48] the empress had sensed the need of improving discipline in her army. She chose generals who were both hard working and capable of introducing discipline among the troops. She also put old officers, little able to do their proper jobs, on pensions and replaced them with young men, who were full of enthusiasm and love for the business of war. The empress herself appeared frequently in the camps of Prague and Olomouc in order to inspire the troops by her presence and gifts. . . . She rewarded those officers who were recommended by their generals, and above all she excited their devotion, talents, and desire to please her. At the same time she formed a school of artillery under the direction of Prince Liechtenstein; he increased this corps to six battalions, and utilized cannon to a degree unprecedented in our day. . . . Finally, in order to neglect nothing that would improve the military, the empress founded near Vienna a college to instruct the young nobility in the arts of war; it included able professors of geometry, fortifications, geography, and history, which constitute the appropriate subjects. This school serves as a seedbed of officers for her army. Owing to all these efforts, the military of this country has achieved a degree of perfection it had never reached under the emperors of the house of Austria, and it was a woman who realized the plans worthy of a great man.

Frederick the Great, *Histoire de la guerre de sept ans,* vol. 1 (Berlin: Rudolph v. Decker, 1847), 7–9, translated by Karl A. Roider Jr., in *Maria Theresa,* edited by Karl A. Roider Jr. (Englewood Cliffs, NJ: Prentice-Hall, 1973), 115–17. Reprinted with the permission of Simon & Schuster. Copyright © 1973 by Prentice-Hall, Inc.

———————————

At this point, the question arises, what was her husband doing all this time? Her father chose a husband to be emperor, but Maria Theresa acted alone. Furthermore, Frederick might seem to be implying that she had lovers, including some of her army officers. She was a sincere Catholic. Her marriage to Francis Stephen of Lorraine in 1736 was monogamous on her part, as Frederick's ambassador, Count Otto Christopher Podewils's 1747 report shows:

One could never accuse her of coquetry. In this respect, she has never given one hint of infidelity. She loves the emperor dearly, but also demands great devotion from him. People claim that her love for this prince is caused partly by her temperament and the good qualities with which he can satisfy it. Among other things they emphasize the little influence which he, despite her love for him, has on her spirit. I have it on good authority that one day during a conference in which the empress had heatedly defended a position against the views of her ministers, she in very sharp words told the emperor, as he made known his opinion, that he should not mix in business he did not understand. The emperor grumbled about this treatment for a few days and complained about it to one of his favorites, a Lorraine colonel by the name of Rosières. This man answered, "Sire, permit me to say that you have handled the empress the wrong way. Had I been in your position, I would have forced her to treat me better, and I would have received her as limp as a glove." "Why should I?" asked the emperor. "I wouldn't be able to sleep," answered the colonel. "Believe me, she loves you in this way, and by refusing her, you could achieve everything." This conversation was reported to the empress, who hounded this officer so unmercifully that he decided to leave the service, despite all the emperor's efforts to get him to stay.

Without doubt she is very jealous of the emperor and does everything to prevent him from establishing a liaison.

Count Otto Christopher Podewils to Frederick II, King of Prussia, in Carl Hinrichs, ed., *Friedrich der Grosse und Maria Theresia: Diplomatische Berichte von Otto Christoph Graf von Podewils* (Berlin: R.v. Deckers Verlag, G. Schenk, 1937), 35–44, translated by Karl A. Roider Jr., in *Maria Theresa*, edited by Karl A. Roider Jr. (Englewood Cliffs, NJ: Prentice-Hall, 1973), 103–4. Reprinted with the permission of Simon & Schuster. Copyright © 1973 by Prentice-Hall, Inc.

In his area of expertise, investments, Francis was very competent. Starting with a small amount of capital, he increased his personal estate to more than 20 million guilders at his death. He successfully invested in real estate, banking, government bonds, and army contracts. At one time during a war between Austria and Prussia, he was providing army supplies to both sides! His reorganization of the Austrian state debt was considered an improvement.

Maria Theresa and Francis were married almost thirty years and had sixteen children. Pregnancies did not seem to reduce her energy. She bore seven children during the eight years Austria was at war, 1740–48. After her husband's death in 1765, Maria Theresa gave her son and successor, Joseph II, the training she lacked by ruling Austria jointly with him for the last fifteen years of her life.

Suggested Further Readings

An introduction to the extensive literature in English on European women in the early modern period is found in articles by seventeen scholars collected in *History of Women in the West*, vol. 3, *Renaissance and Enlightenment Paradoxes*, edited by Natalie Zemon Davis and Arlette Farge (Cambridge, MA: Harvard University Press, 1993). Geoffrey Scarre has written a short introduction to *Witchcraft and Magic in 16th and 17th Century Europe* (Atlantic Highlands, NJ: Humanities Press International, 1987), with a discussion of why women were the focus of persecution. Carol F. Karlsen's *The Devil in the Shape of a Woman: Witchcraft in Colonial New England* (New York: Vintage, 1989) argues that the New England witchcraze was a manifestation of women's resistance to patriarchy. Lyndal Roper's *Oedipus and the Devil: Witchcraft, Sexuality and Religion in Early Modern Europe* (London: Routledge, 1994) explores interactions between belief and reality in shaping masculine and feminine psychology. How women who worked beside men in medieval embroiderers' guilds—when needlework was an art equal to painting and sculpture—were later excluded from the trade, which itself was then transformed into a symbol of femininity, hence a skill less valued, is revealed in Rozsika Parker's *The Subversive Stitch: Embroidery and the Making of the Feminine* (New York: Routledge, 1984). In *Artemisia Gentileschi* (Princeton, NJ: Princeton University Press, 1989), Mary D. Garrard explores the art and life of a seventeenth-century Italian painter who competed with men in a craft inhospitable to women. Other studies of women's economic roles are Barbara A. Hanawalt, ed., *Women and Work in Preindustrial Europe* (Bloomington: Indiana University Press, 1986); Daryl M. Haftner, ed., *European Women and Preindustrial Craft* (Bloomington: Indiana University Press, 1995); and William Chester Jordan, *Women and Credit in Pre-In-*

dustrial and Developing Societies (Philadelphia: University of Pennsylvania Press, 1993). The best study of Maria Theresa is C.A. Macartney, *Maria Theresa and the House of Austria* (Mystic, CT: Lawrence Verry, 1969). How England's Elizabeth I used her femininity to counter opposition to her rule is the subject of Carole Levin's *The Heart and Stomach of a King: Elizabeth and the Politics of Sex and Power* (Philadelphia: University of Pennsylvania Press, 1994). *Women Who Would Be Kings: Female Rulers in the Sixteenth Century* (New York: St. Martin's Press, 1991), by Lisa Hopkins, compares women who reigned with those who were wives and/or mothers of kings.

–5–

GENDER IN THE EUROPEAN COLONIZATION OF THE AMERICAS

English artist John White's sixteenth-century drawings of Algonquians on the North American coast shaped European perceptions of indigenous women. This scene was titled *Theire Sitting at Meale* in a widely circulated book of engravings made from White's drawings by Theodor de Bry in 1590. (Rare Books and Manuscripts Division. The New York Public Library. Astor, Lenox and Tilden Foundations.)

European conquest moved in waves across the continents of the Americas after 1492. The Spanish and Portuguese extended their control beyond the rim of the Caribbean during the sixteenth century. In the seventeenth century, the Dutch, French, English, and Scandinavians successfully invaded the outskirts of Spanish colonial domains. The intrusion of these largely male European invaders into less patriarchal, often complementary and egalitarian Indian societies had profound consequences for the first women of the Americas.

5.1 The Jesuit Attack on Algonquian Women

As Europeans conquered the Americas, inhabitants necessarily adjusted to the invaders' colonization policies and cultures. In seventeenth-century New France (eastern Canada), the struggle over culture was carried out in the starkest form as French Catholic Jesuits sought to convert Algonquian-speaking people, who were hunter–gatherers. Within an Algonquian group, men and women had separate, complementary responsibilities, with cooperation necessary for day-to-day living. Indian women realized that their value in European communities would be lessened and men's status would increase. Consequently, the women, often in conflict with the men, resisted European culture by seeking to retain traditional ways. Carol Devens describes the precolonial society:

These Algonquian-speaking peoples occupied the land from Labrador to Lake Winnipeg. The Ojibwa, Cree, and Montagnais-Naskapi based their economies primarily on hunting, fishing, and gathering, although some more southerly groups of Ojibwa practiced occasional horticulture. . . .

Reports, journals, and travel accounts from New France furnish us with a large, if biased, portrait . . . of native communities. . . . Prominent in this profile is the sexual division that permeated all aspects of the native peoples' world. . . . Each sex played an integral yet autonomous role in the social and productive unit. Males and females had complementary functions that seldom overlapped, though they might be overlooked temporarily when necessary, as during a spouse's illness. As Paul Le Jeune, [Jesuit] superior of the reopened missions, noted of the Montagnais in 1632, the women know what they are to do, and the men also; and one never meddles with the work of the other. The men make the frames of their canoes, and the women sew the bark with willow withes or similar wood. . . . Men go hunting, and kill the animals; and the women go after them, skin them, and clean the hides. . . .

Men . . . focused on the bush. . . . Their primary productive role was hunting large game and furbearers such as moose, caribou, bear, beaver, and deer. . . .

Women usually worked apart from men, either within the commensal unit or in groups, and the communal nature of their work allowed them regular contact with one another. They fished and hunted small game, such as rabbit, marten, and birds, in the vicinity of the camp, providing a good portion of the daily diet. . . . The women of all groups also controlled the distribution of meat; once the men reported a kill, it became the women's property to butcher and process as they saw fit. . . . [Father] Paul Le Jeune described this exchange with amazement: "Men leave the arrangement of the household to the women, without interfering with them; they cut, and decide, and give away [meat] as they please, without making the husband angry." . . .

Women were responsible for processing hides—scraping, stretching, and rubbing them with brains or grease—to be used as furs or made into shirts, leggings, parkas, moccasins, and other items of clothing. . . . Men then received these items in exchange for the meat they provided. Women also controlled the assignment of living space and the selection of campsites. . . .

This system recognized the autonomy of men and women by emphasizing their different needs and concerns. The division was not disruptive, however, countered as it was by the complementarity of social and productive activities. Instead, the different aspects of female and male combined in a vital symmetry upon which the community's survival depended.

Carol Devens [Carol Green-Devins], *Countering Colonization: Native American Women and Great Lakes Missions, 1630–1900* (Berkeley: University of California Press, 1992), 9–13. Copyright © 1992 by The Regents of the University of California. Notes omitted.

Before the arrival of the French, Algonquian men and women received equal respect. Production was for use by the group, which was self-sufficient, and little was traded to outsiders. The French invaders encouraged trade in furs to be sent to Europe. Itinerant French merchants discovered that the Algonquians spent the summers on the shores of the Saint Lawrence, its tributaries, and the Great Lakes. There they traded for the winter fur catch and eventually built permanent palisaded trading posts. In the long run, the French expected to take more than furs: they expected to replace the Algonquian culture with their own. Devens continues:

Missionaries did not face a virgin country when they set out to evangelize the *sauvages*. A fundamental economic transformation already had begun as market-oriented trapping gradually replaced subsistence hunting-gathering. This shift preceded the mission effort, and paved the way for it. . . .

French traders wanted the furs obtained by the men rather than the small game, tools, utensils, or clothing procured or produced by women. . . . Because furs served as the medium of exchange for goods, daily and seasonal life for all came increasingly to revolve around the trade. . . .

The introduction of and growing dependence on European goods obtainable primarily with furs not only reoriented male hunting patterns, but it altered or eliminated many female productive activities as well. . . . For domiciled [living near the French] Indians and those in the trade, subsistence patterns were beginning to change dramatically. European merchandise replaced items [such as clothing and food] whose manufacture had previously constituted some of women's most important productive activities. Where women had been responsible for processing skins and transforming them into garments, hunters now obtained clothing for furs. . . .

Although native people did not, of course, immediately buy all of their clothing from the French, ready-made goods may have seemed a convenient substitute for time-consuming manufacture of native dress. Acquiring such items from traders also allowed women to spend more time readying furs for market. Thus, as women's relationship to the disposal of hides and furs changed, the significance of their direct contribution to the community welfare diminished. As for men, while they too experienced a degree of alienation from the fruit of their labor, their contribution now became the focal one within the economy.

The orientation of many female tasks began to shift from the creation of a useful end product, such as clothing or tools, to assistance in the preparation of furs. . . . They were becoming auxiliaries to the trapping process. . . .

After the introduction of European food items, however, although women continued to gather nuts and berries when available and to fish, the importance of these subsistence foods decreased as French foods became more accessible. . . . Women's direct contribution to communal and family well-being diminished as dried peas, bread, and biscuits became common fare acquired by the trapper in exchange for his furs. . . .

In response to French demands [for furs], an inequality in the productive values of the sexes had developed that Indians were forced to accept, at least in part, if they were to participate in the fur trade.

Carol Devens [Carol Green-Devins], *Countering Colonization: Native American Women and Great Lakes Missions, 1630–1900* (Berkeley: University of California Press, 1992), 14–18. Copyright © 1992 by The Regents of the University of California. Notes omitted.

————————

The Jesuits decided that Indians who trapped furs would not accept Christianity. Christianity required a hierarchical, patriarchal society. They encouraged a sedentary horticultural life similar to that found in French villages.

For security, some bands settled near the French trading posts. Periodic epidemics of smallpox, measles, and influenza killed as much as half the Indian population. Bands whose adults had died could not find enough food to survive in the hunter–gatherer economy and could not effectively defend themselves against Iroquois raids. Huddled near the French posts, with some protection from the Iroquois, they frequently began farming.

Early Europeans in New France were dismayed to find that native peoples placed little value on tangible wealth as a source of status. Their economic system was more communal than competitive; each person gained prestige through contributions to the group's welfare.

Originally, Indians were hard put to understand the Europeans' desire for wealth. "You [the French] are covetous," they reprimanded one missionary, "and are neither generous nor kind; as for us, if we have a morsel of bread we share it with our neighbors." . . .

This careless attitude toward property would change, the French hoped, once they had enticed the Indians to settle, "for anyone who has taken the trouble to cultivate a piece of land does not readily abandon it, but struggles valiantly to keep it." The French saw a direct relationship between native economic concerns and their own missionary work. They were, in fact, much freer with material aid to those who expressed an interest in conversion. . . .

At first the Jesuits focused their proselytizing on men and boys, alternating attacks on male hunting and divination rituals with blandishments of the comforts and virtue of life as a Christian man. Modesty and convenience limited their contact with women. . . . But then, the priests expected the women to convert as a matter of course, if only because the "neophytes" needed Christian wives to minimize the temptation of backsliding. . . . So although the Jesuits needed female converts to meet the goal of establishing sedentary villages based on the nuclear family structure, they initially planned to leave the instruction of women to chance or to male converts. . . .

If they converted, women tended to interpret and manipulate Christianity to serve their own needs. Indeed, Catholic mysticism proved a useful tool in their continued emphasis of the sexual distinctions and female autonomy that had distinguished precolonial society. . . . By the 1670s a virtual cult of the Virgin had developed in some mission communities as women converts focused their ritual attention on that consummate symbol of femaleness in Catholic ideology. Ursuline convents—the ultimate separate institution for females within the church—became gathering places for Christian women. There they continued to stress older values of female autonomy, but now in a format acceptable to the demands of the missionaries.

More frequently, however, to the missionaries' dismay, women declined conversion and instead stressed the importance of older rituals and practices. Women scorned priests and converts alike for flouting tradition, and they had little patience for Christians who threatened eternal damnation to those who clung to heathen practices. . . .

Le Jeune recounted in 1640 that the wife of one convert from Sagné, "a rough and wild creature, who gives a great deal of trouble to the poor man," refused to consider conversion when "Charles" insisted that he must have a Christian wife. The priest described the man's anxiety over the situation: " 'You have told me that those who do evil are very often incited to it by Demons; alas!' said he, 'then I am always with some Demon, for my wife is always angry; I fear that the Demons she keeps in my cabin are perverting the good that I received in holy Baptism.' " The fellow confided that she had hurled a knife at him during an argument over her refusal to convert. The woman spurned his efforts—he even had volunteered to do her chores if she converted—and mocked his faith. " 'Dost thou not see that we are all dying since they told us to pray to God?' " she asked, as would many others throughout New France. " 'Where are thy relatives? Where are mine? the most of them are dead; it is no longer a time to believe.' "

Other male converts had equal difficulty convincing wives to become Christians and grew increasingly aggressive and punitive in their attempts to secure a conversion. Le Jeune found the male converts' zeal gratifying; he observed that "there was nothing they would not do or endure in order to secure obedience to God." Women's husbands and brothers beat them in punishment for defiance, sometimes with the full support of the missionaries, who believed that the Indians were finally learning the importance of exercising justice. The zealous Christian relatives of one unconverted young woman flogged her publicly for not discouraging an unconverted suitor; they forced the other girls in the community to watch the display and warned them that similar punishment awaited further rebellion.

Carol Devens [Carol Green-Devins], *Countering Colonization: Native American Women and Great Lakes Missions, 1630–1900* (Berkeley: University of California Press, 1992), 14–15, 20–23. Copyright © 1992 by The Regents of the University of California. Notes omitted.

The Christian European ideal of permanent, monogamous nuclear families, with women subservient to men, compared unfavorably to the egalitarian Algonquian practice of companionate marriage with easy divorce whenever one of the partners wished to end the union. European domination not only *changed* family life, it could also obliterate Indian familial ties through forced labor or slavery.

Despite various edicts of distant European governments banning enslavement of Indians, Indians were everywhere captured, bought and sold, and forced to endure slavery. On the borders of Spanish Mexico, in what is now the state of New Mexico, women were sought especially to work in settlers' homes.

5.2 Pueblo and Apache Domestic Slaves in New Mexico

Spanish Franciscans were able to convert and live among the Indians of what is today New Mexico from 1581 to 1680. In 1680, the Indians successfully revolted during a long drought and famine. For ten years, the Spanish were content to hold El Paso. Finally, in 1692, fearing the western expansion of the French from the Mississippi River valley, the Spanish reconquered the territory and opened it to settlement by colonists from Mexico.

The most important source of wealth in New Mexico was Indian slaves. Two terms were used to differentiate between Indians first enslaved by other Indians and then purchased by the Spanish, *criados,* and Indians captured in Spanish slave raids, *genízaros.* Eventually, the terms were used interchangeably for detribalized Indian slaves living in Spanish communities. Ramón Gutiérrez describes the life of Indian slaves in New Mexico. Indian women did not labor growing a staple plantation crop, but their lot as domestic slaves was hard.

Within New Mexico households slave treatment ran the gamut from the kind neglect of some to the utter sadism of others. To be a slave or *criado* in a Hispano household was to be a marginal and stigmatized person. At the crack of dawn they were the first to rise to perform their duties. They got the hearth's fire going, braved the morning cold to chop wood and to haul in water for the day's needs. If chamber pots had to be emptied, . . . it was the *genizaro* slave who did it. . . .

Both inside the household and outside of it, *genizaros* were addressed as children, in the second person Spanish informal and personal *tú* (you), but had to address their masters and local citizens with the formal *usted*. In Indian society increasing age brought increasing respect, but not for New Mexico's slaves. They were permanently infantilized, even by the master's own children. . . .

That slaves lacked genealogical ties to the Spanish community and had been torn from their history through violence was humiliation enough in a society that prided itself on ancestry. Some masters compounded the hurt by refusing to allow their slaves to marry, establish families, or retain their own progeny. When slave women bore children while in captivity, the children were sometimes sold or given to another household as gifts.

Excerpted from *When Jesus Came, the Corn Mothers Went Away: Marriage, Sexuality, and Power in New Mexico, 1500–1846* by Ramón A. Gutiérrez (Stanford, CA: Stanford University Press, 1991), 182–83, with the permission of the publishers, Stanford University Press. Copyright © 1991 by the Board of Trustees of the Leland Stanford Junior University.

Women living in the households of Santa Fe were more vulnerable to men's sexual violence than slaves laboring in the fields. Virginity's high value in Hispanic societies heaped shame upon the raped Indian woman as well as on any "illegitimate" children born of the relationship. Gutiérrez relates the example of Alejandro Mora's cruelty to his slave Juana, which was so vicious that his wife complained to the constable.

In 1751 he [Mora] raped his slave Juana "to determine if she was a virgin." Because she had resisted, said Juana, "he hung me from a roof-beam and beat me." . . .

[An investigation] found Juana's body totally covered with bruises. Her neck and body had burns from the application of live coals. Her ankles were scabbed from restraining manacles. Her knees had festering ulcers. Mora had initially broken Juana's knees to keep her from fleeing. The knee wounds never healed because Mora periodically reopened them, mincing the flesh with a sharp flintstone. . . .

Juana was removed from Mora's household and there the matter ended, without even a reprimand. . . .

Slavery was an uplifting privilege, or so some owners convinced themselves. Governor Vélez Cachupín reminded colonists in 1752 that Indian slavery was illegal but was tolerated in New Mexico "so that they [captives] can be instructed in Our Holy Catholic Faith and made cognizant of the Divine Precepts, so that they may win their own salvation in honor and glory of God, our Lord." Slavery "civilized" Indians by giving them the requisites of culture: clothes, life in a European styled home, and knowledge of the one true God. . . .

New Mexico's settlers valued female slaves more highly than males and paid twice as much to acquire them. . . . The preference for female slaves is easy to understand. In a province where only one out of every three children born was likely to reach the age of twenty, female slaves were essential for social and biological reproduction. The pretensions of aristocratic households were hollow without slaves. Who would perform the menial household chores? Corn had to be shucked and wheat threshed, ground into flour, and baked into bread. . . . There were buildings to construct and to plaster—all women's work. When not otherwise caring for household needs female slaves undertook production for the market. Animal pelts had to be tanned and sewn into shoes and saddles. Cotton and wool were spun and knit into socks, gloves, and caps, or woven into blankets and rugs, all of which would be sold in Chihuahua for manufactured goods and luxury items. And the illegitimate children slave women bore often remained in the household as additional working hands.

Excerpted from *When Jesus Came, the Corn Mothers Went Away: Marriage, Sexuality, and Power in New Mexico, 1500–1846* by Ramón A. Gutiérrez (Stanford, CA: Stanford University Press, 1991), 184–87, with the permission of the publishers, Stanford University Press. Copyright © 1991 by the Board of Trustees of the Leland Stanford Junior University.

5.3 African Women in Barbados

African men accompanied Columbus, and African women, both free and slave, came to the Americas soon afterward. In the eighteenth century, the number of African women on the slave ships crossing the Atlantic Ocean soared. Despite European preference for male plantation workers, about 40 percent of all Africans brought to the Americas were women.

The typical slave woman remembered today is not an indigenous American but an African. A common misconception is that African slave women were usually domestic servants; only a small percentage worked in homes. Almost all were purchased as agricultural workers, whether the woman was destined to live on a Chesapeake tobacco plantation or a Brazilian or West Indian sugar plantation. Between 1640 and 1800, the British Caribbean colony on the island of Barbados was important as the first stop of slavers from Africa and as an important sugar producer. Among the African women who reached Barbados, Hilary Beckles concludes that most spent their lives growing sugar:

As field hands in Barbados, black women were subjected to the same exhausting productive employment as men. . . . It has been stated that this pattern of labour organization expressed principles of enlightened equalitarianism, but it also suggests the greater exploitation of female labour on the plantations.

Hilary McD. Beckles, *Natural Rebels: A Social History of Enslaved Black Women in Barbados* (New Brunswick, NJ: Rutgers University Press, 1989), 24. Copyright © 1989 by Hilary McD. Beckles. Reprinted by permission of Rutgers University Press. Notes omitted.

———————

Women also predominated in the eighteenth-century tobacco fields of the Chesapeake and the sugarcane fields of Jamaica. Although Europeans sought to buy two men for each woman, few merchants could consistently obtain that many men. Men composed most of the field labor force only in areas producing exceptional wealth, and everywhere male numbers were depleted by higher mortality and assignment to jobs in the sugar mills, transport on land and sea, and as artisans.

Beckles quotes Richard Ligon, an Englishman, describing the sale of newly arrived Africans to sugar planters in Barbados:

When they are brought to us, the planters buy them out of the ship, where they find them stark naked, and therefore cannot deceive in any outward infirmity. They chose them as they do horses in a market; the strongest, youthfullest, and most beautiful yield the greatest price. . . .

During Ligon's time in Barbados (1647–50), white indentured female servants worked in the field gangs alongside the small, but the rapidly growing number of enslaved black women. . . . By the 1660s, however, . . . slave owners adopted the racially inspired labour policy that . . . white women were no longer to be employed as field hands.

This policy was central to slave owners' attempt to establish the ideology of white racial superiority, and . . . just the beginning of a long-term attempt to elevate white women and degrade black women. . . .

As white female labourers assumed the status of "misses," black women became the symbol of physical, sexual, emotional, and other forms of exploitation. . . . [This] was a conscious attempt to use women, or the image of womanhood, as an important element in the structure of their social ideology. . . .

Africans were subjected to a process of colonial acclimatization and adaptation, generally referred to as "seasoning" . . . [when] they were protected from the full rigours of plantation life. . . . [to] build up some immunity to the new disease environment and learn the routine of plantation labour organization. . . .

Up to 33% of new recruits died within their first three years on the island. . . . Of the African women who survived the seasoning period those of 20 years or more were normally placed in the first field gang, and those between 15 and 19 in the second gang. . . . All gangs were of both sexes and separated mainly by age. . . . Managements' refusal to shelter field women from even the most arduous physical tasks suggests that productivity differentials were not expected to exist between the sexes.

First gang women hoed the soil, dug drains, cut and bundled canes, planted new canes, carried baskets of manure to the fields and performed other physically demanding tasks. Younger women in the second gang did what was considered light work, such as weeding, grass picking, tending cattle, and miscellaneous plantation tasks. The third gang, of female children, looked after stocks, carried water to the fields, as well as other minor tasks. . . .

Placing children and young adults in the hands of women drivers enabled planters to achieve several objectives with one policy. Women drivers were generally selected from the first gang on account of their diminishing productivity and old age, or if they showed signs of a sense of responsibility. . . . For these women, it was a welcome elevation into the supervisory élite, the top echelon of which was dominated by men. It was the one avenue for mature field women to achieve status in production. Masters, however, conceived of the promotion in different terms: not only as a way of conferring rank and privilege, but also the most effective way of attempting to inculcate the acceptance of slavery in the minds of children. These women were seen as agents in the socialization of the young, who, on becoming adults, would replace them in the first gang; they also mothered and nursed the young under their whip as part of the labour preparation plan. . . .

The working year was divided into two parts—"crop time" and "hard time". . . . During crop time, in spite of the hard labour required for harvesting, slave women tended to appear healthier and stronger than in the hard time, when provisions were scarce and diet reduced . . . [and when] they looked "emaciated" from starvation and cumulative malnutrition. . . .

Before the 1780s pregnant women in the first gang were given a short respite from labour in their advanced stages. . . . When [William] Dickson arrived in Barbados during the early 1770s he was:

> Astonished to see some women far gone in pregnancy, toiling in the field, and others whose naked infants lay exposed to the weather sprawling on a goat skin, or in a wooden tray. I have heard with indignation, drivers curse both them and their squalling brats, when they were suckling them.

The tendency to express hostility to pregnant women emerged during Ligon's time (1647–50) when planters were convinced that given the large profits of sugar cultivation, and the reasonable prices of slaves, it was cheaper to buy than to reproduce them naturally. . . . As a result, neither pre- nor post-natal care was provided for field women. . . .

Women, in both gangs, were whipped by male drivers for what were considered insubordinate actions. Women drivers of the second gangs were similarly required to use the whip: and they did. . . . For women who resisted, ran away or were violent, irons were used to enforce subordination and labour. Management considered it unsatisfactory to imprison slaves, and preferred the use of chains and irons to secure them while they laboured in the fields. . . .

The commonest form of punishment inflicted on field women in Barbados, until the late 1820s, was for drivers to tie their hands to a pole or tree above their heads and flog them upon the back. . . .

Corporal punishments were reserved for what masters considered to be minor offences. For more serious crimes, such as murder of whites, attacks upon white overseers, persistent running away or theft, punishment took a more "dreadful and excruciating" form. When, for example, in 1774 a field woman was accused and convicted for participation in the murder of a white overseer on a St. Philip cotton plantation, . . . she was chained to the gallows in a public place and starved to death; she died within four days. . . .

There was also a sexual dimension to the practice of physically punishing defenseless field women. . . . Violent sexual abuse and punishments for non-cooperation at the hands of masters, managers, overseers, poor-white labourers and, at times, black drivers and other élite male slaves, were part of field women's life experiences. . . . The basis of male assumptions that field women were, or should be, available for sexual exploitation was slave owners' attribution of social inferiority and lack of "honour" to these women, and therefore a degradation of the value of their sexuality. . . . In Barbados, as elsewhere in the British Caribbean until the closing years of slavery, the rape of an enslaved black woman was not an offence by law. Only white women could be raped as far as the judiciary was concerned. Some black men lost their lives on being convicted for raping white women, but neither white men nor black men were similarly punished for the rape of black women. . . .

Whereas field women achieved limited status in the production system as drivers of the second, third, and fourth gangs, and as special attendants to male drivers of the first gang, it was in relation to slave owners' households that slave women achieved their highest material rewards, social status, and human rights. . . .

There were also male slaves in the domestic labour force, but female housekeepers were considered the principal house slaves, and as such, were invested with special rights and "semi-freedoms." In terms of social status and power, they were on a par with head drivers of first gangs and chief artisans; together, they constituted a distinct labour aristocracy. . . .

In white households by the end of the [seventeenth] century, black slaves had replaced white servants and dominated occupational roles from washerwomen to housekeepers. . . .

Probably the most emotional aspects of house women's duties

were those of suckling, weaning, and the socialization of their owners' children. . . . As it was common for élite white women to consider the suckling of their own children unseemly, this task became an important function of slave nannies, who were intended to be responsible for these children into their adulthood. . . .

Domestic slaves, however, considered themselves better placed to survive the slavery system than were field women. Not only were their life experiences more varied, but their chances of manumission were infinitely greater. . . . Based on economic and social indicators, and on their own and their infants' mortality rate, house women were part of the labour élite. Nobody knew the true value attached to this status better than the house women themselves, though the clue possibly lies in the fact that many would rather risk life and limb in resistance than be sent back to the fields.

More African women came to the Americas before 1800 than European women. The number of African slave women forced into involuntary migration to North and South America is estimated at over two and one-half times the number of women who freely migrated from Great Britain, Scandinavia, Germany, the Netherlands, France, Spain, and Portugal. Far fewer women than men settlers came to the colonies of Spain, Portugal, and France. England's colonies—particularly those settled by Puritans, Quakers, and Pietists—had larger proportions of English and German girls and adult women. Yet in the context of the entire population of the Americas, their numbers were insignificant. Everywhere the relative scarcity of European women affected their status. How it did so depended on historic and cultural circumstances in various colonies.

5.4 Honor and Shame in New Spain

Three centuries of Spanish dominance implanted Iberian gender values deeply in the colonial cultures of the Western Hemisphere. Ramón Gutiérrez discusses what this meant in colonial New Mexico.

Don Francisco Armijo arrived at the Albuquerque home of his mother-in-law, Doña María Antonia Durán, in a very agitated mood at about nine in the evening of March 12, 1816. In one hand he had his whip, in the other a knife. He demanded to see his wife, Doña María Rosalía Maestas, who had been staying with her mother while he was out of town. When his wife entered the room Don Francisco began whipping her violently. He threw her to the floor, put his foot on her throat, and with the knife cut off her braids and hair. Don Francisco hurled the braids at his mother-in-law and dragged his wife out of the house. Why such violent treatment? Don Francisco said that it was "to protect my honor." He had heard that during his absence Juan García had propositioned his wife to adultery, giving her two sheep as a present, and had taken her in his carriage to the fiesta at Los Ranchos. For this Doña María Rosalía had brought scandal to his reputation "because she will not live in seclusion . . . she is shameless." . . .

When Don Francisco Armijo complained that his wife was shameless and whipped her and cut off her hair to guard her honor, [he was] . . . expressing the basic tenets of what Spaniards said constituted a virtuous life. The nexus between personal public behavior and a social structure predicated on conquest and force was provided by honor and shame, the values that most fundamentally defined virtue in colonial New Mexico. . . .

Honor also belonged collectively to one's family and to one's kindred as a group. . . . The patriarch of a family or household was responsible for the actions of all of his dependents. The conduct of children reflected on the father. . . . The honor of one reflected on all, just as the honor of one tarnished all.

Honor-virtue prescribed gender-specific rules of proper social comportment. Honor *(honor)* was strictly a male attribute while shame *(vergüenza)* was intrinsic to females. Infractions of behavioral norms by males were dishonoring, in females they were a sign of shamelessness. The shamelessness of a female reflected on the male head of the household and dishonored him and the family as a group. . . . Men were honorable if they esteemed honesty and loyalty and were concerned for their reputation and that of their family. Women embodied the sentiment of shame and were considered honorable if they cherished these same values. . . .

Women displayed *vergüenza* when they were sexually pure and displayed the utmost discretion around men. *Vergüenza* brought a blush to a woman's face when lewd matters were discussed and called for timidity around men. . . . Men were honorable if they acted with *hombría* (manliness) and exerted authority over their family. . . .

Because God had created woman as the weaker of the sexes and rendered her helpless before the desires of men, male authority enforced through seclusion was one way to guarantee female virtue and maintenance of the family's honor. . . . Doña María stated, "My daughter had that unfortunate frailty to which all the feminine sex are exposed." Frailty to the ploys of men and the desires of the flesh meant that it was necessary to seclude women to protect their virtue. Men could win and enhance their honor through action, but a woman's virtue was something that could not be won, only maintained or lost. . . .

Yet only in aristocratic households, where servants and retainers abounded, could resources be expended to assure that females were being properly restrained. The maintenance of virtue among aristocratic females was possible only because Indian and *genizaro* women could be forced or persuaded to offer sexual service. . . .

The landed peasantry prized honor-virtue just as much as the nobility because it signified participation in the values and ideals of Spanish society. No matter how lowly the peasant, he prided himself on being a Spaniard and thereby a player in the game of honor. Like men of the nobility, his sport was the conquest of Indian and *genizaro* women, his boast, the capacity to maintain the purity of his own women intact. . . .

The required participation of all able-bodied [peasant] household members at planting and harvest meant that there were periods when constraints on females of this class were less rigorously enforced. Juana Carrillo of Santa Fe admitted as much in 1712, when she confessed enjoying the affections of two men her father had hired for the spring planting. In households where men were frequently absent, such as those of soldiers, muleteers, shepherds, and hunters, cultural ideals were necessarily less rigid. The fact that females married to such men had to supervise family and home by themselves for large parts of the year, stave off Indian attacks, and care for the group's public rights meant that it was difficult for them to lead sheltered and secluded lives. Indeed, it was not uncommon to hear these women lament that they had been assaulted, raped, or seduced while their husbands or fathers were away from home.

Excerpted from *When Jesus Came, the Corn Mothers Went Away: Marriage, Sexuality, and Power in New Mexico, 1500–1846* by Ramón A. Gutiérrez (Stanford, CA: Stanford University Press, 1991), 207–9, 213–15, with the permission of the publishers, Stanford University Press. Copyright © 1991 by the Board of Trustees of the Leland Stanford Junior University.

Whether a woman was assaulted or seduced, the fault was presumed to be hers. Single women who willingly engaged in premarital intercourse frequently believed they were engaged to be married. If pregnancy occurred and the lover refused to marry, either the woman or her family might sue him to preserve the family honor. To win such a case required the woman to produce evidence both of a formal betrothal and of her virginity. Even if the engagement was proved, a man who successfully impugned his victim's reputation by charging promiscuity was excused from his promise of marriage.

Reputation was a public evaluation of how well someone personified the ideals of the honor code. Just as it was in the self-interest of men to have their sexual feats and prowess proclaimed, it was also to the benefit of women and particularly of their fathers and brothers to keep the knowledge of any frailty that might occur as secret as possible. In this task they often had the help of parish priests, who felt a primary responsibility for protecting the virtue of women and attenuating public scandal. To have it known that a daughter had been seduced and lost her virginity was to significantly alter her symbolic value on the marriage market. Familial resources could be severely taxed by marrying such a woman. If a father was going to secure her an honorable husband, a significant dowry would have to be offered, one that adequately remunerated the male for the acceptance of a spoiled woman. If the economic means to counter-balance the loss of virtue did not exist, parents might have to consent to someone of a lower status becoming their son-in-law, or face the possibility of never marrying off their daughter. . . .

The best way to assure that familial considerations in marriage would be placed above all else and that personal likes and desires did not complicate the matter was to preclude the expression of love. Perhaps the easiest way this could be done was to arrange a marriage while the candidate was still in infancy. By the time the child reached adolescence he or she would be faced with a fait accompli. There would be little choice but to do as parents ordered, and certainly the issue of love was unlikely to surface. One New Mexico folk poet described this practice thus:

> On the day of my birth
> They christened me
> They found me a wife
> And they married me

Equally common was the use of threats, intimidation, and force to convince a child to marry a person the parents or guardians considered advantageous. . . .

Although it was technically contrary to canon law for a parent to force a marital partner on their child, the practice was not all that uncommon in colonial New Mexico.

Excerpted from *When Jesus Came, the Corn Mothers Went Away: Marriage, Sexuality, and Power in New Mexico, 1500–1846* by Ramón A. Gutiérrez (Stanford, CA: Stanford University Press, 1991), 222, 228, with the permission of the publishers, Stanford University Press. Copyright © 1991 by the Board of Trustees of the Leland Stanford Junior University.

5.5 The Independence of Sor Juana Inés de la Cruz

A woman's physical sign of virtue—her virginity—was ideally claimed by her husband, who jealously guarded her reputation afterward. Not all women did marry. Some remained unmarried in the family homes of their parents or siblings. Others joined communities of women in convents as brides of Christ. By the seventeenth century, Catholic institutions for religious women dotted the cities and towns of Spain's American colonies, as well as those of Portuguese Brazil and French Canada. Nuns were cloistered and their lives regulated by rules adopted at the Council of Trent, where the male hierarchy reformed the institutions of the Catholic Church in the sixteenth century. In Mexico and Peru, the classes of secular society were replicated in religious communities. Elite convents provided a refuge for privileged women who chose neither marriage nor family dependency. Sor Juana Inés de la Cruz (1648–95) chose an intellectual life in the convent of St. Jerome in Mexico City. Born Juana Asbaje on a farm managed by her mother, she began her self-education in her grandfather's library. Since she could not enter a university, her education continued in Mexico City at the court of the Spanish colonial governor (or viceroy), where Juana was a lady-in-waiting to the viceroy's wife. At court, she met educated, aristocratic Spanish women, under whose patronage her career as a writer would flourish. After spending her teen years at court and publicly proving herself an intellectual prodigy in an examination organized by the viceroy, Juana Asbaje took the veil in 1668.

Although she could not leave her convent, hers was not a vow of solitude. Instead, her studies and writing were interrupted by streams of visitors: male priests and scholars, as well as women of the court. Like twelfth-century Hilda of Bingen, Sor Juana conducted a wide correspondence. She held offices in her order.

And she earned money to support her private servants by commissions for religious and secular poetry, songs, and dramas. Between 1689 and 1700, three volumes of her collected writings were published in Spain. Sor Juana's poetry eventually became part of the classic canon in Hispanic America.

But her scholarly prominence was contested for decades by male clerics in Mexico. With a sharp tongue, she defended her reputation in a private letter to her confessor in 1681 or 1682. But in that decade, when the viceroy and his wife visited her almost daily, she was relatively free to write. In the 1690s, Juana boldly spoke and wrote in defense of women's right to read, to think, and to criticize anyone, couching her argument not in terms of her own precocity or hopes of salvation, but in broad feminist strokes. Drawing upon a long tradition of biblical and classical sources similar to those used by Christine de Pisan in *The Book of the City of Ladies,* Sor Juana cited some forty cases of women who, rather than being silent and submissive, were vocal, public scholars, teachers, or leaders. She directly refuted contemporary interpretations of St. Paul's injunction that women should keep silent in churches and learn only from their husbands by citing the active roles women took in early Christianity. Ignorance in women was not a virtue, for she believed learning and knowledge were essential to understanding Christianity. Furthermore, Sor Juana argued that attempts to censor women's intellect were in vain, using a time when she was prohibited from reading by her mother superior as an example:

I obeyed her (for the three months or so that her authority over us lasted) in that I did not pick up a book. But with regard to avoiding study absolutely, as such a thing does not lie within my power, I could not do it. For although I did not study in books, I studied all the things that God created, taking them for my letters, and for my book all the intricate structures of this world. Nothing could I see without reflecting upon it, nothing could I hear without pondering it, even to the most minute, material things. . . . Well, and what then shall I tell you . . . of the secrets of nature that I have learned while cooking? I observe that an egg becomes solid and cooks in butter and oil, and on the contrary that it dissolves in sugar syrup. Or again, to ensure that sugar flow freely one need only add the slightest bit of water that has held quince or some other sour fruit. . . . I often say, when I make these little observations, "Had Aristotle cooked, he would have written a great deal more."

Reprinted by permission, from Sor Juana Inés de la Cruz, *The Answer/La Respuesta: Including a Selection of Poems,* critical edition and translation by Electa Arenal and Amanda Powell (New York: The Feminist Press at The City University of New York, 1994), 73, 75. Copyright © 1994 by Electa Arenal and Amanda Powell.

———————

Paralleling arguments more familiar in Europe than in the Americas, Sor Juana maintained that, through reading, she had learned that historically women were the equals of (and perhaps superior to) men. But such equality could be achieved only by educated women. Accepting Hispanic sexual seclusion of young women, Sor Juana stressed the importance of women teachers.

Oh, how many abuses would be avoided in our land if the older women were as well instructed as Leta [an early Christian women whom St. Jerome had advised on the education of her daughter] and knew how to teach as is commanded by St. Paul and my father St. Jerome! Instead, for lack of such learning and through the extreme feebleness in which they are determined to maintain our poor women, if any parents then wish to give their daughters more extensive Christian instruction than is usual, necessity and the lack of learned older women oblige them to employ men as instructors to teach reading and writing, numbers and music, and other skills. This leads to considerable harm, which occurs every day. . . . For this reason, many parents prefer to let their daughters remain uncivilized and untutored, rather than risk exposing them to such notorious peril as this familiarity with men.

Reprinted by permission, from Sor Juana Inés de la Cruz, *The Answer/La Respuesta: Including a Selection of Poems,* critical edition and translation by Electa Arenal and Amanda Powell (New York: The Feminist Press at The City University of New York, 1994), 85. Copyright © 1994 by Electa Arenal and Amanda Powell.

Under pressure from her church, Sor Juana silenced herself with a vow of faith and repentance in 1694, immediately after publishing her bold feminist statement. She died during an epidemic in Mexico City on April 17, 1695, when she was forty-seven years old. Sor Juana's published scholarship earned her recognition as a New World intellectual and as one of the finest lyric poets of the Spanish language.

Suggested Further Readings

Kathleen M. Brown's review article "Brave New Worlds: Women's and Gender History," *William and Mary Quarterly,* 3d ser., 50, no. 2 (April 1993): 311–28, is a useful guide to the extensive literature on North America and the Caribbean in the seventeenth and eighteenth centuries. Karen Anderson, in *Chain Her by One Foot: The Subjugation of Women in Seventeenth Century New France* (London: Routledge, 1991), argues that Huron and Montagnais women resisted the Jesuits' teachings and accepted the French feminine ideal only when their societies were nearly destroyed by war, epidemics, and famine. Sylvia Van Kirk contends, in *"Many Tender Ties": Women in Fur Trade Society, 1670–1870* (Winnipeg: Watson & Dwyer, 1980), that

Indian women's marriages to French fur traders formed the critical cultural link between their peoples. Nancy Shoemaker's study
of the saintly Mohawk woman Kateri Tekakwitha finds that Iroquois women adapted Christian symbols brought to New
France by the Jesuit priests to subvert patriarchy. Shoemaker's
introduction to the volume she edited, *Negotiators of Change:
Historical Perspectives on Native American Women* (New York:
Routledge, 1995), is a useful brief summary of key issues in
interpreting early contact between Europeans and North Ameri-
can women. A powerful woman who confronted the English in
Virginia in the seventeenth century is discussed by Martha W.
McCartney in "Cockacoeske, Queen of Pamunkey: Diplomat and
Suzeraine," in *Powhatan's Mantle,* edited by Peter H. Wood,
Gregory A. Waselkov, and M. Thomas Hatley (Lincoln: Univer-
sity of Nebraska Press, 1989). Irene Silverblatt, *Moon, Sun, and
Witches: Gender Ideologies and Class in Inca and Colonial Peru*
(Princeton, NJ: Princeton University Press, 1987), differentiates
between the impact of Spanish colonization on women of the
Inca nobility and peasants. Another study of indigenous women
of the Andes is Ann Zulawski's article "Social Differentiation,
Gender and Ethnicity: Urban Indian Women in Colonial Bolivia,
1640–1725," *Latin American Research Review* 25, no. 2 (1990):
93–114.

*More Than Chattel: Black Women and Slavery in the Ameri-
cas,* David Barry Gaspar and Darlene Clark Hine, eds. (Bloo-
mington: Indiana University Press, 1996), surveys the conditions
of African and African-American women's lives throughout the
Western Hemisphere. Marietta Morrissey, in *Slave Women in the
New World: Gender Stratification in the Caribbean* (Lawrence:
University Press of Kansas, 1989), and Barbara Bush, in *Slave
Women in Caribbean Society, 1650–1838* (Bloomington: Indiana
University Press, 1990), discuss the experiences of slave women
in the British West Indies. For British North America, see Jacque-
line Jones, "Race, Sex, and Self-Evident Truths: The Status of
Slave Women during the Era of the American Revolution," in
Women in the Age of the American Revolution, edited by Ronald
Hoffman and Peter J. Albert (Charlottesville: University Press of
Virginia, 1989).

For further exploration of Hispanic concepts of shame and
virtue, see Patricia Seed, *To Love, Honor, and Obey in Colonial
Mexico: Conflicts over Marriage Choice, 1574–1821* (Stanford,

CA: Stanford University Press, 1988). Two collections of articles edited by Asunción Lavrin present a range of scholarship: *Sexuality and Marriage in Colonial Latin America* (Lincoln: University of Nebraska Press, 1989) and *Latin American Women: Historical Perspectives* (Westport, CT: Greenwood Press, 1978). Among the most useful of many studies of white women in British North American colonies are Laurel Thatcher Ulrich, *Good Wives: Image and Reality in the Lives of Women in Northern New England, 1650–1750* (New York: Knopf, 1987); Carol F. Karlsen, *The Devil in the Shape of a Woman: Witchcraft in Colonial New England* (New York: Norton, 1987); Lois Green Carr and Lorena S. Walsh, "The Planter's Wife: The Experience of White Women in Seventeenth-Century Maryland," *William and Mary Quarterly,* 3d ser., 34 (1977): 542–71; and Mary Beth Norton, *Liberty's Daughters: The Revolutionary Experience of American Women, 1750–1800* (Boston: Little, Brown, 1980).

–6–

AFRICAN WOMEN IN A NEW ERA OF COMMERCE AND STATE BUILDING

West African mother and child. (Mali, Bamana, nineteenth-twentieth century. The Metropolitan Museum of Art. The Michael C. Rockefeller Memorial Collection.)

The Portuguese sailors who ventured along West Africa's coast in the fifteenth century opened new trade routes that initiated Western Europe's mastery of seaborne world trade. The ships that later carried Catholic missionary priests to Angola's shores brought back ivory, gold, and slaves. As the wealth of Africa enticed competitors from France, the Netherlands, Prussia, Denmark, and England, resident European agents wrote accounts of the people with whom they traded, much as foreign Muslim merchants had begun doing more than five hundred years earlier.

Christian European men arrived in Africa with many of the same gender prejudices as their Muslim predecessors: favoring virginity, shyness, and sexual modesty in women; regarding nudity as obscene; expecting men to dominate farming and trade, as well as war, hunting, and fishing. Though permeated with bias of cultural ethnocentrism and Christian contempt for "heathen" beliefs, European accounts written before 1700 seldom express the racial contempt for Africans that arose in later centuries of colonial conquest. By the end of the seventeenth century, in both West and Central Africa, accounts of literate Africans and oral histories complement European documents, allowing nuanced commentaries on relationships between free and slave women, as well as biographies of individuals such as Queen Njinga and Betsey Heard.

For more than 4 million African women, expanding trade between 1480 and 1850 meant estrangement from family and community in forced exile to a life of slavery in the Americas. Many more millions of African women experienced changing, and sometimes chaotic, economic and political circumstances within their own countries during that period.

6.1 Fetu Women on the Coast of Ghana, 1662–69

Wilhelm Johann Muller was a Lutheran pastor for the European employees of a Danish trading company in a West African coastal town of the Fetu nation in what is today Ghana. Although he compared the customs of the Fetu with those of Europeans, sometimes unfavorably, his observations of Fetu women's appearance are reliable. For example, he was aware that women's ordinary clothing varied according to their social rank.

Women of low status wear only an under-garment, consisting of one or two farthoms of linen cloth or say. They tie it round their body with a belt, in such a way that the lower part of the garment reaches down to the knee or below it. They go around with the upper part of their body naked. They do not specially adorn themselves, except that, like the men, they wash their body daily and smear it with palm oil, so that they shine the whole day.

They plait their hair elegantly and may hang just one large blue bead in it. Around the neck, arms and legs they have a string of common beads and perhaps an elegant little cord woven from bark.

Those who are of high status and possess a large fortune, however, put on much more magnificent clothes and other women's ornaments. . . .

Important ladies cover the upper part of their body with the most precious silk garments that money can buy. The most marketable are those made in the East Indies and brought in large quantities for sale on the Guinea coast. . . . With such silk garments many women, out of modesty, cover their breast. Others tie them below their naked breast, as decoration. . . .

In adorning their heads, they plait their hair into several fairly long frizzy locks, and, like distinguished gentlemen, hang precious stones and golden ornaments on it. . . .

On their arms, fingers and legs they wear gold and silver rings and other gold ornaments, as far as their fortune stretches.

This is the everyday costume and finery in which important ladies let themselves be seen daily. . . . This could be stately and magnificent enough for these black, heathen people. Nevertheless, they appear in far more stately and magnificent apparel when they hold a day of celebration.

"Wilhelm Johann Muller's Description of the Fetu Country, 1662–69" in *German Sources for West African History, 1599–1669,* edited and translated by Adam Jones (Wiesbaden, Germany: Franz Steiner Verlag GMBH, 1983), 205–6. Notes omitted.

The wealth of the important families clearly impressed Muller, and he was not critical of the Fetu marriage ceremony. As a Christian, Muller was shocked by African polygyny. Wives and slave concubines in Fetu were forced to adhere to a double standard of chastity not imposed on males, but, as Muller notes, these women shared little else in a status-conscious society.

As soon as the wedding day arrives, the bride goes out with her playmates to bathe and anoint herself. She adorns herself as splendidly and elegantly as she is able to do and can afford, with clothes, golden necklaces and bracelets, rings, beads, . . . etc., and then goes back and forth in her finery, to display herself at public dances. . . .

Towards noon she goes with her companions into the compound or house in which the bridegroom and the friends he has invited are gathered. Then something to eat is brought, or the bridegroom just treats people to palm wine and perhaps spirits. They enjoy themselves, dancing, singing and capering till late in the night. When the time comes to go to bed, the bride goes with some of her friends to a bedroom in which the wedding bed is prepared, but they bar the bedroom door. A short while afterwards the bridegroom comes and knocks on the barred door; but it is not opened for him unless he has previously promised to treat people again the following day. Then he is permitted free entry and all the wedding guests go away. No-one remains in the bedroom except the bridegroom and his bride, together with a young girl aged seven or eight, who must sleep in between them and watch out that they do not touch each other for seven days. It is hard to believe, however, that this really happens. At daybreak a group of old women—relatives of the bridegroom and of the bride—come in and bring the young people warm water to wash in. If the bridegroom then treats these old women to plenty of spirits, or some gold for palm wine, they call out that he is a handsome, generous man; but if he shows himself miserly, they spread the word in the open market and street that he is a *quiteriqui,* a stingy niggard, who does no-one any good.

The aforementioned wedding festivities are only held when someone marries his first wife, whom he wishes to regard as the principal wife among all the others. If he takes others in addition, the marriage takes place quite quietly and no special wedding-day is celebrated.

Here it is to be noted that if someone wants to take a wife, she must first, in the presence of the bridegroom and her friends, . . . [make an oath] that she will remain faithful to him and not go near any stranger. If she afterwards does not keep the oath she has sworn, he has the power to proceed against her according to the law. . . . He divorces her as an ografo (a faithless wife), insulting and mocking her.

The husband, however, is not bound by such an oath. Even if he is unfaithful to his wives, this is not held against him. He likewise gives *summán* to [requires an oath from] his concubines, in order that they shall not lie with anyone. If they break their oath, he is free to sell or even kill them, as his bondswomen.

The Blacks make this distinction between their many wives: they regard some as proper wives and some as concubines. This distinction was also made in antiquity.

Proper wives are free women, born of free, highly respectable parents.

Among these, the first wife, who is called *odufù*, is the most important.

She is honoured above everyone by the husband and concubines. In her daily dress and ornaments she outdoes all other wives, and she has charge over the concubines and domestic servants. The other wives, though free people and of high birth, are considered inferior to this *odufù;* and as a sign of their subordination, they must say '*Acjù'* to the first-chosen wife and obey her orders.

The concubines are not free women but slaves. Consequently they are not considered equal to the proper wives and must perform all the heavy housework, including cooking, carrying wood and water, baking, washing etc., as befits bonds-women. As regards their dress and female ornaments, too, they are treated as nothing but bondswomen, unless the husband, out of special affection, makes one or other of them the present of a piece of clothing.

"Wilhelm Johann Muller's Description of the Fetu Country, 1662–69" in *German Sources for West African History, 1599–1669*, edited and translated by Adam Jones (Wiesbaden, Germany: Franz Steiner Verlag GMBH, 1983), 214–15. Notes omitted.

African women's domination of local markets impressed European travelers in the seventeenth century as much as it had Muslims centuries before. Although the spread of Islam in West Africa would eventually drive women from market stalls in

Muslim towns, female traders were encountered widely when Wilhelm Muller lived in Ghana.

As regards the trade they conduct among themselves, they have their general markets at Fetu, Cabo Corso and Friederichs-Berg, at which they sell their wares every day. Apart from the peasants who bring palm wine and sugar-cane to market every day, there are no men who stand in public markets to trade, but only women. It is remarkable to see how the market is filled every day with stark naked women, selling large and small *milie, canties,* fresh fish and fish fried in palm oil, *anassas, baccofes, enjamos, bananses, crosse, malaguetta* etc.

In one spot stands a woman who has a large wooden dish of chopped tobacco, which grows in the Fetu country, with tobacco pipes [which have bowls] the size of a fist. In another is a woman with fowls, eggs and palm oil in large pots for sale.

Besides the aforementioned trade in livestock, the Fetu people conduct great trade in salt, which they know how to boil in their country themselves; for they fill large earthenware pots with the stagnant water which is brought inland when the salty sea overflows and which then settles there. They place the pots on a large fire, let the water become hot and boil it till the brine has completely dried up and turned into salt. Then they tip the salt out in the sun and stir frequently, till it is dry, fine and good. Fetu salt is so strong and white that it is not inferior to the best European salt in taste or colour. . . .

Not only is this salt sold daily in the market by black women, but large quantities are also carried a great distance inland in special baskets for sale.

The Fetu tradeswomen devote great energy to selling the goods they have carried to market before the day is over, so that nothing is left over for the following day, or is spoilt, or must be consumed by them themselves. Consequently one hears women vying with one another to attract passers-by with persuasive words, and they do not willingly let these passers-by out of their hands until they have bought something.

"Wilhelm Johann Muller's Description of the Fetu Country, 1662–69" in *German Sources for West African History, 1599–1669,* edited and translated by Adam Jones (Wiesbaden, Germany: Franz Steiner Verlag GMBH, 1983), 243–44. Notes omitted.

6.2 Slave Wives, Free Sisters: Bakongo Women

Gold was the most valuable African export, initially sought by Europeans to enable them to trade in Asia. Trade in slaves, at first of minor importance, grew rapidly in the seventeenth century, and by the eighteenth century, Europeans came to Africa only to buy people. For powerful Africans, the trade in slaves—usually people regarded as "other," foreigners whose ethnic identity and language distanced them from their African captors—meant earnings to purchase imported products. The scramble to obtain this wealth of highly valued Asian cloth, Indian Ocean cowrie shells, European iron and copper bars, and guns disrupted kingdoms and villages. Some communities were devastated by slave raiders, even as new African empires of Oyo, Asante, and Dahomey consolidated power, offering protection from the slave trade to their own peoples as their wars of expansion produced more slave prisoners at their peripheries.

Within Africa, the most prized slaves were women whose value was higher than that of men. There was a tendency, therefore, for captive women to be retained within Africa, whereas men were sold to Europeans, who prized and paid more for them. After 1600, slavery, though an ancient African institution, increased within the continent under stimulation from the Atlantic slave trade. Distinctions between free and slave women grew, although any woman and her children added the numbers to a household that increased its community influence and status.

These distinctions are evident in the kingdom of Kongo, a Central African coastal nation that eventually raided the interior for slaves but sold very few of the people living within its own borders. The intensity of the slave trade in Central Africa not only sent millions of men, women, and children to the Americas, it also greatly increased the numbers of slaves owned by the indigenous nobility of Kongo.

The kingdom of Kongo, where the Bakongo lived, administered an extensive territory in 1483 when the Portuguese landed. Located on the south bank of the Zaire (Congo) River, the kingdom controlled the Atlantic coast almost as far south as Luanda (today a part of Angola) and about as far into the interior. Kongo's kings welcomed Portuguese merchants, converted to Christianity, and urged the pope to send Roman Catholic priests to serve their people. Catholicism spread rapidly, especially among the Kongo aristocracy. Both educated Kongolese and resident priests wrote in Portuguese. Their writings have provided scholars with unusual sources on the history and lives of the inhabitants.

The Bakongo's lineage system was matrilineal. Naturally, free women's relationships were different from those in the average patrilineal society. Inheritance and kin identity were traced through the female line. The children of a marriage were seen as members of the mother's family. Her older sisters might have influence on decisions made by the lineage, and her brothers had more power over her children than her husband did.

Susan Broadhead uses concepts from an analysis of several African patrilineal societies made by Karen Sacks to explain relationships within the matrilineal Kongo:

In examining the role of women in Bakongo society and their relation to slavery, the most helpful theoretical model is that developed by Karen Sacks. . . . Sacks divides women's roles analytically into two categories, one associated with the status of sister and the other with that of wife. In general she links sisterhood with positions of autonomy, ownership, solidarity, and power; while wifehood is linked with positions of subordination, dependence, and isolation. The bulk of her case studies involve societies practicing what she terms a "kin corporate mode of production," an analytical model which also is useful for looking at Bakongo society in this era. The central feature of Sacks's model is that the means of production are owned collectively by groups of kin, lineages, or lineage segments, whose essential relationships are those obtaining among siblings. Women in such a system participate in the ownership of the means of production through their status as sisters. In most of the [patrilineal] cases described by Sacks, young women in their childbearing years are confined to the wife role, producing children for their husbands' lineages and laboring in their husbands' fields and compounds. Older women, on the other hand, are often more able to assume the role of sister, helping to advise on the affairs of their lineage and commanding the services of daughters-in-law. Through these cases Sacks demonstrates that there is a major contradiction between woman's place as wife and sister.

From Susan Herlin Broadhead, "Slave Wives, Free Sisters: Bakongo Women and Slavery, c. 1700–1850," in *Women and Slavery in Africa,* edited by Claire C.

Broadhead expands on the concepts Karen Sacks developed to distinguish between free sisters and free wives to illustrate who has rights to both productive and reproductive capacities of women and men when some are free and many are slaves.

In this matrilineally oriented society a free woman's reproductive capacity was not ordinarily transferrable by marriage. Thus, in contrast to the case of women in most patrilineally organized societies, for free Bakongo women the tension between spouse and sibling roles was lessened because the role of wife was secondary. The primacy of sister status at the expense of the wife role is epitomized in the lifestyle of royal princesses in Loango in the eighteenth century. They could choose any man for a husband, even if already married, and dismiss him at will. For most women, however, the primacy of sister status during the reproductive years basically meant access to divorce.

Slave women, by contrast, enjoyed no legal rights as siblings. Despite the fact that . . . they served as "sister surrogates" in the reproductive sphere, they had no recognized birth lineage. Thus, following Sacks's model, they functioned exclusively in the role of wife or dependent within the lineage which owned them. This means that the greatest contradiction in the spouse-sibling roles in the case of Bakongo women appeared not during the different stages in a single woman's life, but rather between the roles of different categories of women. The most obvious distinction was between that of free and slave women, with the latter confined, as we have seen, to a permanent wife position. There were also class distinctions in "women's places," with noblewomen generally having greater access to positions of power based on their status as sisters in ruling families. Like their brothers, at least in some circumstances, they could aspire to head households, and this apparently was the key to power within the aristocracy.

Bakongo men could only use their reproductive capacities on behalf of their lineage through marriage to, or cohabitation with, a slave woman. The offspring of slave wives of male slaves also normally belonged to the lineage owning the woman. A freeborn woman could be reduced to de facto slavery if her lineage deserted her, defaulted in its obligations, or otherwise lost its rights in her offspring. A woman without legally recognized ties of sisterhood was a slave, often to her husband's lineage.

Although it did not affect her reproductive services, marriage did transfer a part of a free woman's productive services: specifically, it obligated her to grow and prepare food for her husband, her children by him, and sometimes his relatives as well. Marriage also served to join two lineages and create a unit of production which combined the specialized labor of males and females. The marital household was the fundamental unit of Bakongo society. To the daily needs of their households women contributed grains and vegetables; pots and baskets; and cooking of the major daily meal. Men provided the hoes with which their wives farmed, goods obtained through trade or the hunt (salt, meat, fish, imported items), and tree products (bananas, palm oil, palm wine, building materials, buildings, and the cloth woven from tree fibers). Both spouses ordinarily participated in child-rearing.

Almost all women in Bakongo society spent their reproductive years functioning on a daily basis mainly in the role of wife. This applied equally to slave or free women, with the exception only of aristocratic women during the seventeenth and part of the eighteenth centuries. Male slaves owed only their reproductive services to their owner. Although they generally participated in the male productive sphere, they were sometimes required to do normally female farming tasks. They were socialized in the role of sons (albeit perpetual ones).

From Susan Herlin Broadhead, "Slave Wives, Free Sisters: Bakongo Women and Slavery, c. 1700–1850," in *Women and Slavery in Africa,* edited by Claire C. Robertson and Martin A. Klein (Madison: University of Wisconsin Press, 1983), 161–62. Copyright © 1983. Reprinted by permission of The University of Wisconsin Press. Notes omitted.

Bakongo male aristocrats had multiple wives, including many slave wives. Noblewomen who held office could also marry more than one husband, but the growth of slavery offered them even greater privileges. They gained political influence and power, some administering territories within the kingdom. For such noblewomen, slaves were essential to household size, prestige, and independence.

As was the case among peasants, the household was the fundamental social unit for the aristocracy. However, noble households differed significantly from peasant ones. They did not support themselves. Also they were quite large—that of a seventeenth-century king was a city within the city. Membership consisted largely of women and children, both slave and free, organized under the supervision of a highborn principal wife or wives.

Slave wives were widely kept among the nobility. In the first half of the seventeenth century such wives and their royal children figured prominently in the intricacies of royal succession politics. In this period noble status, including eligibility for the throne, was not calculated matrilineally but bilaterally from the founder of the Christian dynasty, the sixteenth-century king, Affonso I [1506–43]. By either set of rules, the children of slave wives belonged to the lineage of their father, since they had no separate lineage on their mother's side under Kongo law.

Not all noble households were headed by men. Prominent noblewomen sometimes headed their own households and participated directly in political life, joining or organizing noble factions and even governing districts or provinces. Some women, such as the Queen Mother and the female members of the royal council, were granted lands of their own for a living. Others appear to have inherited land and governing positions through their position as sisters within a particular branch of the various noble lineages. Such noblewomen, like their brother household heads, had control of both household slaves and agricultural workers. Details of the marriage patterns of such women are not known, although there are reports indicating that in some cases spouses settled in different places, each maintaining his or her own household.

From Susan Herlin Broadhead, "Slave Wives, Free Sisters: Bakongo Women and Slavery, c. 1700–1850," in *Women and Slavery in Africa,* edited by Claire C. Robertson and Martin A. Klein (Madison: University of Wisconsin Press, 1983), 166. Copyright © 1983. Reprinted by permission of The University of Wisconsin Press. Notes omitted.

By the end of the seventeenth century, Kongo had too many aristocrats. The nobility who traced their descent from Affonso I through either their matrilineal or patrilineal ancestors increased at fantastic rates in a polygynous society. Unfortunately, Kongo did not have sufficient communities requiring the administration of an aristocrat. Unemployed nobles sought power by attempting to displace rivals within the kingdom, a process encouraged by representatives of competing European nations that stood ready to arm Kongo factions.

In the last quarter of the seventeenth century and the first decade or so of the eighteenth century the Kongo countryside was racked by a long series of civil wars. The capital was abandoned, and noble households dispersed to provincial bases. Slaves and other clients followed their noble masters, or decamped, attaching themselves for safety to new households, providing soldiers and retainers for the wars and agricultural labor for their new patrons. As the condition of war continued, many Bakongo retreated into the forests and hills where they built stockaded villages to avoid the perils of endemic unrest.

During the eighteenth century the international slave trade became the principal form of long-distance commerce for the area. Many of the slaves, shipped in increasing numbers and at escalating prices from the coastal states' well-organized markets, came from interior sources beyond Kongo borders. . . .

The slaves preferred for export were young adult males. Enslaved females found a ready market within Kongo, usually as slave wives. A late-century missionary maintained that ten to twenty wives elevated a husband to the status of "great man." Only the poor had just one wife. Even slaves could have more than one. Further, his informants maintained that many more men than women were exported, leaving a surplus of women of marriageable age in the population. A recent study of the area affected by the Angolan slave trade (including parts of Kongo) suggests that the practice of exporting more males indeed led to heavy concentrations of adult females in the population of the region. However, it seems just as likely that a growing local demand for slave wives led instead to a surplus of males for export. Since Kongo was mainly a transit area for the eighteenth-century trade, a net population gain seems likely. . . . If, as seems likely, there was a trend toward a predominance of females in the work force and a fairly strict division of labor by gender, some changes might be expected in levels of production in the subsistence sector. A change in the diet as a result of the availability of more field crops (produced by women) and fewer tree crops (produced by men) might be postulated. However, there is little evidence for this one way or the other. Among male-sphere food products, only salt is specifically mentioned as scarce, and there is no evidence that this was connected to a shortage of men. However, there is evidence of change in productive patterns outside the realm of food production. Such traditionally male-manufactured goods as cloth and hoes were gradually replaced in the Kongo economy by imported European and Asian versions. This particularly affected the production of cloth money in this period. Production of cloth for personal use continued in the interior well into the nineteenth century. However, the wearing of imported cloth was a status symbol, which slowly spread from its restricted place among the aristocracy. . . .

Although European observers of the period saw women only in their status as wives, or occasionally rulers with female slave entourages, they nonetheless make it clear from their observations that women were actively involved in the community life of the times. Women are noted as traditional healers and diviners and as patrons of the Christian church. Women participated in the councils of the elders and in the communal festivals which were occasioned by the arrival of a missionary. Women served as the commissariat for armies and, of course, cultivated two crops a year, cooked the food, and participated in the distinctively female aspects of such community events as initiation, childbirth, marriage, and funerals. With the exception of those functions which required full membership in a lineage, such as council membership or kanda leadership, slave women apparently participated in the normal sphere of women's activities. Under this circumstance it is not hard to imagine how the question of slave origins could become subject to debate within a couple of generations as, on the one hand, success in reproduction, production, and alliance building created opportunities for slave branches to better themselves, and, on the other hand, lack of children, poor productivity, or witchcraft convictions reduced some free families to slave status.

From Susan Herlin Broadhead, "Slave Wives, Free Sisters: Bakongo Women and Slavery, c. 1700–1850," in *Women and Slavery in Africa,* edited by Claire C. Robertson and Martin A. Klein (Madison: University of Wisconsin Press, 1983), 166–67, 171, 173. Copyright © 1983. Reprinted by permission of The University of Wisconsin Press. Notes omitted.

6.3 Queen Njinga of Ndongo and Matamba, 1624–63

Among all the women who gained power in Central Africa in the wake of the seventeenth-century civil wars that raged not only in Kongo but also in adjacent states, the most famous was Njinga (or Nzinga), Queen of Ndongo and Matamba. Queen Njinga figures in African history as a positive symbol of mythical proportions embodying both heroic resistance to Portuguese colonialism and female power. As a monarch who wielded power for nearly four decades, Njinga's story is known from oral tradition and the writings of Portuguese priests and diplomats resident at her court. That Njinga's central dilemma of legitimating her political power arose from her being a woman is not contested.

The kingdom of Ndongo lies on the Atlantic coast, bordering Kongo to the north. Matamba was adjacent to Ndongo's eastern border. Armed by Portugal, the rulers of Ndongo gained independence from Kongo in the sixteenth century. The coastal town of Luanda in Ndongo became the home of many Portuguese traders and the base for Portuguese efforts to colonize Ndongo and Matamba after 1571. Portuguese interventions in the following century took the form of support for pliant clients in African civil wars as well as direct invasion. Eventually, the entire region would fall under Portuguese governance as the colony of Angola. But that was long after Queen Njinga's reign.

When the king of Ndongo died in 1623, his sister Njinga became regent for his heir, an underage son. She had the heir killed and assumed power in Ndongo. For the next thirty-two years, she conducted an extraordinary series of campaigns and alliances to secure the throne. Not until she successfully negotiated a 1656 treaty with the Portuguese could she afford to relax. The fact that she was a female ruler made her struggle much more difficult—so much so that, in the 1640s, she decided to "become a man" in an attempt to broaden general acceptance of her administration.

The legitimacy of her succession depended on the "constitution" of Ndongo. Ndongo was not a modern state with a written constitution but rather a decentralized entity in which relative power sometimes centered upon a strong monarch, sometimes upon the noblemen who headed family-based coalitions. Legitimacy of office and political acts was based on widely known traditions and historical precedents, whose meaning was open to varying interpretations. John Thornton explains:

In seventeenth-century Ndongo these [constitutional] issues . . . could be settled by the emergence of a powerful ruler or stable polity which would enforce law and ensure that the historical precedents supporting his or her claims were accepted as legitimate. But at the time of Njinga, and for some years before her succession, this comfortable situation of clearly defined constitutional precedent was far from being established and various rival social groups struggled to create a constitution that favored them. . . .

Ultimately, of course, the real resolution of the constitutional problems lay as much in who could win the struggles in the material field, through marshalling supporters or armies, as in who could convince their rivals of the truth of historical or legal precedents. . . .

Although we cannot know all the details of raw political power in Njinga's time, the limited source material describing the structure of Ndongo from the mid-sixteenth century gives us an idea. When the earliest Portuguese arrived in Ndongo in the 1560s they found a fairly decentralized state. The king ruled along with a number of powerful, territorially based nobles (the *makota,* singular *dikota*), who represented a check on his absolute power. . . .

But the kings of the later sixteenth and early seventeenth centuries moved to centralize their authority, especially making use of royal slaves, the *ijiko* (singular *kijiko*). They had also perhaps asserted the right to hereditary succession according to the rules of kinship rather than election by the *makota*. Late sixteenth-century kings drew substantial revenues from villages of their slaves planted throughout the country, and at the same time slave officials managed affairs at court and formed the elite and officer corps of the royal army. Moreover, they placed the *ijiko* as judicial and military supervisors over the territorial nobles, thus reducing their power while insuring the collection of taxes. This use of slaves greatly enhanced royal revenues and probably allowed the rulers to take in many members of the lesser nobility as clients. Royally appointed officers could be sent on missions to collect taxes from the nobility, thus becoming enriched.

It was this growing and increasingly powerful class of court slaves that supported Njinga in her quest for power, and her struggle against rivals over who controlled the military slaves (*kimbare,* plural *imbare*) was the crux of her early relations with Portugal. What is more, Njinga's first rival, Hari a Kiluanji, was essentially a *dikota* [nobleman] who might benefit from reversing the tendency to centralization under royal slaves that benefited Njinga. As Fernão de Sousa, the Portuguese governor of Angola, put it, when speaking of the [royal slaves] . . . who were "captives of the king," one could dispense with the ruler were it not for them, and the country might revert to rule by [nobles] . . . each of whom was "lord of his *morinda* [group of free people] and lands where they live." Indeed, it was perhaps this fundamental struggle, more than the fact that Hari a Kiluanji had sought Portuguese support, in exchange for giving the governor his vassalage, that set him and his Portuguese supporters against Njinga, who had herself initially offered to swear vassalage to Portugal and to accept the terms of her predecessors.

The war of the Ndongo succession in the early 1620s was thus as much a struggle over the fundamental constitution of Ndongo as simply an episode in the Portuguese invasion of Angola, and Hari a Kiluanji and [her second rival] Ngola Hari were therefore more than simply Portuguese puppets. . . . [The essential issue was] did the *ijiko* [royal slaves] have the right to enthrone Njinga against the wishes of the *makota* [nobles], or did the *makota* have the final say in succession? Could these electors abandon hereditary succession should they choose, especially if an eligible heir were lacking? If hereditary factors had to be considered, what determined who was eligible to succeed? Finally did the precedents exclude females from power, as partisans of Hari a Kiluanji assured Fernão de Sousa . . . ?

John K. Thornton, "Legitimacy and Political Power: Queen Njinga, 1624–1663," *Journal of African History* 32 (1991): 28–31. Reprinted with the permission of Cambridge University Press. Notes omitted.

The complete story of what followed is too long to include here. Njinga was driven out of Ndongo and retreated to Matamba, where her capital was taken in 1626 and 1628, only to be re-taken by Njinga each time. She made an alliance with the Im-bangala, mercenaries who were located to her southeast. In 1628, they switched sides, joining her opponents during a battle. Njinga responded by reorganizing her army on the Imbangala model. She kept that organization until 1640, when—after she defeated the nobles contesting her legitimacy—she returned to Christianity. She made alliances then with the king of the Kongo, at least twice. John Thornton describes her effort in this period to "become a man":

At some point in the 1640s Njinga decided "to become a man". . . . Njinga's husbands became her "concubines," and she took several at the same time. She required these husbands to dress in women's clothes and to sleep among her maids in waiting. Should they touch these maids sexually they would be instantly killed.

Njinga reinforced this maleness by engaging in virile pursuits. She led her troops personally in battle. . . . She equipped a battalion of her ladies in waiting as soldiers and used them as her personal guard as well, and she was quite dexterous in the use of arms herself. . . .

Njinga's gender change was not simply a personal quirk or a psy-chological reaction to her illegitimate situation. There were prece-dents for gender change among powerful women in central Africa, where the distinction between sex as a biological condition and gen-der as a social condition is made clear in law. In Kongo, for example, women who obtained or were given positions of political power had the right to marry several men and also had the right to dispose of them whenever they saw fit. This form of polyandry was only for the upper class and certainly did not occur in other settings.

The various twists of Njinga's coping with the barrier of her fe-male sex, and even the assertions of maleness by which she finally overcame it, demonstrate that, as powerful as Njinga became, she could not simply create the constitutional precedents she needed to establish her power. . . .

The epilogue to the case of Njinga confirms the role of precedent in African constitutional law. Obviously, once Njinga had secured her power and based it on historical precedent, and once she and her successors had defeated those who challenged her claim, she became a historical precedent herself. While Njinga had obviously not overcome the idea that females could not rule in Ndongo during her lifetime, and had to "become a male" to retain power, her female successors faced little problem in being accepted as rulers.

The combined kingdom of Ndongo and Matamba (a title still in use in 1756), which she had ruled, had numerous queens in the following century. . . . In the period of 104 years that followed Njinga's death in 1663, queens ruled for at least eighty of them. . . . Indeed there are few examples in history of a country ruled so consistently by a queen as Matamba in the century after Njinga.

John K. Thornton, "Legitimacy and Political Power: Queen Njinga, 1624–1663," *Journal of African History* 32 (1991): 38–40. Reprinted with the permission of Cambridge University Press. Notes omitted.

6.4 Eur-African Women Slave Traders

Temporary marriages have been a social institution in world history for centuries. They were frequently contracted between an outsider male and an indigenous female. A foreign male merchant gained access to markets by marrying a local woman. Male religious pilgrims, soldiers of an occupying army, and employees on temporary assignments also married women during their travels. Free women entered such marriages for economic or social reasons. Where women were severely subordinated to men or enslaved, they might be "given" to travelers as wives or concubines by their fathers or brothers.

Islam provides rules to protect both parties in a temporary marriage (especially at its conclusion). Christianity condemned temporary marriage, but Christian men in Africa often married local women on this basis. The children of such marriages shared the languages and cultures of both parents. However, they were marginal people, not assured acceptance in either family. On the West African coast, African wives and their daughters born of marriages to European traders could exploit their marginality to become influential in the Atlantic slave trade. Bruce L. Mouser describes Eur-African women slavers who lived in what is now Guinea.

Along the rivers of coastal Guinea-Conakry, a number of women were active participants in the slave trade during the late eighteenth and early nineteenth centuries. Among the more prosperous women

slave traders were three who became as well known to champions of
the anti-slave trade movement as they were to ship captains plying
the coast. These women were Betsy Heard of Bereira on the Bereira
River, Elizabeth Frazer Skelton of Victoria on the Rio Nuñez, and
Mary Faber of Sangha on the Rio Pongo. . . .

Successful women entrepreneurs along these rivers were not unusual on the windward coast at the time. Perhaps the most famous of
the early women traders was Bibiana Vaz of Eur-African ancestry
who operated out of Cacheu on the Cacheu River during the seventeenth century. Bibiana Vaz had married a Portuguese captain,
Ambrosio Gomez, and had drawn into her commercial empire other
Luso-Africans who proclaimed a brief republic in 1684. Less spec-
tacular but certainly more visible were the women traders of Gorée
and Saint Louis [Senegal], some of whom were of Eur-African descent, others of indigenous background. These African traders, the
signares, attached themselves to European traders or civil servants
for the purposes of obtaining commercial and political advantages as
well as social status. Europeans were attracted in turn by the expert
knowledge and the ties to the local market which these "culture-bro-
kers" represented. Europeans also were drawn by the chance to escape from the tedium of life on the coast and by the desire to
establish a household, if only for a short period. Such a system of
"mutual concubinage" benefited both parties. . . .

Betsy Heard of Bereira [Guinea] . . . was born c. 1759 of mixed
African and European descent. Her father probably was attached to
the Liverpool entrepôts on the Iles de Los, a group of islands located
a little over two miles off Cape Sangara (Conakry). English merchants from Liverpool, like others before them, had found the islands
an ideal place to warehouse merchandise which they then carried
coastward and retailed in local markets lining the coastal rivers or
sold to traders who came from the coast to the islands. Heard was
born of a liaison which her father established with a local woman.
Although the circumstances of this particular relationship are unknown, it was common along these rivers for European traders to
arrange a tenancy agreement with a local landlord for the use of land
for a factory or trading post. This agreement involved a record of
fees, range of mobility, and expectations required from the
"stranger" and a corresponding agreement by the landlord to protect

property and rights of inheritance. As often as not, the landlord arranged for a daughter by a slave wife to marry this new stranger. This arrangement provided the landlord with an informant who kept him abreast of events at the factory, and at the same time guaranteed that any children would have minimal political or inheritance rights among indigenous peoples. Although Betsy Heard was freeborn by virtue of her father's status, her minuscule matrilineal ties did not afford her the security of land and/or people who would claim her as kin. . . .

Leaning to her father's side, Betsy Heard had little option but to enter the life available to outsiders like herself. Heard's father provided her with the necessary commercial training by sending her to England, where she remained for several years. Most likely she lived in or near Liverpool, where the number of male and female African students fluctuated between fifty and seventy annually. The Africans learned reading, writing, mathematics, and, of course, religion. Primarily, though, they were there "to learn Sense and to get a good Head". . . .

The precise circumstances of Heard's return to Africa are uncertain, but clearly she inherited the property and position of her father at Bereira as well as his involvement in the slave trade. By 1794, Betsy Heard was well enough known on the coast to be noted specifically in the Sierra Leone Company Report as a successful slave merchant who had studied in England. Adam Afzelius, botanist of the company at Freetown, described her as something of an expert on native medicine.

Betsy Heard both achieved her greatest commercial and political influence and decided to retire during the decade 1800 to 1810. Employees of the Sierra Leone Company who visited Bereira in 1802 described it and the neighboring area in some detail. Richard Bright used Heard's factory as his headquarters while he was in Bereira and in his report noted that her house was furnished in the European style. Her commercial power at Bereira and along the coast was considerable. In addition to operating trading vessels which plied the coast, she owned the principal wharf at Bereira. Long-distance traders from Futa Jalon, the Upper Niger, and the headwaters of the Sierra Leone River frequented her factory. In 1801, for example, such a large group arrived and demanded customary hospitality that her financial resources were nearly exhausted before the local headman rescued her with contributions of rice with which to feed her guests. . . . By 1807, she had built a new house. And Englishmen now were describing Bereira in terms normally reserved for the more important political centers of Wonkapong and Forekaria. At the same time, however, her monopoly at Bereira was under challenge from competition by two other traders: Mrs. Williams and Mrs. Crowdson. . . .

Although Heard's political influence was strong early in this decade, her exact status in local and regional politics is less than clear. . . . Whenever emissaries from surrounding towns came to Bereira, they inevitably sought out her factory. In one instance, when traditional gifts were distributed to headmen and other political elites at Bereira, she also received a share. Neighboring headmen brought her gifts, a clear indication of the wide respect for her wealth and for her effective sociopolitical status, if not actual position.

Perhaps even more interesting than her unofficial but probably important role in internal Bereira politics was the role she played in regional conflicts. From 1800 to 1807, for example, the Sierra Leone Company and certain chiefs in Moria, Sumbuya, and Moricania had been in dispute over the role which a few Morian chiefs had taken not only in the Nova Scotian insurrection at Freetown but also in subsequent wars between the company and neighboring Temne peoples. King Tom and several Nova Scotian rebels had taken refuge in Moria following those wars, and the company wanted them turned over for trial. In this instance, Betsy Heard acquired great influence by playing a mediating role between the parties. Sattan Tumani, ruler of Moria, turned to Heard first when it became clear both that a controversy between Moria and the Sierra Leone Company was escalating and that she was the person best qualified to mediate, to act as broker. Other headmen and chiefs accepted her position on the understanding that as long as discussions between Moria and the Sierra Leone Company were peaceful, a woman could participate and play a principal role. Should they change to a war palaver, however, the proceedings would then become man's business. Heard thereafter engaged in "shuttle diplomacy," interceding between parties, recommending compromises, and translating proposals. Respected by all parties concerned, including the company, Heard apparently retired from active participation in the slave trade after the 1800–1807 negotiations.

From Bruce L. Mouser, "Women Slavers of Guinea-Conakry," in *Women and Slavery in Africa,* edited by Claire C. Robertson and Martin A. Klein (Madison: University of Wisconsin Press, 1983), 320–25. Copyright © 1983. Reprinted by permission of The University of Wisconsin Press. Notes omitted.

Mouser, interested in the reasons that these women—probably themselves daughters of slaves—became slave traders, accepts that they were intelligent and that they were in the place and circumstances to pursue their careers. The Atlantic slave trade peaked at the end of the eighteenth century. But after 1807, when England began its campaign to end international commerce in slaves, the scope for independent women traders narrowed. What factors in the heritage of Betsy Heard, Elizabeth Skelton, and Mary Faber differentiated them from other West African women and enabled them to enter the male preserve of slave trading?

Heard, Skelton, and Faber were all born free of traditional responsibilities to extended families or lineage and held marginal positions in coastal society. . . . [This] meant Heard, Skelton, and Faber were able to seek out economic alternatives not available or permitted to local women. The traditional domain of women along the coast had included the house, the fields, and the wells: the care of babies, preparation of food and fetching water, and conduct of local markets. Heard and Skelton could be part of this domain [Faber's family was in Sierra Leone], but because of their marginal status they lacked the economic security which family ties and levirate would give in difficult times. To obtain economic self-sufficiency and security and to escape those restrictions attached to women as a caste, they were forced to lean "to their father's side," to identify primarily as traders by occupation. . . .

Another theme common to the biographies of Heard, Skelton, and Faber is the importance of education and experience in dealing with Europeans. Both Heard and Skelton had lived in England for several years and during that time acquired tastes different from those of the coast. Both had factory houses furnished in the English fashion and served meals to Europeans in the English manner. The factories of both became mandatory ports-of-call for important European visitors, and this contact undoubtedly increased their volume of trade.

That both could speak English was an important asset. . . . Balancing their "Western" education, which made them acceptable to European visitors, was their knowledge of African practices and languages, which kept them from making uncorrectable errors with their hosts. As intermediaries in the slave trade, these women could engage in local as well as long-distance trade.

Suggested Further Readings

Karen Sacks, in *Sisters and Wives: The Past and Future of Sexual Equality* (Westport, CT: Greenwood Press, 1979), discusses historical evidence of women's status in several African societies. The ability of elite women to exploit the changing trade patterns and/or political instability of the seventeenth and eighteenth centuries is explored by several authors: George Brooks, "The *Signares* of Saint-Louis and Goree: Women Entrepreneurs in Eighteenth-Century Senegal," in *Women in Africa: Studies in Social and Economic Change*, edited by Nancy J. Hafkin and Edna G. Bay (Stanford, CA: Stanford University Press, 1976), 19–44; Nakanyika B. Musisi, "Women, 'Elite Polygyny,' and Buganda State Formation," *Signs* 16, no. 4 (summer 1991): 757–86; Anne Hilton, "Family and Kinship among the Kongo South of the Zaire River from the Sixteenth to the Nineteenth Centuries," *Journal of African History* 24 (1983): 189–206; and John Thornton, *The Kingdom of Kongo: Civil War and Transition, 1641–1718* (Madison: University of Wisconsin Press, 1983). Thornton explains the key roles of women of the nobility in the civil strife of Kongo, but one of his most fascinating characters is Dona Beatrice Kimpa Vita, whose claim to be Saint Anthony reincarnated had profound religious and political impact.

Two authors explore legal records to show how eighteenth-century economic development in Sudan and Ethiopia resulted in women's loss of productive roles and land ownership: Jay Spaulding, "The Misfortunes of Some—The Advantages of Others: Land Sales by Women in Sinnar," and Donald Crummey,

"Women, Property, and Litigation among the Bagemder Amhara, 1750s to 1850s," in *African Women and the Law: Historical Perspectives,* edited by Margaret Jean Hay and Marcia Wright, Boston University Papers on Africa VII (Boston: Boston University, 1982), 3–18, 19–32. Anyone interested in the complexity of women's relationships to African slavery should consult *Women and Slavery in Africa,* edited by Claire C. Robertson and Martin A. Klein (Madison: University of Wisconsin Press, 1983). Although many of its chapters concern the nineteenth century, those in "Part I: Demographic and Theoretical Perspectives" stimulate thought about the connections between gender and slavery anywhere at any period, while Edna G. Bay's "Servitude and Worldly Success in the Palace of Dahomey," 340–68, illustrates how elite and warrior women benefited from and controlled the ruler's slaves.

PART 2
1800–Present

–7–
WESTERN EUROPE
Equality and Equity
for New Women

English woman campaigning for suffrage on London streets, 1907.
(Photograph © Museum of London.)

A few women in the French Revolution tentatively raised some of women's grievances, including their desire for equal education for young women, civil rather than religious marriages, and the right of divorce. Even these modest proposals were repudiated in Napoleon's codification of French law, in which women were defined as noncitizens, without control of their property and, among other repressive measures, were not allowed to testify as witnesses in court. The ancient doctrine of women's subordination, *femes covert,* remained triumphant in Europe.

Countering early nineteenth-century oppression of European women was the work of female novelists, such as Jane Austen, Mme. de Stael, George Sand, and Emily and Charlotte Bronte. In a period when everyone was reading novels, women novelists had a large readership among both sexes. In examining relationships within families between husband and wife, children and parents, fiction personalized the unjust treatment of women with an emotional impact on middle-class readers.

Women in the working class seldom found time to read as they sought to adjust to an industrializing economy. At first, young women and children almost monopolized the workforce in the expanding textile factories. Living at home, they accepted wages lower than men's. Women's pay remained poor throughout the nineteenth century as they were relegated to urban service industries or segregated in tasks and trades stigmatized for being female. Furthermore, throughout the nineteenth century, the notoriously ill-paid farm and domestic occupations employed many women.

As the middle-class urban ideal of the nurturing wife and mother who did not work outside the home gained dominance, working-class men demanded equity for their wives and children. Rather than supporting higher wages for women, labor unions sought a higher male wage—*the family wage*—that would obviate his wife's or children's needing earnings. Skilled men won the family wage; unskilled men did not. Their wives continued to work for miserly pay. Ambivalence between commitment to equal pay for women and to the family wage characterized the rising socialist parties, although they eventually pioneered in demanding equal political rights for women.

By the twentieth century, femininization of retail and office work offered women new jobs in fields where their respectability was not sacrificed to career. At the same time, falling birthrates in many countries led to a new political focus on motherhood. Origins of the welfare state can be found in the nation's assumption of the husband's role in providing a family wage via payments to encourage women to pursue motherhood as a career. The immense toll of death in two world wars accelerated development of European welfare states, which, after 1945, assumed responsibility for health care, pensions, and payments to all women for birth of a child.

European states gradually extended the franchise to men, even men without property, during the nineteenth century. Women exercised substantial political influence through men long before their claims to vote themselves were organized in the suffrage movement. By the 1890s, the rising clamor of women's public demands for reform of law, education, the family, and the franchise so impressed public consciousness that the terms *feminist* and *feminism* were invented to identify them. Norwegian women were the first Europeans to win the unrestricted right to vote in national elections, in 1913; Swiss women were the last, in 1971.

7.1 The French Revolution

Although the French Revolution began before 1800, for European women, it unmistakably marks the beginning of the modern period. In the early years of the Revolution, women participated in the attack on the Bastille and street demonstrations, then organized influential political clubs. Although female revolutionaries lost power after 1793, when their clubs were disbanded and their public activities restricted, nevertheless, that short burst of political power gave European women precedents on which they subsequently built.

Women were a public revolutionary force in the first months of 1789, although they could neither vote nor seek seats in the National Assembly. Their most impressive demonstration of numbers was the seven thousand women seeking cheaper bread who walked to Versailles in October 1789 and forced the king and the National Assembly to return to Paris. European women had a long tradition of rioting when they suspected speculators of hoarding food to drive up prices. Authorities seldom arrested the women rioters. Frenchwomen's food riots, called *taxation populaire,* typically involved crowds seizing merchandise from shopkeepers and grocers, distributing it equally to the crowd at what

they determined was a just price, and returning the proceeds to
the merchants.

Women's success in organizing demonstrations against high
food prices gained them political influence, which some of their
leaders then sought to use for further legal reforms of education,
marriage, divorce, and widows' rights. As their revolutionary objectives moved beyond traditional rioting to protect their families
in the early 1790s, Parisian women's influence was at first exercised through male relatives. Darline Gay Levy, Harriet Branson
Applewhite, and Mary Durham Johnson explain:

The common women of Paris were acknowledged as a central political force during 1792.... Common women were able to increase
their political power steadily in 1792 and 1793 because political institutions in Paris were coming more and more under the control of the
popular classes. Men were still the leaders, but now they were husbands, fathers, fellow members of the working and artisan classes. As
the political institutions democratized, they also became more autonomous, no longer subservient to the middle-class Jacobins and deputies.
The Paris Sections [wards] were the most important of these institutions. The Section assemblies, originally set up as forty-eight administrative bodies, took on deliberative functions to protect the interests of
sans-culottes [common people] and their families.... Women were
admitted to the spectator galleries. Leadership in the Sections passed in
1793 from rich lawyers and merchants to small shopkeepers, revolutionary journalists, and the less wealthy lawyers and clerks....

The fraternal societies changed along with the Sections. They now
became truly popular societies which called upon women to take an
active role in Paris politics. Expanding their educational functions,
they became independent political bodies whose members debated
issues, sent petitions, and championed the interests of war widows,
soldiers and needy citizens....

Middle-class radicals continued pressuring authorities for legislation to remove inequalities in other dimensions of women's lives.

Women in Revolutionary Paris, 1789–1795: Selected Documents, translated with
notes and commentary by Darline Gay Levy, Harriet Branson Applewhite, and
Mary Durham Johnson (Urbana: University of Illinois Press, 1979), 106–7.

The persuasion of the radicals and the power of the women were temporarily successful in enacting reform legislation in the years from 1790 through 1793. In order to reduce interference of the Roman Catholic Church and family in marriages, civil marriages were prescribed. Divorce was allowed, even if the couple's families opposed it. And finally, all children, including illegitimate children, were to inherit equally. The summer of 1793 was the high point of women's political influence in France.

In the fall of 1793, the revolutionary government, under the pressure of civil war and rural reaction against restrictions imposed on the Catholic Church, began a retreat that eventually eliminated women's participation in politics. By 1804, women were as powerless and submissive as they had been before they marched to Versailles in 1789. Their subordination was ordained by the French search for stability in repudiating equalitarian ideals and reinstating patriarchal values. The instrument that marked their fall was the Napoleonic Code of 1804, a set of laws proudly sponsored by Napoleon Bonaparte that influenced many legal systems in Europe and the New World. One of the important outcomes of the Revolution, the Napoleonic Code symbolized for women the conservative reaction against revolution. Under the code, married women returned to the status of *femes covert,* permanent legal dependents of men. Hence, 1804 can represent better than most other dates the nadir of European women's power and status. Bonnie Smith summarizes key aspects of the code:

First, women acquired the nationality of their husbands upon marriage. This made a woman's relationship to the state an indirect one because it was dependent on her husband's. Second, a woman had to reside where her husband desired. Women could not participate in lawsuits or serve as witnesses in court. . . . Men were no longer susceptible to paternity suits or legally responsible for the support of illegitimate children. . . . Female adultery was punished by imprisonment and fines unless the husband relented and took his wife back. Men, however, suffered no such sanctions unless they brought their sexual partners into the home. . . .

The Napoleonic Code also defined the space women would occupy in the new regime as marital, maternal, and domestic—all public matters would be determined by men. . . . In general, a woman had no control over property. Even if she was married under a contract that ensured a separate accounting of her dowry, her husband still had administrative control of funds. . . . This kind of economic control of women held in all classes. Women's wages went to their husbands, and market women and others engaged in business could not do so without permission from their husbands. . . . She had no control of her profits—these always passed to her husband.

Bonnie G. Smith, *Changing Lives: Women in European History Since 1700* (Lexington, MA: D.C. Heath, 1989), 120–21. Copyright © 1989 by D.C. Heath and Company. Used by permission of Houghton Mifflin Company.

7.2 George Sand, Novelist

Having little access to political power, women intellectuals began examining their grievances and publicizing their analyses to test public reaction. Women writers, especially novelists, took the lead in this campaign. George Sand (1804–76) is a good example.

Married couples sometimes discover that they do not like each other and would prefer to get "unmarried." Under the Napoleonic Code, divorce was not a choice, but separation was. Wives were at a great disadvantage in seeking a legal separation, since the laws favored husbands. The marriage of the famous female writer George Sand (Aurore Dupin) and Casmir Dudevant is a good illustration of the dangers separation posed, even for a wife like Aurore who became a financially successful author.

When Aurore Dupin married in September 1822, at the age of eighteen, she had inherited from her grandmother two pieces of income-producing property: an apartment house in Paris, the Hotel de Narbonne, and a rural chateau, Nohant, in Indre, which included rental property. Casmir Dudevant brought less to the marriage, for his familial income ceased with his nuptials, though he inherited a modest sum of money.

Although Aurore had been administering her estate with the aid of her grandmother's manager, she gave control of her properties to Casmir as the law required. The properties were not transferred to Casmir but remained in her name. Casmir also managed the couple's investments, apparently mostly unsuccessfully.

Their interests in life were so different that they had little to share with each other. She tried to get him to read, to talk of poetry and ethics, but he knew nothing of the authors. He fled when she played the piano. She liked Paris. He liked Nohant, shooting, drinking, and local politics. After the first child, Maurice, was born, she gradually lost respect for Casmir. By 1828, both were having affairs; hers produced a daughter, Solange. Although each had committed adultery, only she was liable to be imprisoned if it could be proved.

In 1830, upon accidentally reading Casmir's will, she discovered how much he hated her. Immediately, she proposed a new arrangement of their lives. Both would be free to do as they pleased; she would live six months in Nohant and six months in Paris, on an annual income that was adequate for a student. He agreed, and she went to Paris in 1831. The next year, she wrote and published two novels, which immediately established her reputation and increased her income, so that Solange could come with her mother to Paris.

Aurore and whoever was her current lover were frequently seen in public. There was a danger she might be charged with adultery, but her social reputation had been ruined when she accepted payment for her writing, even though she published her work using a male pseudonym, George Sand.

Finally, in February 1835, Aurore and Casmir decided to seek a legal separation. He would get life interest in the Paris apartment house and custody of Maurice. Aurore would take over Nohant and her daughter. Aurore requested the local court to issue a separation on the grounds of her husband's physical abuse, his affairs, and his indifference to her. As promised, Casmir did not contest, and the court agreed to the separation but gave custody of both children to their mother. This order returned control of her inherited properties to Aurore.

However, Casmir had second thoughts and appealed, arguing that she was unfit as a mother by alleging her adultery with at least seven men. Had the court considered the allegation seriously, Aurore might have been sent to prison. Instead, the judge told Casmir that he was acting ridiculously. The separation was seen in law as an expedient to prevent the dissolution of the marriage, but he was trying to achieve just that. The judge sustained the original judgment. After an appeal to a higher court, the February 1835 agreement was accepted. Aurore's national fame certainly gave her access to expensive legal advice and a much better chance for success than the average woman.

In the early novels that Aurore wrote using the name George Sand, she argued that marriage for money, without love and without the possibility of divorce, was in fact prostitution, which society enforced with its legal system. She cried out for freedom in this excerpt from her first novel, *Indiana* (1832). When the heroine was locked in a room to make her obey her husband's commands, she crawled out a window; in a later confrontation, she declares her moral position:

I know that I am the slave and you the master. The laws of this country make you my master. You can bind my body, tie my hands, govern my acts. You have the right of the stronger, and society confirms you in it: but you cannot command my will, monsieur; God alone can bend it and subdue it. Try to find a law, a dungeon, an instrument of torture that gives you any hold on it! you might as well try to handle the air and grasp space.

George Sand, *Indiana*, translated by George Burnham Ives (Philadelphia, 1900), 204–8. Quoted in *Women, the Family, and Freedom: The Debate in Documents*, vol. 1, edited by Susan Groag Bell and Karen M. Offen (Stanford, CA: Stanford University Press, 1983), 149.

George Sand was just one of an extraordinary outburst of women authors in nineteenth-century Europe. No other previous century in world history produced publication of so many serious female writers. They wrote plays, novels, poems, tracts, essays, and newspaper or magazine articles. The novelists are best known today, as they were then. This was the century of the novel in Europe, and women were the greater part of the readers. Because novels focused upon private lives, the authors were able to discuss the tensions within families, as well as between the individual and the state, with a public openness that was otherwise prohibited in this period of censorship and political suppression. Social criticism generally began in England or France but quickly spread through the Continent, Scandinavia, Russia, Poland, and the Americas, being translated as needed.

Female authors were not taken seriously in this period when all women were considered emotional and irrational. Bonnie

Smith explains why some women took precautions to have their work fairly judged by publishing under male names:

Great women novelists in England and France filled the bookstores with their works. Although female novelists were commonplace, women's writing of a more serious sort sometimes was not accepted for publication or was not regarded as fitting. . . . The high seriousness with which male writers were regarded contrasted sharply with the characterization of women novelists as "scribblers" and authors of "silly" works.

As if in acknowledgment of their misfit status, many women writers, including the best, took men's names as their pseudonyms: George Eliot, Currer Bell (Charlotte Bronte), Ellis Bell (Emily Bronte), Acton Bell (Anne Bronte), Daniel Stern, George Sand, Otto Stern (Louise Otto-Peters), and Paul Grendel (Julia Bécour). They adopted men's names because maleness gave legitimacy to their writing, especially if they were writing on serious subjects such as politics. . . .

Women writers were clearly in an ambivalent position. As women, they often admired many traditional values ascribed to womanhood, but by having a profession, they stepped beyond these values and moved into the world of men. Many women writers fulfilled the ideal of motherhood. . . . Some authors . . . filled their letters with stories of their bouncing, blissful children. Other women writers were concerned about moving out of their sphere: for example, Charlotte Bronte worried about having written something "unfitting." The woman writer understood woman's world yet was separated from it by her writing, which gave her a man's perspective. Although active in the world of men, women writers were able to see its problems, particularly its immorality and lust for gold.

Bonnie G. Smith, *Changing Lives: Women in European History Since 1700* (Lexington, MA: D.C. Heath, 1989), 227–28. Copyright © 1989 by D.C. Heath and Company. Used by permission of Houghton Mifflin Company.

7.3 Socialist Women: Clara Zetkin

After Napoleon's defeat in 1815, conservative European governments sought to prevent social change. At a time when European women had very little freedom, women novelists kept women's dependency before the public eye. Before midcentury, the "woman problem" emerged as a political issue, especially in France, where women's issues reappeared in the revolutions of both 1830 and 1848. Yet on the whole, few political reforms can be noted in France or elsewhere until late in the nineteenth century. Nonetheless, social changes were taking place that had important, and often adverse, effects on women.

Industrialization, which began in England about 1750 and moved eastward across Europe, instigated many economic changes. New employment for women arose in the lead industry of industrialization, textile manufacturing of cotton and silk. Other new factories attracted male laborers and their families to growing urban centers. The wages of male factory and mine workers were insufficient to support their families, so their young children and unmarried daughters and sons had to work and bring their wages home. Eventually, many wives had to find income for family survival. Instead of the agricultural or artisanal family working together, now urban working family members worked in different places during the long working days. Employers benefited from the low wages, and a newly influential middle class arose among the managers, engineers, and professional men of the cities.

Bonnie Smith explains how urban class differentiation affected women:

During the course of the [nineteenth] century a great divide opened between those women who worked and those in the respectable middle class who did not. In place of the aristocratic woman and her pleasures, the middle-class woman developed the culture of domesticity resting on her household and family. The comforts of this way of life depended on servants and more abundant goods. But domesticity also involved an array of rituals such as charity work and upper-class etiquette that were closed off to working women. The high culture of the theater attracted the wealthy, whereas working-class women enjoyed a neighborhood culture of their own. Separated in new ways, both played their part in the intense urbanization then in progress, and both contributed to the lively life of the nineteenth-century city.

Industrialization and urbanization produced tensions, inequities, and anxiety, while also making for experimentation and adventure. Dislocated and impoverished, many urban newcomers lived in the utmost misery. Many kept alive the language and dreams of revolutionary Europe in an ongoing series of strikes, political movements, and new waves of revolution. Filled with ambition for liberty, working women started political groups of their own and engaged in political struggle. Simultaneously, middle-class women began organizing a mass feminist movement to obtain education, property and marital rights, and the vote.

Bonnie G. Smith, *Changing Lives: Women in European History Since 1700* (Lexington, MA: D.C. Heath, 1989), 135–36. Copyright © 1989 by D.C. Heath and Company. Used by permission of Houghton Mifflin Company.

Working women began organizing in the nineteenth century in trade unions and in populist, anarchist, and socialist parties. One of their most articulate spokespersons was Clara Zetkin (1857–1933). As editor of the paper *Gleicheit* (Equality) from 1891 to 1916, she directed the women of the German Social Democratic Party (SPD), the largest revolutionary Marxist party in Europe with the largest female membership (175,000 in 1914), until the Russian Revolution. She played a key role in committing socialists to women's equality, even though they often failed to do more than give lip service.

Clara Zetkin was born into a progressive German middle-class family and educated to be a teacher, the only work acceptable for women of her class. She was attracted to feminism but was converted to socialism partly through the help of Ossip Zetkin, a Russian émigré. Her decision to become a socialist brought personal and financial sacrifice, a break with her family and friends, and made her a semioutlaw in Germany. In 1881, Ossip was forced to leave Germany and went to Paris. Clara followed, and they had two children. The couple continued their political work while working as freelance writer and tutor, but their health deteriorated. Clara returned to Germany when her mother offered reconciliation and a trip back home. There her health improved, and she returned to Paris to support her family and nurse Ossip until he died in 1889. Her Paris years of poverty marked her with a deep sympathy for working women. Even while living in France, she continued to correspond with socialist leaders on women's education and trade associations. They dispersed her articles throughout Germany. So when she returned to Germany after Ossip's death, she was eventually able to take over editing *Gleicheit.*

She worked hard to influence German socialists to oppose the *family wage* (a wage for husbands high enough to support the family without the children's or wives' working). Zetkin's argument convinced the SPD not to support the family wage and instead to support organizing women:

It is not just the women workers who suffer because of the miserable payment of their labor. The male workers, too, suffer because of it. As a consequence of their low wages, the women are transformed from mere competitors into unfair competitors who push down the wages of men. Cheap women's labor eliminates the work of men and if the men want to continue to earn their daily bread, they must put up with low wages. Thus women's work is not only a cheap form of labor, it also cheapens the work of men and for that reason it is doubly appreciated by the capitalist, who craves profits. . . .

The economic advantages of the industrial activity of proletarian women only aid the tiny minority of the sacrosanct guild of coupon clippers and extortionists of profit. . . .

Given the fact that many thousands of female workers are active in industry, it is vital for the trade unions to incorporate them into their movement. In individual industries where female labor plays an important role, any movement advocating better wages, shorter working hours, etc., would be doomed from the start because of the attitude of those women workers who are not organized. Battles which began propitiously enough, ended up in failure because the employers were able to play off non-union female workers against those that are organized in unions. These non-union workers continued to work (or took up work) under any conditions, which transformed them from competitors in dirty work to scabs. . . .

Certainly one of the reasons for these poor wages for women is the circumstance that female workers are practically unorganized. They lack the strength which comes with unity. They lack the courage, the feeling of power, the spirit of resistance and the ability to resist which is produced by the strength of an organization in which the individual fights for everybody and everybody fights for the individual. Furthermore, they lack the enlightenment and the training which an organization provides.

"Women's Work and the Trade Unions," in *Clara Zetkin: Selected Writings*, edited by Philip S. Foner (New York: International Publishers, 1984), 54–56.

7.4 The Right to Vote and Govern

Feminists supported various reforms, but especially suffrage for women. Progress was slow. Some indication of male opposition can be inferred from the fight Clara Zetkin waged in the SPD for its adoption of support for political rights for everyone, without regard to gender. Many male socialists opposed woman suffrage because they believed women would be conservative voters opposed to socialism. Most socialist women supported suffrage, and Zetkin was able to get the SPD endorsement in 1891. Suffrage also faced opposition from conservative men who thought women should not be involved in politics, as well as from conservative women who were content in their dependency and domesticity.

Etta Palm d'Aelder and Olympe de Gouges were leaders in the struggle for equal rights in the early years of the French Revolution. In the nineteenth century, the long campaign by Englishwomen for suffrage provided leadership for European women. Beginning in 1832, when Parliament explicitly restricted voting to males, a century-long campaign followed. In 1869, Englishwomen won the right to vote in municipal elections if they were taxpayers. Many exceptional women were involved in the struggle for individual rights equal to men's. Harriet Hardy Taylor Mill had been an early leader of women's rights before she married John Stuart Mill. He, as a member of Parliament, was able to speak for her on the issue. After her death in 1858, Mill published the classic *Subjugation of Women* (1869) based on her ideas. Englishwomen over thirty won the right to vote in parliamentary elections in 1918, and the vote was extended to women over twenty-one in 1928.

Bonnie Smith examines the origins of the suffrage movement:

The suffrage movement developed from a base of varied public activities and a wide-ranging array of issues. Settlement house workers, proponents of social purity, temperance reformers, vegetarians, and other types of activists considered themselves part of the "woman movement"—the term "feminist" was only just beginning to be used. Some of these activists were "new women," [who did not accept standard roles] but many were middle-class housewives or working-class mothers. . . . Broadly conceived around a range of property, marital, and cultural issues, the woman movement experienced a deliberate refocusing by the end of the nineteenth century, which produced a variety of suffrage groups. The vitality of these groups sprang from women's prior experience with reform. In fact, for many activists the emphasis on suffrage would unify the dispersed efforts that earlier reform seemed to engender and would resolve the intense debate over gender relations. The drive for the vote grew out of the liberal principles that by 1900 influenced most governments. Many women also saw the vote as a new broom for doing some social housekeeping in order to improve the conditions of motherhood. All the social service that had already been accomplished by women and the century of their raising citizens served as their credentials, their claim to the franchise. If that did not suffice, they were prepared to use the expertise at organizing, publicizing, raising funds, influencing politicians, and political analyzing that had been gained over the decades.

Bonnie G. Smith, *Changing Lives: Women in European History Since 1700* (Lexington, MA: D.C. Heath, 1989), 348–49. Copyright © 1989 by D.C. Heath and Company. Used by permission of Houghton Mifflin Company.

After World War I, women gained the vote in the United States, the U.S.S.R (Russia), Great Britain, Germany, Denmark, Sweden, Austria, Czechoslovakia, Poland, the Netherlands, Spain, Turkey, and Romania. After World War II, they gained the vote in France, Italy, Yugoslavia, Hungary, and Bulgaria. By the early 1960s, as former European colonies gained independence in Asia and Africa, millions more women had gained the franchise. South Africa extended the vote to African women in 1994. Today, women lack the power for minimal participation in government through voting mainly in those few monarchies or dictatorships where no one votes.

The right to vote only slowly drew women into positions

where they had an effective voice in governing. Few European women attained the highest government posts—and those only after 1979. In the near century between 1900 and 1994, there have been only twenty-four elected female presidents or prime ministers heading governments throughout the world. Seven of these were in Europe: Edith Cresson of France (1991–92), Margaret Thatcher of Great Britain (1979–90), Mary Robinson of Ireland (1990–), Gro Harlem Brundtland of Norway (1981, 1986–89, 1990–), Hanna Suchocka of Poland (1992–93), Maria de Lourdes Pintasilgo of Portugal (1981–85), and Milka Planinc of Yugoslavia (1982–86). Margaret Thatcher's eleven-year tenure as prime minister was longer than that of Winston Churchill. Yet Thatcher was no friend to women: she tried to dismantle the welfare system and never described herself as serving women. Although Sweden has not chosen a woman to head its government, after the 1994 elections, 52 percent of ministerial (cabinet rank) posts were held by women.

Still, even by 1994, no European state had a number of women proportionate to their population serving in the legislature. Many countries had fewer than 10 percent of the seats held by women. Women were most successful in Scandinavian electoral politics in the 1990s. Noting that female candidates, like Margaret Thatcher, could be indifferent to the needs of the women who helped elect them, Norwegian feminists worked to have female candidates compete for votes only against other women. They were able to get all parties to promise to nominate a minimum of 40 percent female candidates. In 1994, 39 percent of Norwegian legislators were women.[*]

7.5 Relational and Individual Feminisms

For two centuries, Europeans have been involved in a discourse over women's roles in society. Various theories of feminism and reform agendas have been advanced. European feminists often supported reforms that strengthened the family in addition to improving women's lives. Some advocated that the state pay mothers a monthly "salary" to stay home with their small chil-

---

[*]Information on elections of women to European legislatures and as heads of state or government from United Nations, *The World's Women, 1995: Trends and Statistics* (New York: United Nations, 1995), 150–52, 171–72.

dren. Karen Offen argues that most of the different forms of feminism can be classified into two general categories—"relational" and "individualist" feminism—and that relational feminism, which especially supports women's function in procreation and nurturing, was dominant in most of Europe before the twentieth century:

Recent scholarship bearing on the history of feminism in Europe strongly suggests that relational feminism represents the dominant line of argument prior to the twentieth century throughout the Western world. Indeed, relational arguments dominate European continental debate on the woman question until very recently. Individualist feminism also has deep historical roots in European culture, but it has become increasingly characteristic of British and American discourse since ... 1869 and has reached its most expansive development in twentieth-century Anglo-American thought. . . .

Viewed historically, arguments in the relational feminist tradition proposed a gender-based but egalitarian vision of social organization. They featured the primacy of a companionate, non-hierarchial, male-female couple as the basic unit of society, whereas individual arguments posited the individual, irrespective of sex or gender, as the basic unit. Relational feminism emphasized women's rights *as women* (defined principally by their childbearing and/or nurturing capacities) in relation to men. It insisted on *women's* distinctive contributions in these roles to the broader society and made claims on the commonwealth on the basis of these contributions. By contrast, the individualist feminist tradition of argumentation emphasized more abstract concepts of individual human rights and celebrated the quest for personal independence (or autonomy) in all aspects of life, while downplaying, deprecating, or dismissing as insignificant all socially defined roles and minimizing discussion of sex-linked qualities or contributions, including childbearing and its attendant responsibilities. . . .

These two modes of argument certainly reflect the self/other dualism characteristic of Western thought, but they continue to be meaningful because they reflect profound differences of opinion that have long existed within Western discourse about basic structural questions of social organization and, specifically, about the relationship of individuals and family groups to society and the state. Both modes must be accounted for if one is to understand feminism historically.

The Anglo-American individualistic tradition of feminism is nevertheless the model on which much discussion of feminism by historians has been based. Individualist arguments have served especially the cause of single women to justify an independent, non-family-based existence in a world that remains male defined. . . . Individualistic arguments inevitably rested on the emulation of a model of the individual that seemed to others functionally male. . . . As recently as the early 1970s, this notion of feminism seemed to be the only "politically correct" form available to American women. Individualist feminism placed political priority on enactment of the Equal Rights Amendment and on dismantling the gender-stratified educational system and economy that disadvantage women through occupational segregation. . . .

Relational feminism, with its couple-centered vision, has led historically to very different interpretations of women's circumstances and needs . . . especially in the arena of state action on behalf of mothers. In the experience of nineteenth century France in particular, the key arguments of relational feminism culminated historically in the seemingly paradoxical doctrine of "equality in difference," or equity as distinct from equality. The fundamental tenets included the notion that there were *both* biological *and* cultural distinctions between the sexes, a concept of womanly or manly nature, of a sharply defined sexual division of labor, or roles, in the family and throughout society following from that "difference" and that "nature," and of the centrality of the complementary couple and/or the mother/child dyad to social analysis. As these ideas were elaborated in conjunction with the discourse surrounding the democratic and industrial revolutions of the last two centuries, "relational feminism" could and did incorporate demands for women's right to work outside the household, to participate in all professions, and to vote, alongside demands for equality in civil law concerning property and persons. This it did in tandem with older demands for equal access to formal education and for unimpeded moral and ethical development. In other words, relational feminism combined a case for moral equality of women and men with an explicit acknowledgement of differences in women's and men's sexual function in society. . . . Increasingly, relational feminists called for governmental programs that would bolster and enhance women's performance of procreative functions even as they argued that other avenues for life-work must also be available to women.

Karen Offen, "Defining Feminism: A Comparative Historical Approach," *Signs: Journal of Women in Culture and Society* 14:1 (1988): 135–39. Copyright © 1988 by The University of Chicago. All rights reserved. Note omitted.

7.6 The Welfare State

Katti Anker Møller (1868–1945) was a Norwegian activist who was a model relational feminist. She was able to use two themes in conventional wisdom for her purposes. First, people believed women were uniquely given the task of creating and educating future generations. Theirs was the responsibility for the ethical and moral education of the children, and to do that, they should stay home, not work for wages. Second, by 1900, all of Europe was concerned with the declining birthrates and seeking measures to raise fertility. Møller used these concerns to seek redress of some of women's injustices while arguing for their increased self-confidence and self-realization. Ida Blom describes Møller's theories:

Her theories about motherhood rested on two pillars: first, motherhood should be voluntary, and therefore women needed free access to contraception and abortion. Secondly, motherhood should be given equal status to a profession, presupposing formal schooling in all necessary knowledge about pregnancy, childbirth and child care. The state should be responsible for the economic independence of mothers, making it possible for mothers and children to subsist without the direct support of the husband/father. . . .

She persistently argued for abolishing the differences between unmarried and married mothers. The state should take over economic responsibility for all mothers, paying them for the work they were doing when producing and raising children. A monthly state-financed salary [from taxes] from the very beginning of pregnancy, sufficient to keep mother and child healthy, should continue until the school system took over some of the responsibility for the child.

Ida Blom, "Voluntary Motherhood, 1900–1930: Theories and Politics of a Norwegian Feminist in an International Perspective," in *Maternity and Gender Policies: Women and the Rise of the European Welfare States, 1880s–1950s,* edited by Gisela Bock and Pat Thane (London: Routledge, 1991), 23.

It is unlikely that many Norwegian women would have agreed with every reform Møller supported, but they accepted laws that implemented some of her theories. She had many supporters and opponents; however, her influential brother-in-law, Johan Castberg, was the most useful. As a member of parliament and twice a cabinet minister, he was a very effective player in the legislative process. After a fourteen-year campaign, she helped write a law giving children born out of wedlock rights to parental inheritance and rights to their father's family name. In another campaign, she helped get economic assistance for unmarried mothers in 1909 and then helped get it extended to married mothers in 1915. For the education of mothers, she helped get a chapter on female health in schoolbooks.

Møller's early success in providing state aid that was paid directly to mothers was unusual. Before 1914, when European governments developed the first programs of the welfare state, payments were normally made to adult males covered by state social insurance funds. If payments were made for women's needs, such as for maternity leave, they were given to the husbands. These early national social policies were subsidies to men to bring their incomes to the level considered adequate for the family wage and to insure against sickness, disablement, old age, and unemployment. Gisela Bock and Pat Thane summarize the parts of these programs related to maternity.

[At the introduction of early social insurance schemes,] they were everywhere conceived as assisting the male who could no longer assist himself and his wife by his paid employment. . . .

In most European countries, including the classic welfare states of Britain, Germany and the Scandinavian countries, early and particularly later welfare reforms had an important meaning for, and impact on, mothers and maternity. Their indirect impact was to reinforce women's dependency on husbands who benefited from the welfare measures, and hence also to reinforce the gender gap in terms of income and (relative) poverty. On the other hand, certain welfare provisions . . . were aimed directly at women and contributed to re-lieving some aspects of female misery and poverty, particularly those related to maternity. . . . Under the German health insurance law of 1883, female factory workers could obtain modest benefits for three weeks of maternity leave after the birth of a child, . . . but the bene-fits were minimal, optional and rarely paid, and only in 1924 were maternity benefits extended to non-employed wives of insured hus-bands. The British National Insurance Act of 1911 included cash maternity benefits for insured women and for the wives of insured men. . . . In France, too, several laws of 1913 on maternity benefits, on support to needy families with many children and on child allow-ances to civil servants preceded by far the introduction of a com-prehensive national insurance scheme in 1928. . . . Payments during maternity leave for women employed in the formal labour market were generally modest, and the provisions often differentiated be-tween different fields of employment. . . .

Whereas these measures, which were introduced in the period be-fore and during the First World War, aimed only at specific groups of mothers (mostly the needy and the employed), the period between the wars and shortly after the Second World War brought about innovations which had been hardly conceivable for most of the nine-teenth century: state child allowances and a range of further maternal welfare provisions.

Maternity and Gender Policies: Women and the Rise of the European Welfare States, 1880s–1950s, edited by Gisela Bock and Pat Thane (London: Routledge, 1991), 4–5.

In western European countries, state child allowances along the lines of Katti Møller's monthly state-financed salary were intro-duced in France (1932), Germany (1935), Italy (1936), Spain (1938), Britain (1945), and finally Denmark (1952). Most coun-tries initially restricted eligibility to specific groups, such as wid-ows with children or mothers whose husbands were in the military. After World War II, allowances were paid directly to the mothers and made universal, though payments were rare for the first child. About the same time, income-tax relief for depen-dents, including children and wives, was provided, usually for the husbands and fathers, as it was in the United States. European welfare programs were not, however, usually restricted to poor women as in the United States.

Suggested Further Readings

The best introduction to women's topics in European history can be found in the introductory essays and headnotes in *Women, the Family, and Freedom: The Debate in Documents,* vol. I, 1750–1880, and vol. II, 1880–1950, edited by Susan Groag Bell and Karen M. Offen (Stanford, CA: Stanford University Press, 1983). For the French Revolution, many titles are available, but a good introduction to current research is Joan B. Landes's review essay, "Women and the French Revolution," *Gender and History* 6 (August 1994): 280–91. One of the latest essays in a debate about the feminism of George Sand is Naomi Schor, "Feminism and George Sand: *Lettres a Marcie,*" in *Feminists Theorize the Political,* edited by Judith Butler and Joan W. Scott (New York: Routledge, 1992). A comprehensive discussion of *Reluctant Feminists in German Social Democracy, 1885–1917,* by Jean H. Quataert (Princeton, NJ: Princeton University Press, 1979), is excellent. Not to be overlooked are essays by Karen Offen and Ellen Carol DuBois in the collection *Suffrage and Beyond: International Feminist Perspectives,* edited by Caroline Daley and Melanie Nolan (New York: New York University Press, 1994). The welfare state in Great Britain and the United States is compared in chapter 9 of *Faces of Feminism: A Study of Feminism as a Social Movement* by Olive Banks (New York: St. Martin's Press, 1981).

–8–
AFRICA
The Colonial Legacy

African Woman and Child in Cornfield, Nigeria, Africa, 1989.
(Photograph by Benita Keller. © B. Keller 1989.)

Almost all of Africa experienced European conquest and political administration by the end of the nineteenth century. However, this alien control did not last very long for most African nations. It is true that European trading stations could be found along the coast as early as the fifteenth century, but the bulk of the continent's population was free from European rule until the 1880s. In the first reading, Baba, a woman who lived in present-day northern Nigeria, saw, in her lifetime, the beginning of British occupation in 1903 and died just nine years before its end in 1960. Most African nations became independent around 1960.

Baba also recounts some of the changes that British rule caused. The abolition of slavery within Africa is among the most important. The process that led to ending African slavery began a century earlier. The British prohibited Englishmen from engaging in the Atlantic slave trade in 1807 and actively sought the cooperation of other countries in banning international trade in slaves. By 1850, few slavers ventured onto the Atlantic Ocean, although the slave trade in the Indian Ocean continued into the twentieth century. The British passed an emancipation act for their empire in 1833. But for northern Nigeria, emancipation was not proclaimed until 1903.

During colonial rule, African economies were partially forced into world markets. Their main contribution was exporting raw materials. Agricultural products were the most valuable, including cocoa, ground nuts (peanuts), wild rubber, tea, and cotton. Mineral exports included copper, gold, and diamonds. Some aspects of European culture were adopted by Africans, especially business practices, Christianity, schools, and national judicial systems. Many changes were detrimental for women, but some were welcomed.

Women's political power suffered during alien rule. Europeans worked almost exclusively with those members of the male African political elite who were willing to cooperate with them. Most Europeans did not appreciate the functions of traditional councils of women elders or queen mothers. When female African officials asserted their power against European interests, they were often summarily removed from office. This was the fate of the Asante queen mother at the end of the nineteenth century. Yaa Akyaa became queen mother when she installed her minor son Prempe I on the gold stool that symbolized rule of the Asante. The opposition of mother and son to British imperialism ended with defeat and exile from Ghana in 1896.

During the twentieth-century independence struggles against Europeans, women participated on all levels, from organizing demonstrations to soldiering. Since independence, African governments have included women as cabinet ministers, and by 1994, there was at least one woman minister in almost every nation. Still, women have not regained the status they had before the European colonial era and traditional patriarchal practices like female genital mutilation have continued.

8.1 Baba, a Hausa Woman of Nigeria

In the late nineteenth century, major European nations undertook the conquest of the nations of Africa. Between 1880 and 1900, the Europeans overpowered 90 percent of the continent. Their desire for power was intense, and they acted so quickly that historians have labeled the episode "the Scramble for Africa."

When Europeans conquered an African nation, the inhabitants had to adjust to the demands of an alien power. Africans variously considered the changes in their lives as both good and bad, and resisted when they felt a change was too great. Initially, Europeans sought African acceptance of their new regimes. They offered privileges to Africans who cooperated with them, thereby creating new class and gender divisions among Africans.

In West Africa, the British, French, Portuguese, and Germans competed to acquire territory. The Hausa lived on the savanna in northern Nigeria. In 1804, Fulani nomad cattle herders had conquered the agricultural Hausa and remained as their overlords. The sultan of Sokoto was the Fulani ruler in 1903, when he was defeated by the British. In each province of Sokoto, the British forced the local Fulani lords to swear allegiance to the British monarch but delegated them power to govern and did not interfere with Islamic law, customs, or religion.

Baba (1890–1951) lived in the old Hausa city–states of Kano and Zaria, now in Nigeria. She was a member of the Habe nation, whose members spoke Hausa. During the period of the British conquest, Baba, an adolescent, lived with her family in the village of Karo. In times of danger, her father and his brothers moved their families to the safety of their joint compound in the walled town of Zarewa. Just a year or two before her death, Baba recalled the events of almost a half a century before, when the Habe experienced the disruptions of the conquest:

When I was a maiden the Europeans first arrived. Ever since we were quite small the *malams* [Muslim scholars] had been saying that the Europeans would come with a thing called a train, they would come with a thing called a motor-car. . . . They would stop wars, they would repair the world, they would stop oppression and lawlessness, we should live at peace with them. We used to go and sit quietly and listen to the prophecies. . . .

I remember when a European came to Karo on a horse, and some of his foot soldiers went into the town. Everyone came out to look at them. . . . Everyone at Karo ran away—"There's a European, there's a European!" . . .

At that time Yusufu was the [Fulani] king of Kano. He did not like the Europeans, he did not wish them, he would not sign their treaty. Then he saw that perforce he would have to agree, so he did. We Habe wanted them to come, it was the Fulani who did not like it. When the Europeans came the Habe saw that if you worked for them they paid you for it, they didn't say, like the Fulani, "Commoner, give me this! Commoner, bring me that!" Yes, the Habe wanted them. . . .

The Europeans said that there were to be no more slaves; if someone said "Slave!" you could complain to the *alkali* [judge] who would punish the master who said it, the judge said "That is what the Europeans have decreed." . . . When slavery was stopped, nothing much happened at our *rinji* [the farm where their slaves lived] except that some slaves whom we had bought in the market ran away. Our own father went to his farm and worked, he and his son took up their large hoes. . . . They farmed guineacorn and millet and groundnuts and everything; before this they had supervised the slaves' work— now they did their own. When the midday food was ready, the women of the compound would give us children the food, one of us drew water, and off we went to the farm to take the men their food at the foot of a tree.

Mary E. Smith, *Baba of Karo: A Woman of the Muslim Hausa* (New Haven, CT: Yale University Press, 1981), 66–68. Notes omitted.

Baba's family immediately lost the income from the slaves who ran away. Balancing that loss was the abolition of many taxes her family previously paid. Taxes had been paid in cowries (small seashells) to the chief of Zarewa:

The Chief of Zarewa would send his men to collect the money. His courtiers went to each house and collected the money for tax. In those days there was not only the household tax . . . , there were also taxes on all sorts of different farming—groundnut tax, sweet potato tax, sugar-cane tax, and others; . . . there were craft taxes, too, for instance, a dyer paid 2,000 cowries for every dyepit he had. Only the household tax went to the king of Kano, the other taxes were kept by the town chiefs. If they used up all the money themselves, the common people had to pay.

Mary E. Smith, *Baba of Karo: A Woman of the Muslim Hausa* (New Haven, CT: Yale University Press, 1981), 81.

———————————————

The British abolished all the taxes except the household tax. They also prevented the Fulani officials from simply taking any daughter they liked from the common people and keeping her in the chief's compound. The British also ended slave raids, but not before raiders had taken Baba's father's wife, who was working in the rice fields. Her father raised the ransom money to buy her back, but she died before it was all paid.

The British had little interest in Sokoto at that time. Its capital, Kano, was more than five hundred miles overland from the Atlantic port of Lagos. They did not see any immediate commercial prospects in the agricultural and cattle society of Sokoto. As long as the inhabitants were peaceful, there was little interference.

In areas the Europeans decided to exploit economically, they took land without paying the African owners, paid laborers minimal wages, forced African merchants out of markets in favor of their own nationals, and coerced farmers to plant specific crops even if the farmers lost money. Some colonies became international scandals, as was the Independent State of Congo in 1904–5. The colonial government of the Belgian king forced Africans to tap rubber from wild trees to pay a village tax that was payable only in wild rubber. Villages with shortages were punished, sometimes by amputation of hands or feet. The tax was so high that starvation became rampant as villagers lacked time to grow crops to feed themselves.

8.2 Divorce among the Hausa

Hausa women were comparatively fortunate. Divorces were easy to obtain, and most women had two or three during their lives. Parents usually arranged a woman's first marriage, preferring a cousin. When a woman was barren, as was Baba, it was a great sorrow for her, but a relative often offered her a child to adopt. She might raise several adopted children during her lifetime. Baba's aunt, Rabi, provides an example of the marriages of an attractive woman.

Our Aunt Rabi was our father's elder sister. She was adopted by her father Dara's [Baba's grandfather's] younger sister, Rakia. When Rabi reached marriageable age ... , Rakia married her to her co-wife's son Rabi'u, because Rakia had no children herself, and if her adopted daughter Rabi married her co-wife's son in the same compound, she hoped to acquire grandchildren. Rakia and her co-wife liked one another. When Rabi and Rabi'u had had seven children, she left him and married Malam Barau, a man from Doka, a hamlet like Karo. She had more children by him. ... Then Rabi left Barau and married Mai Koko, the *jakada* [agent] of the king of Kano. He used to come to fetch the tax of the country. ... One day he saw Aunt Rabi carrying her baby on her back, looking very handsome. He desired her. She also liked him, so she broke up her marriage with Malam Barau and when Mai Koko returned he married her and took her away to Kano City, where he shut her up. All the men of Kano City lock up their wives completely, so that no one shall see them. He brought her nice food to eat, he brought her lovely clothes to wear, but she could not visit her kinsfolk, she could not see her children. When he came to Zarewa to collect the tax we used to make him porridge and cook chickens for him, we would ask him "How is Rabi?" and he answered "Very well," but he would not bring her to see us. After four years in Kano she slipped out one night and ran away to a village; in the morning she asked the way home. She walked and walked, there were no lorries then as there are now; she passed about fifteen walled towns before she came to Zarewa. ... She had returned to her kinsfolk and her children, she couldn't bear to stay away there and not see them.

Mary E. Smith, *Baba of Karo: A Woman of the Muslim Hausa* (New Haven, CT: Yale University Press, 1981), 80. Note omitted.

Rabi married one more time before she was captured by slave traders and never returned.

8.3 Widows "Sold," Men Migrate

Divorce was infrequent in those societies that required the groom's family to give to the bride's family considerable wealth, called bridewealth, as part of a marriage contract. Before a husband would relinquish his legal rights to one of his wives, he would usually demand repayment of the bridewealth. If the value of the bridewealth was great, her family might be reluctant or unable to repay it.

Societies requiring payment of bridewealth were patrilocal, patrilineal, and polygamous. They were, and are, common in East Africa, but less so in West Africa. Young men could not accumulate adequate bridewealth, so most waited to marry until they inherited their father's wealth. In these societies, young brides usually married older men. Consequently, many women became widows.

Jane Guyer discusses the alternatives facing Beti widows. The Beti people lived in West Africa in southern Cameroon. She begins by describing the society before European conquest:

The precolonial economic system was defined in terms of social adults, the men who had passed through the initiation ritual, married and founded their own village. All other people—women, children and slaves—formed part of the wealth of the man they belonged to and their main economic function was to increase his fortune. Wives were the key people in the process of accumulation because they contributed in several ways: they bore children, they produced food for daily subsistence and for the feasts which accompanied exchange, certain of their agricultural and artisanal products could be exchanged against indigenous money, and their presence alone cemented political alliances between clans. All the wealth generated by a wife automatically belonged to her husband. . . . The widows a man left when he died were the most valuable part of his estate, especially young women who could still bear children. . . . They were inherited by his successors [male relatives], and became their wives. . . .

Wives past menopause were also inherited, although their value was diminished. . . . Old women still contributed to the agricultural economy of the inheritor, and could be very important to his prosperity through the practice of medicine, midwifery, and particularly through expertise in the women's ritual *mevungu* which counteracted failing productivity in human reproduction, in agriculture, in hunting, or any of the activities which were basic to the economy. . . .

All widows, regardless of their value, were attributed to an inheritor. . . . In their inheritor's village all wives had the right to a house to live in, land which they could cultivate and basic security of life in case of illness and attack. . . . A woman past childbearing age whose son was already a social adult generally went to live in his village where she was respected and looked after by her son's wives. An old woman with no children or only daughters who had married away was much more vulnerable to neglect; she might get land, but no help with the clearing, a house, but no help with repairs. . . . All this depended on the personal character of her inheritor and her own relationship to him. The relative abundance of both time and subsistence goods probably meant that no one was seriously neglected.

Jane I. Guyer, "The Economic Position of Beti Widows Past and Present," working paper no. 22, Boston University, African Studies Center (Boston, 1979), 3–5. Beti words omitted.

After World War I, when the Beti became part of the French colonial empire, Cameroonian exports of cocoa were increasing. Before the planting of cocoa trees, when Beti women practiced a shifting farming system, wives had use rights to the land on which they had planted crops at any time. With the increasing production of cocoa, men acquired permanent ownership and exclusive use of the land planted in cocoa. The value of adult women who tended the trees increased. In this situation, consideration of the interests of widows was often ignored, and widows were almost sold to the highest bidder.

Christian missionaries opposed remarriage of Christian widows. They wanted Christian widows to become independent rather than marry a pagan inheritor. But a serious obstacle to allowing widows their freedom was meeting the demand for repayment of bridewealth to their dead husbands' families.

Jane Guyer continues:

The conditions of the late nineteenth and early twentieth centuries provoked extreme exaggerations in some of the characteristics of the Beti marriage system. . . . The pressures on the rural population to intensify agricultural production for the world market and to supply labor to colonial enterprises, meant that the work which wives did for their husbands became more important. The result was a system of exchange of women which many observers and participants found differed little from servitude. With respect to widows, the [French] administrator Bertaut wrote in 1935 that the main aim of the inheritor amongst the Bulu was "to sell her again to the highest bidder," and Owono's novel *Tante Bella* documents the life of a widow during the 1920s and 1930s who was inherited and re-inherited, regardless of her welfare, because of the high value her daughter commanded in bridewealth.

The manner in which women were transferred from one "owner" to another became one of the polemic battlegrounds between the [European] administration . . . , the church and the indigenous elite. The church was intransigently opposed to widow inheritance since it automatically returned Christian converts to polygamous marriages with pagans. But even the Christian chiefs refused to accept the rupture of marriage without repayment of the bridewealth. Because it depended on the chiefs, the [colonial] administration accepted their position, and issued a series of decrees granting widows free choice to remarry under various more or less complex conditions of the return of bridewealth.

Jane I. Guyer, "The Economic Position of Beti Widows Past and Present," working paper no. 22, Boston University, African Studies Center (Boston, 1979), 5–6. Note omitted.

In much of Africa, women did most of the farming, except for seasonal cutting of trees to clear new fields. As the colonial economies were integrated into world markets, inevitably some regions prospered and others were impoverished. Women's defenseless position as legal minors often left them to bear the brunt of recessions or droughts. When male elites had to make difficult group decisions, women's interests were often sacrificed.

When colonialism began in Africa, agriculture was the basic economic activity. Beti males, blessed with a favorable climate for growing cocoa and rising international prices, prospered if they acquired women to farm without even traditional protection for their well-being. In East Africa, European settlers seized the best lands in the early twentieth century. Africans, pushed to western Kenya, found the land and the climate unfavorable. The value of a typical farm's production became increasingly inadequate to buy the new products people began to want and need. Men then migrated to urban areas. At first, they brought their families, but after World War II, they came by themselves, leaving the families behind. Margaret Jean Hay explains:

The years of British colonialism, 1895–1963, witnessed profound social and economic changes in western Kenya, including the rise of striking inequalities within rural societies. . . . Most areas of western Kenya today are characterized by land fragmentation, male labor migration, and rural impoverishment. Within this broad context of rural differentiation and increasingly scarce resources, it is also clear that the economic position of rural women has declined. We can see that limiting women's access to property has been a principal means of social control for the Luo, Luyia, and Gusii peoples of western Kenya. . . .

One important . . . point for western Kenya is the impact of labor migration on women's roles in protecting and managing land and other property. There are clearly global elements in the migrant situation, a desire to hold onto one's stake in the rural areas. Property rights in the rural areas come to be protected by reliable women, as occupants. Mothers are already assumed to be reliable, because of their structural dependence on their sons, while wives are made reliable by the strictness of the legal situation. . . . In rural areas experiencing a general decline . . . as was the case for most of western Kenya during the later decades of the colonial period, the need for effective occupancy became a vise holding marriage in its old patterns. . . .

In the context of historical western Kenya, as in much of sub-Saharan Africa, it would be incorrect in most cases to assert that either men or women "owned" land. Men had rights to land for cultivation and grazing simply by virtue of their membership in a patrilineage . . . , whereas women obtained access to land only through marriage, and enjoyed these rights only so long as their marriages continued. . . .

Traditionally land was held corporately by the patrilineage, and men were allocated agricultural and grazing land according to the needs of their extended households. The male household head would assign particular fields for cultivation and particular cattle to the house of each of his wives according to their productivity and the number of their children.

Margaret Jean Hay, "Women as Owners, Occupants, and Managers of Property in Colonial Western Kenya," in *African Women and the Law: Historical Perspectives,* edited by Margaret Jean Hay and Marcia Wright. Boston University Papers on Africa, vol. 7 (Boston, 1982), 110, 112, 115. Note omitted.

For rural wives, the thought of their husbands' death always stirred appalling images that they might have to marry one of his relatives and be treated disgracefully. Their natal families had no obligation to take them back if their husbands died or they were separated. A widow's best prospect was to live with an adult son and his family, where she would be cared for and treated with respect. Consequently, the relationship between mother and sons was much closer than that between husband and wife. The colonial economy initially offered jobs to men, but at wages too low to support a family. In contrast to Western industrialization, which drew wives and children into factories to supplement minimal male wages, African colonialism left mother, wives, and children working in the agricultural sector to achieve the same results. Margaret Jean Hay describes the effects of male migrations:

As early as 1910, colonial administrators lamented the growth of male labor migration from western Kenya, complaining about the social and economic consequences of the migrants' absence from home. . . . In the early period of labor migration, married men from western Kenya often took their wives and families with them to Nakuru or Mombasa or Nairobi. After the Second World War, however, the pattern of leaving wives and children on the land was clearly established, both to protect male rights to particular parcels of land, which could theoretically be reallocated if not used, and to subsidize migrant wages. Women were expected to produce enough grain and vegetables to feed the family in the rural areas as well as to send regular contributions of food—grain, sometimes chickens—to the urban workers. . . . Rural women's subsistence production thus allowed the colonial capitalist sector to pay workers less than a subsistence familial wage, enabling it to extract greater surplus [profit]. . . . The presence of women on farm land served as both a validation and a protection of men's rights in land—and their presence was seen as critical in a society where the only form of social security most workers have is to be able to return to their rural homes in times of illness, unemployment, and after retirement. . . .

On the other hand, it is important to acknowledge that this rather rigid system of marriage as control carries with it distinct rights for wives and a certain bottom-line security. It is clear that women's welfare depends on a great deal more than simply access to land, and that not all security is material. On the whole, it is still accepted that women must be provided for in the sense of making available to them parcels of land for their own farming, if little else. Married women who have borne children for the lineage are almost impossible to dislodge, despite the vigorous attempts of a husband seeking divorce.

Margaret Jean Hay, "Women as Owners, Occupants, and Managers of Property in Colonial Western Kenya," in *African Women and the Law: Historical Perspectives,* edited by Margaret Jean Hay and Marcia Wright. Boston University Papers on Africa, vol. 7 (Boston, 1982), 119–20.

Independence brought little change to social and economic patterns forged under colonialism. Throughout East Africa, women, though gaining citizenship in new nations, continued to be denied ownership of the land they farmed. African men called upon women to accept patriarchal subordination in the name of nationalism and defense of an often dubious customary tradition against Western imperialism.

8.4 Urban Women Migrants

Luo men had been one of the first large migrant groups arriving in Kampala, Uganda, in the 1940s. Following the first migrants were single Luo women. Fearing a loss of control of the women, Luo males in the 1950s organized the Luo Union, which developed various programs to benefit the migrants, such as building low-cost housing. It gained fame in East Africa by labeling some women in Kampala a disgrace to the Luo nation and forcing them to return to their rural homes wearing a jute sack over their bodies. However, a few Luo women, who migrated alone or were separated from their husbands once they were in town, refused to join the Luo Union. These the Luo Union could not discipline.

The organization crumbled when a military government took over Uganda in 1971 and began expelling foreigners. By 1972, the Luo Union was underground and had little power over the women. Luo men tried to regain their authority by other means. Christine Obbo describes one attempt in which they sought to discourage Luo women's independent acts through a small Christian religious cult:

Some churches, such as the Legio Maria (a breakaway from the Catholic Church), attempted to preserve the Luo family and marriages by discouraging women from acquiring independent incomes which would weaken the position of men. The method used was making women confess to such sins as keeping some of the household management money for themselves. What was intriguing was the fact that the confessions were held during prayer fellowships with husbands in attendance.

One such woman was Atieno, and each time she confessed I would wait a week and then ask her whether she had returned the money to her husband. Each of the four times she just smiled sweetly and told me I should ask other women who confessed too! . . .

While women confessed to wanting to start or having started trading, the men confessed to being angry with the Lord for not dealing satisfactorily with their employment situation.

Christine Obbo, *African Women: Their Struggle for Economic Independence* (London: Zed Press, 1980), 111–13.

Many rural women migrants, often unskilled and uneducated, managed to survive in Kampala. One common pattern was to pool their resources and invest in joint ventures: women gin distillers were often in joint ventures. Women in a venture usually lived in neighboring rooms or houses and were on eating and visiting terms. They borrowed clothes and kitchen utensils from each other, baby-sat, and were concerned with each other's welfare.

Christine Obbo describes an example of a slightly different joint arrangement in Kisugu, a suburb of Kampala, which incidentally illustrates some of the experiences migrant women—in this case, Ganda women—often had in the city:

Namu, aged 22, Nankya, aged 35, and Najjingo, aged 46, had not always lived on the same block as they did in 1972. Namu had been at Kisugu for only a year, and had at first worked as a barmaid. Her salary of 30 shillings a month was just enough to pay the rent and feed her two small children. She decided that she would supplement her inadequate salary by selling curried pancakes and brewing and selling pineapple beer during the day, while she still worked as a barmaid in the evening. At night she also sold her sex services for money. After four months of this kind of life, she felt dissatisfied but also felt that she had little option but to go on. She was particularly distressed at the violence of the men in the bars. By this time she had met Najjingo who advised her to stop working in the bar if she did not want to end up every month in the hospital nursing her injuries. Najjingo had two large rooms and suggested that Namu come and rent the back one while she kept the front one that served as a shop.

Najjingo herself had experienced a very unhappy marriage, and used to visit her married daughter at Kisugu for long periods whenever the daughter was ill or pregnant, or if one of the grandchildren were ill. Each time she came, she used to leave the daughter with some money which she had obtained by selling bananas and coffee while her husband was away visiting friends. Soon the money amounted to 600 shillings, enough to open a shop. One day in 1968 she came to visit her daughter carrying a large cloth bundle and a wooden suitcase, and announced that this time she was not returning to her husband. At first she rented a small room for 35 shillings a month, and sold soft drinks and cigarettes "under the bed" [illegally]. Before long her son-in-law had found her an old . . . refrigerator for cooling the drinks. Since her room was next door to a school, a stand pipe [water source] and a church, her drinks were in constant demand, and after two years she was ready to move into two large rooms next door which a Nubi houseowner had just finished building. Within a few months she realized that the rent was too much for her and this was when she invited Namu to share with her. By this time Namu had borrowed some money from her friends and established herself in the food selling and brewing businesses.

A month later a third woman, Nankya, moved into two large rooms next door. She too was a shopkeeper, but had been born and raised in Namuwongo [a Kampala suburb]. Her parents owned some land so she never had to buy food. . . . Meanwhile Namu would sit on Najjingo's verandah every day after work watching the dinner cooking and passersby conversing with Najjingo and the customers at her shop, but above all watching the goings on at Nankya's rooms.

After two months Nankya was a close friend of both Namu and Najjingo. Namu called Najjingo "mother" and her children called Najjingo "grandmother." Najjingo's own grandchildren, who stayed with her or who occasionally came to visit her, were told to call Namu "mother." Namu, on the other hand, addressed Nankya as "paternal aunt." . . .

Namu, Nankya and Najjingo looked after each other's welfare and economic interests. When Nankya's children were ill, which they often were, it was Najjingo and Namu, rather than Nankya's real relatives, who would be asked to look after the shop while she took the children to the hospital. Namu often had to leave her pancakes in baskets at Nankya and Najjingo's shop to sell for her while she went to sell food or beer somewhere else and, if she were going to be selling late, they would baby-sit for her. Najjingo always entrusted her shop to her two friends, but never left it open when her brother or nephew were visiting. If one of the three were late, the others would keep some food for her. . . .

However, unless absolutely necessary, they stayed out of each other's arguments, not interfering even when Namu's ex-husband tried to kidnap one of her sons. But they did defend Namu against the landlord's insinuations, since they could attest to her virtue.

Christine Obbo, *African Women: Their Struggle for Economic Independence* (London: Zed Press, 1980), 114–16. Ganda words omitted.

8.5 Female Genital Mutilation (FGM) in Kenya

In the late twentieth century, women in Uganda and neighboring Kenya struggled against male-dominated political and judicial systems. Kenya, which won independence from British rule in 1963, established a nominally democratic government; women voted but seldom won elective or appointive offices. Examples of the prevailing male ideology within Kenya's governing institutions can be found in statements made by male members of parliament (MPs) during debates over a proposed Law of Marriage and Divorce, as reported by Maria Nzomo and Kathleen Staudt:

The law fully addressed household relations; it strengthened women's right to own property, to be protected from corporal punishment, and to avoid polygamy. . . . MP's said corporal punishment was necessary to discipline wives, and wives should be beaten, for it is "a pleasure to her . . . a way of expressing love in Lubha custom." A woman MP's query on why women providers did not have the right to punish their husbands invoked a defense of bridewealth: "because she has not bought [her husband]." The most vigorous debate occurred over polygamy, with lengthy rationales being offered in support of the practice: what if the first wife was childless, old, or rude? What if a man needed a nurse in his old age?

Maria Nzomo and Kathleen Staudt, "Man-made Political Machinery in Kenya: Political Space for Women?" In *Women and Politics Worldwide*, edited by Barbara J. Nelson and Najma Chowdhury (New Haven, CT: Yale University Press, 1994), 423.

Within Kenya, approximately one-half of contemporary women have undergone female genital mutilation. This percentage is not the highest in the world. FGM is practiced almost universally in the nations of the Horn of Africa: Somalia, Ethiopia, and Eritrea. Elsewhere in Africa and Asia, FGM is a traditional practice among some peoples—including both Christians and Muslims— but not among others. It is done to girls in city hospitals as well as in rural homes. Dr. Nahid Toubia, a Sudanese pediatrician, explains the operation:

An estimated 130 million girls and women in the world are genitally mutilated. Most live in Africa, a few in Asia, and increasingly, there are more women in Europe, Canada, and the United States who have suffered female genital mutilation. These women and girls experience pain, trauma, and frequently, severe physical complications, such as bleeding, infections, or even death. . . . For those with the severest form of FGM, infibulation, the trauma of mutilation is repeated with each childbirth. . . .

FGM is one of the traditional rituals that prepare girls for womanhood, although the age at which it is practiced varies widely. In some cultures girls are circumcised as early as infancy, while in others, the ceremony may not occur until the girl is of marriageable age. . . .

Although many studies refer to several different types of female genital mutilation, the different operations can be incorporated into three basic types: Type I: Clitoridectomy. In this operation a part or the whole of the clitoris is amputated and the bleeding is stopped with pressure or a stitch. . . . Type II: Excision. Both the clitoris and the inner lips are amputated. Bleeding is usually stopped with stitching but the vagina is not covered. Approximately 85 percent of all women who undergo FGM have either Type I or II. Type III: Infibulation. In this group of operations, the clitoris is removed, some or all of the labia minora are cut off and incisions are made in the labia majora to create raw surfaces. These raw surfaces are either stitched together and/or kept in contact by tying the legs together until they heal as a "hood of skin," which covers the urethra and most of the vagina.

Since a physical barrier to intercourse has been created, a small opening must be reconstructed for the flow of urine and menstrual blood. . . . If the opening is more generous, sexual intercourse can take place after gradual dilation, which may take days, weeks, or even months.

Nahid Toubia, *Female Genital Mutilation: A Call for Global Action,* 2nd edition (New York: Research, Action, & Information Network for Bodily Integrity of Women [Rainbᵎ], 1995), 5, 9–10.

FGM is condemned worldwide, but discussion continues about which campaigns are effective in ending the pain and suffering of young females. Attacks on FGM by Western feminists have provoked defenses of it as an ancient customary religious practice. Such defenses of FGM came not only from men. In the past, older African women have supported FGM because it was an important part of initiation ceremonies into female organizations that were beneficial to women. Claire Robertson explains why support for and practice of FGM have decreased since the 1920s among the Kikuyu and Kamba women traders of Nairobi, Kenya:

The old form of Kikuyu women's organization centered around their age-sets . . . and a solidarity induced by their common initiation ritual. Part of the ritual was genital mutilation in the form of clitoridectomy. . . .

Initiation . . . has often been viewed as the most important old Kikuyu custom, and it was also universally practiced by the Kamba. Boys and girls underwent a series of ceremonies with the ultimate aim of initiating them into adulthood. . . . Boys were circumcised during initiation . . . when they were sixteen to eighteen years old. Girls had the clitoris and sometimes the labia removed [during initiation] . . . usually between the ages of ten and fifteen on the first appearance of breasts. . . .

An extremely important part of initiation everywhere was the knowledge imparted to the initiates by their elders, which involved traditions, laws, manners, the duties of adults, ideas of appropriate behavior regarding sexual intercourse, in particular, child rearing, or generally any knowledge necessary to function as a successful adult in Kikuyu society. . . .

The pain endured at initiation was to prepare a girl to endure pain in childbirth. A respected woman elder acted as her sponsor and held her during the operation. Afterward she was supposed to be well cared for along with her mates. They stayed together while healing, which helped solidify lifelong friendships.

Claire Robertson, "Grassroots in Kenya: Women, Genital Mutilation, and Collective Action, 1920–1990," *Signs: Journal of Women in Culture and Society* 21:3 (spring 1996): 620–22. Copyright © 1996 by The University of Chicago. All rights reserved.

The age-sets had power over women's activities and could punish men who committed offenses against women. The age-sets had a hierarchy, in which the senior age-sets had significant authority. As women in an age-set got older, they were supposed to move up to a higher level after payment to the women elders. The highest level was the council of women elders. The activities of the women's councils were described by a local British colonial official:

They dealt with "purely domestic affairs," he said, such as agricultural matters like food crops, rainfall, and land use, and the discipline and regulation of the social life of girls and women or other offenders. They punished men who maltreated women by levying fines . . . ; by the men's wives withdrawing their services; by ostracism; or, if the offense was very bad, by a curse placed by baring the private parts toward the object of the curse and hurling genital insults, accompanied by other antisocial behavior.

Claire Robertson, "Grassroots in Kenya: Women, Genital Mutilation, and Collective Action, 1920–1990," *Signs: Journal of Women in Culture and Society* 21:3 (spring 1996): 625. Copyright © 1996 by The University of Chicago. All rights reserved.

One of the important functions of the council of women elders was to organize *ngwatio,* cooperative agricultural work parties. These might prepare the fields for planting—heavy work that passed more quickly and productively with gang labor. Parties might also weed the cornfields or harvest grains. Such cooperative work parties were common in Africa.

Some researchers have concluded that clitoridectomy and age-sets have disappeared in Kenya. Claire Robertson conducted a survey of Nairobi market traders in 1987–88. In her survey, all the older women aged fifty and over had had clitoridectomies, but each younger cohort had fewer, and in the critical group, ages ten to fourteen, only 20 percent had undergone the operation. The reasons given for the decline fell into three categories:

(1) Clitoridectomy and the associated ceremonies were seen as being uncivilized and counter to the Bible; (2) it was no longer the style and difficult to find operators to do it; and (3) it was expensive and undesirable for health reasons.

Claire Robertson, "Grassroots in Kenya: Women, Genital Mutilation, and Collective Action, 1920–1990," *Signs: Journal of Women in Culture and Society* 21:3 (spring 1996): 630. Copyright © 1996 by The University of Chicago. All rights reserved.

Robertson argues that the age-sets of the Nairobi women traders have been merged into women's groups dealing with contemporary problems:

If among the Kikuyu and Kamba the practice of clitoridectomy is diminishing sharply, membership in contemporary women's groups is rising and has emerged seamlessly from the older versions. This transition took place in the late 1940s and 1950s, which saw the formation or modification of women's groups for new purposes, using *ngwatio* as their base. . . .

[In the late 1980s,] many of the associations were targeted in purpose. The pooled money was to be used to buy land to be worked cooperatively by members; to buy roofing for members' houses . . . , water tanks, home equipment, and grade cattle; to keep poultry, pigs, or goats; or to do handicrafts like basketry. . . . But most [rotating savings] associations placed no restrictions on the use of funds, so women could use the money as they wished.

Claire Robertson, "Grassroots in Kenya: Women, Genital Mutilation, and Collective Action, 1920–1990," *Signs: Journal of Women in Culture and Society* 21:3 (spring 1996): 630, 634. Copyright © 1996 by The University of Chicago. All rights reserved.

———————————

Within these organizations, age seniority or an initiation rite has almost no function, as Robertson explains:

The democratic multiethnic basis of leadership was evident in the market-based rotating savings organizations, which existed in both urban and rural areas. The leaders of the market-based organizations were usually not elderly women, but, rather, women whose competence was widely recognized, some of whom were quite young—in their late twenties or early thirties. Knowledge, which used to come more from experience, now comes more from education; literate skills were highly prized. Very old women traders were more often in the category of near-beggars and not particularly venerated by others. The prime leadership positions were elective and usually held by women in their forties, who were active traders.

Claire Robertson, "Grassroots in Kenya: Women, Genital Mutilation, and Collective Action, 1920–1990," *Signs: Journal of Women in Culture and Society* 21:3 (spring 1996): 637. Copyright © 1996 by The University of Chicago. All rights reserved.

———————————

The women in these market organizations are very similar to Namu, Nankya, and Najjingo of Kampala, described in reading 8.4. Robertson concludes:

Women's age-sets have transformed themselves into peer-based environmental groups and rotating savings or market associations of various kinds. In the process, initiation with its associated clitoridectomy is disappearing, along with the gerontocratic authority that upheld it. Among Nairobi market women, age seniority as a primary aspect of female leadership has fallen by the way as it has elsewhere in Kenyan society. A rotating savings association may name its business Nyakinyua Enterprises after the authority-bearing female age-set, but in the markets it is survival skills, not age, that count the most. And, the shared experience of an underclass . . . is more important than ascribed characteristics in generating solidarity. The economic basis of solidarity is most important. Most women traders rely for help on neighbors who trade . . . rather than on their families. . . . Their peers are most reliable; they help by watching commodities, giving loans, subbing during necessary absences, conveying necessary information, and so on. In essence, the transgenerational family and locational linkages emphasized at initiation have diminished in favor of stronger peer links. . . . The irony of the situation is that clitoridectomy, now widely recognized as very dangerous to women physically, was a part of a firm authority structure through which some women gained power, which has now been replaced by a status system that contains fewer guarantees for women.

Claire Robertson, "Grassroots in Kenya: Women, Genital Mutilation, and Collective Action, 1920–1990," *Signs: Journal of Women in Culture and Society* 21:3 (spring 1996): 638. Copyright © 1996 by The University of Chicago. All rights reserved.

Kenya banned FGM in 1990. Ghana, Egypt, and Ivory Coast have also prohibited the practice in the 1990s. These actions respond to years of condemnation of FGM by African women's organizations and health professionals and to increasing international pressure to define FGM as a fundamental violation of children's and women's human rights.

The World Conference to Review and Appraise the Achievements of the United Nations Decade for Women brought thousands of women from every continent to Nairobi, Kenya, in 1985. Many Nairobi sessions spotlighted the dismal prospects of African girls and women. A brighter future seemed possible, however, because international experts finally recognized that African economic development depends on women's education, cooperation, and active participation in all sectors of labor.

A decade later, their conditions have worsened, according to a 1995 report by the United Nations. Health and education have declined, and women's literacy is 43 percent, the lowest in the world. At approximately six children, fertility, as measured by the average number of children per mother, is the highest in the world. Estimates of HIV infections are soaring, and more women than men are estimated to be infected, in contrast to other regions of the world. Participation in the labor force has dropped, and this is the only region where this has occurred.[*]

Suggested Further Readings

For information on nineteenth-century African women, there are few sources. Two focus on South Africa: Pamela Scully's "Rape, Race, and Colonial Culture: The Sexual Politics of Identity in the Nineteenth-Century Cape Colony, South Africa," *American Historical Review* 100, no. 2 (April 1995): 335–59; and Cherryl Walker's *Women and Gender in Southern Africa to 1945* (Cape Town: David Philip Publishers, 1990). Elizabeth Schmidt discusses traditional oppression of women in the context of the impact of colonial rule and missionary activity in *Peasants, Traders, and Wives: Shona Women in the History of Zimbabwe, 1870–1939* (Portsmouth, NH: Heinemann, 1992).

For the twentieth century, two anthologies offer studies of women in various societies: Claire Robertson and Iris Berger, eds., *Women and Class in Africa* (New York: Africana Publishing Company, 1986); and Sharon B. Stichter and Jane L. Parpart, eds., *Patriarchy and Class: African Women in the Home and the Workforce* (Boulder, CO: Westview Press, 1988).

Important studies that focus on women in a single society include Iris Berger's *Threads of Solidarity: Women in Southern African Industry, 1900–1980* (Bloomington: Indiana University

---

[*]United Nations, *The World's Women, 1995: Trends and Statistics* (New York: United Nations Publications, 1995), xvii.

Press, 1992). Ifi Amadiume, *Male Daughters, Female Husbands: Gender and Sex in an African Society* (London: Zed Books, 1987), examines a woman's power in her natal family among the Igbo of Nigeria. Sarah Mirza and Margaret Strobel, eds., in *Three Swahili Women: Life Histories from Mombasa, Kenya* (Bloomington: Indiana University Press, 1989), record interviews with Muslim women in the early 1970s.

African women's roles in armed resistance and political organization for independence are told in Amrit Wilson's *Women and the Eritrean Revolution: The Challenge Road* (Trenton, NJ: Red Sea Press, 1991), and Stephanie Urdang's *And Still They Dance: Women, War, and the Struggle for Change in Mozambique* (New York: Monthly Review Press, 1989). Urdang analyzes reasons for the failure to realize promises of equality given to women fighting for national liberation. In "Collective Action and the 'Representation' of African Women: A Liberian Case Study," *Feminist Studies* 15, no. 3 (fall 1989): 443–60, Mary H. Moran argues the basis in tradition for African women to demand separate representation as women in a modern democracy.

–9–
THE SYMBOL OF THE VEIL IN MODERN ISLAM

Yomut woman plying yarn for carpet. Iran, 1966–67.
(Photograph by William Irons.)

The Turkish Ottoman dynasty's power diminished after 1800 as it lost control of the peripheries of its empire in North Africa and the Balkans. The Iranian Qajar and Pahlavi dynasties of the nineteenth and twentieth centuries found their borders and power limited by the expanding Russian and British states. Rising Western military and economic strength that accompanied weakening of Turkish and Iranian domination of the Middle East reached its peak after World War I, with Turkey reduced to its Anatolian provinces; France and Great Britain in control of Syria, Lebanon, Iraq, Palestine, Jordan, and Egypt; and concessions for Iran's new oil fields firmly under European control. Pervasive European imperialism was met by a tide of nationalism, whose leadership was secular and committed to emulating aspects of Western success in education, law, and economy that were perceived as necessary to independent nationhood. Feminism developed in conjunction with Middle Eastern nationalist movements and, like them, was both influenced by European ideals of schooling for women, gender equality, and individualism and repulsed by European arrogance and contempt for Islamic societies. For twentieth-century Muslim women, the veil became a prime symbol: first in the act of removing the veil to signify their feminist ideals, then in voluntarily or involuntarily donning scarf or *chadur* to prove their allegiance to Islam.

Before women were forced to choose political allegiances, many faced changes in daily life instigated by expanding international trade stimulated by nineteenth-century construction of railways and the Suez Canal; development of new steamship lines and banking consortiums; demands in Europe for workers, grain, opium, and cotton; and concentration of land ownership that forced many nomadic families to abandon their pastures and forced farmers to work as sharecroppers. The indirect impact of industrialization in Europe and the United States on traditional women artisans was dramatically evident in the rise of the "Oriental" or "Persian" rug to the status of an art object prized by Western museums.

9.1 Nomadic Carpet Weaving

Books written to identify different "Oriental" carpets often picture women knotting yarn on a loom, a skill that has been practiced by pastoral and village Central Asians for more than twenty-five hundred years. Examples of the principal knotting techniques still used in hand manufacture of pile rugs are found in textiles excavated by archaeologists from frozen kurgans in Russia near the Mongolian border and dated to the sixth and fifth centuries B.C.E. Although these ancient remnants do not reveal the gender of their makers, when, more than fifteen hundred years later, documentary accounts of Turko-Mongolian invaders describe their use of carpets of felt, flat-woven *kilims,* and knotted piles, these rugs are usually attributed to rural women's labor in their households. By the sixteenth century, knotted carpets were important in both the internal and export trade of the Ottoman and Safavid Empires. Court patronage may have supported urban workshops, but village and nomadic women continued to tie rug knots on home looms. By the nineteenth century, many European travelers passed through the rural regions of Turkey, Iran, and southern Russia, often contrasting the poverty of the women and girls who made the rugs with the sophistication and beauty of their product. Twentieth-century anthropological field studies describe similar work, paying attention to the processes of each task and to its importance to the family. William Irons tells about a Yomut Turkmen nomadic group, to which he gave the fictitious name of Ājī Qūī, who were living near the southeastern coast of the Caspian Sea in 1966 and 1967:

The division of labor in the Turkmen households of Ājī Qūī is one in which men do the work which takes them far away from the family tent, whereas women do the work which can be done in or near the family tent. Women are engaged in child care, in the preparation of meals, sewing, washing, carding and spinning wool, and in the making of felts, the weaving of flat woven pieces (*palas*) and the weaving of carpets. Men care for livestock, do agricultural labor, and haul water. . . . Men are also the ones who carry on market transactions, another activity which takes them away from the family tent.

According to the 1973–74 demographic survey I [and two others] conducted . . . the average Turkmen woman at that time could expect to have seven or eight children. This means that between the ages of nineteen and forty, a typical Turkmen women has one child approximately every three years. It is thus not surprising that the economic activities of Turkmen women are those which can be done near the family tent and hence are compatible with child care. Each child is usually breast-fed until the birth of the next child. Because childbearing and the care of older children absorbs a large portion of a woman's effort, other work must be fitted in. . . .

Washing, carding, spinning, and dyeing the wool for carpets fits in nicely with child care. . . . It can be done at home and interrupted periodically.

In Ājī Qūī . . . the amount of weaving done by each family depended on its supply of female labor and wool. Most weavers used only wool from their own family flock rather than buying wool from other families with extra wool from larger flocks. . . . Often several families would pool their resources (in female labor and wool) with close relatives or neighbors to produce large carpets or to balance the available supplies of labor with their supply of wool. . . .

Weaving was usually limited to a period of a few months after the spring shearing. After that, the wool was used up. The fall shearing rarely yielded wool suitable for carpets.

While wool was available, women spent all their spare time at the loom. Most could weave and nurse a baby at the same time. The older women of the household would decide on the pattern and supervise the work of the younger women, especially those who were still learning. The elders, of course, did their share of weaving as well. They had names for the various elements in the design, so that any woman could do a reasonable job of explaining to another woman what sort of design she intended for a particular rug.

They relied upon memory to produce the elaborate designs of their carpets as they wove. Unlike urban carpet weavers in Iran, they never used patterns traced on paper although occasionally they would use another rug to provide a pattern to copy. This latter procedure was followed when learning a new pattern. Their ability to produce an elaborate design purely from memory seemed amazing to outsiders, like my wife and myself. One woman told my wife that the ability to weave a Turkmen carpet was like literacy. It is a skill acquired over many years, one that beginners cannot hope to master in a short time. Our ability to scan a page covered with small letters and produce words and sentences seemed as amazing to a Turkmen woman as her ability to weave an intricate pattern from memory seemed to us.

Most families in Ājī Qūī wove one or two carpets a year. The men of the family would take a completed carpet to the market town of

Gunbad-i Kāvūs where it would be sold to middlemen who transported them to the Tehran bazaar or sold to local shops in Gunbad-i Kāvūs. Most carpets from Ājī Qūī at that time were sold to middlemen for around fifteen *tumans* (unit of currency) an *ayak* (square foot). I calculated that one woman could weave roughly one Ayak in a day of heavy weaving, about twelve hours at the loom. Subtracting the price of wool and dye at 1966 and 1967 prices, the value of the woman's labor came to about five tumans (U.S. $0.66). This was a high return on labor in Ājī Qūī at that time.

For the most part, only young women who had not yet had their first child could devote twelve hours a day to weaving. Older women with children to care for, and with more domestic chores to do, devoted less of their day to weaving. In a large extended family with many female members, the women would often take turns at the loom. Smaller families, with only one female adult, simply did less weaving.

Most of the carpets woven in Ājī Qūī were produced to supplement family income rather than as furnishing for their own tents. At the time of my residence in Ājī Qūī (1966–67), a family of median wealth had a per capita income of $29 in a bad year, and $80 in a good year. . . .

Although most carpet weaving was commercial in motivation, most families would also have one or two carpets and perhaps a Palas or two in their household possessions, which they would bring out as a floor covering for their tents on festive occasions. Other than these occasions, however, floor covering consists of felts. Such luxury items which were used only occasionally were also a form of savings, since in time of need these could be sold.

William Irons, "The Place of Carpet Weaving in Turkmen Society," in *Turkmen: Tribal Carpets and Traditions,* edited by Louise W. Mackie and Jon Thompson (Washington, DC: Textile Museum, 1980), 32–36. Note omitted.

In the forty years from 1875 to 1914, the manufacture of hand-knotted pile carpets became a major industry in Iran (then called Persia). Growth was fed by increasing demand for the carpets in Europe and the United States, where possession of an "Oriental" rug defined the prosperity and respectable taste of middle-class families. By 1914, carpets were Iran's largest export and remained so until displaced by oil exports; carpets retained second place in the value of Iranian exports until the 1978 revolution. As in other textile industries throughout the world, the modern carpet industry depended upon female labor.

To meet rising Western demand, Iranian and foreign merchants expanded their purchases from home workers and set up factories in towns and cities—often distant from the traditional carpet-producing areas. Factories were not mechanized, for despite development of power looms that had transformed the weaving of cloth and carpeting throughout much of the world, technology found no substitute for human fingers to tie knots in piled carpets. Costs were reduced by replacing independent female artisans who created their own patterns with harshly exploited children, some as young as four, poor women, or occasionally, men. Social demands for seclusion created problems for adult women workers. Veiled Muslim women could not tie more than a thousand knots per hour. In villages, mothers and daughters worked in the privacy of their homes. Christian and Jewish women staffed urban factories until economic necessity drove poor Muslim women into shameful public employment.

Working conditions were harsh. To keep the threads from breaking, the preferred work space was damp and dark, and the hours were as long as the managers could keep the workers awake on the looms. A supervisor, reading a pattern, called out a cadence and thread color for rapid knotting. After 1900, Christian medical missionaries began reporting deformities among the children and young women: gnarled fingers, hands, wrists, and arms, as well as legs too crippled to walk. Pelvises of young girls frequently became deformed so that childbirth by caesarean operation was necessary to save the mother's life.[*] Efforts of missionaries, the International Labor Organization, and the Iranian government have had little impact on working conditions. Since the 1979 hostage crisis, imports into the United States from Iran have been banned; however, Iran is not the only country where scandalously low wages and long hours still prevail in the carpet industry.

---

[*]Leonard Helfgott, *Ties That Bind: A Social History of the Iranian Carpet* (Washington, DC: Smithsonian Institution Press, 1994), ch. 9.

9.2 Autobiography of Huda Shaarawi,
Egyptian Feminist

Soon after 1900, daring Egyptian feminists published their demands for education and control of their lives—and a few refused to veil themselves in public spaces. Huda Shaarawi (1879–1947), the founder of the Egyptian Feminist Union, describes personal resentments at the root of her feminism. Her generation was the last to experience harem life from childhood to maturity. Shaarawi's father, Sultan Pasha, was a wealthy Egyptian administrator who eventually became president of the Chamber of Deputies. Her mother was a beautiful Circassian woman from the Caucasus and the last of several wives of Sultan Pasha.

As a child, Huda sought answers for her serious questions from her father's principal wife, Hasiba, who was affectionately called *Umm Kabira* (Big Mother):

I loved *Umm Kabira* immensely, and she returned that love and showed compassion toward me. She, alone, talked frankly with me on a number of matters, making it easy for me to confide in her. She knew how I felt when people favoured my brother over me because he was a boy. She, too, occasionally fanned the flames of jealousy in me, but without diminishing my love for my brother. . . .

I used to imagine that I was not my mother's daughter—that my real mother was a slave girl who had died, and the truth was being withheld from me. Firmly convinced of this, I suffered all the more. I could keep everything suppressed until nightfall but as soon as I laid my head on the pillow, I was overcome by anxieties and frightening thoughts moved me to tears. This inner turbulence provoked nightmares that woke me in terror, with heart beating so hard I feared it would escape from my chest. I dreamed often that huge beasts were pouncing on me, baring their fangs in my face, and that when I sought refuge with my mother I would find that she had taken my brother in her arms and turned her back on me. "I am not your child!" I would scream, "You have lied to me! Tell me the truth! I am not your child! I am not your child!" . . .

In these states of agitation I sometimes confessed my sufferings to *Umm Kabira* and she consoled me. . . .

I once asked *Umm Kabira* why everyone paid more attention to my brother than to me. "Haven't you understood yet?" she asked gently. When I claimed that as the elder I should receive more attention she replied, "But you are a girl and he is a boy. And you are not the only girl, while he is the only boy. One day the support of the family will fall upon him. When you marry you will leave the house and honour your husband's name but he will perpetuate the name of his father and take over his house." This straightforward answer satisfied me. I began to love my brother all the more because he would occupy the place of my father. . . .

My brothers and I and our two companions began our daily lessons early in the morning and finished at noon. We took up various subjects with tutors who came to the house under the supervision of Said Agha [an Ethiopian eunuch freed from slavery, who supervised the harem]. I was devoted to my studies and became completely absorbed at lesson time.

Of all the subjects, Arabic was my favourite. One day when I asked the teacher why I was unable to read the Koran without making a mistake he said, "Because you have not learned the rules of grammar." I pressed him, "Will I be able to read perfectly once I have done so?" When he said yes I asked him to teach me. The next day, when he arrived carrying an Arabic grammar under his arm, Said Agha demanded arrogantly, "What is that?" to which he responded, "The book Mistress Nur al-Huda has requested in order to learn grammar." The eunuch contemptuously ordered, "Take back your book *Sayyidna Shaikh.* The young lady has no need of grammar as she will not become a judge!" I became depressed and began to neglect my studies, hating being a girl because it kept me from the education I sought. Later, being a female became a barrier between me and the freedom for which I yearned. The memory and anguish of this remain sharp to this day. . . .

From the time we were very small, my brother and I shared the same friends, nearly all boys, most of whom were the children of our neighbours. The boys remained my companions until I grew up—that is, until I was about eleven—when suddenly I was required to restrict myself to the company of girls and women. I felt a stranger in their world—their habits and notions startled me. Being separated from the companions of my childhood was a painful experience. Their ways left a mark on me.

Reprinted and excerpted, by permission, from Huda Shaarawi, *Harem Years: The Memoirs of an Egyptian Feminist (1879–1924)*, translated, edited, and introduced by Margot Badran (New York: The Feminist Press at The City University of New York, 1987), 34–36, 39–40, 52. Copyright 1986 by Margot Badran. Note omitted.

Huda Shaarawi was fortunate in her education. Schools for girls established in the nineteenth century, as well as private tutoring, created a small literate group of women among elite and urban middle-class families. By World War I, Western Christian mission schools were rapidly expanding educational opportunities for women in Egypt and Turkey. Still, the prevalence of teenage marriage for girls meant that few educated women could pursue professional careers. Shaarawi's experience was not unusual.

Huda's father died when she was five. The guardian designated by her father to look after the family and administer the estate was Ali Shaarawi, a cousin in his forties. Eight years later, her mother decided to arrange a marriage for Huda, then thirteen.

One day when I was dozing while recovering from an illness, I was suddenly roused by excited voices coming from the far end of the room. My mother and 'Aunt' Gazibiyya Hanim, were talking. Gazibiyya Hanim said, "I have heard that the khedive's family is going to ask for her and if that happens you will have to bow to their will." She continued, "However, if necessary, we could arrange a marriage with her cousin [Ali Shaarawi]." My mother said angrily, "It would be shameful for her to marry a man with children of his own who are older than she is." Gazibiyya Hanim replied, "He is the son of her father's sister and 'lord and master' of all." My mother answered, "We shall see what happens."

The room began to spin and the remarks of the nurses and the slaves made whenever my cousin [Ali Shaarawi] called came echoing back. . . . "Go and greet your husband." It angered me but I dismissed it as a mischievous taunt. When the truth behind this became apparent, I wept long and hard, and the shock caused my illness to worsen and persist for a long time afterwards.

My cousin began to come to Cairo with greater frequency and passed many hours in the company of my mother. At times, I feared they were about to reach an agreement over my future but my forebodings vanished when I detected anger in my mother's speech. Gradually I paid less attention to the matter and it eventually slipped from my mind altogether. . . .

Not long after that, repairs began on our house. During that time my mother decided to pass the winter months in Helwan [Egypt] and so she took a small villa. . . .

After we were there for some time one of my friends came to spend a few days with us. One afternoon as I was taking her on a promenade to show her the delightful sights, we were startled by the appearance of Said Agha, who was accompanying some gentlemen. "Where are you going?" he scowled. "Return to the house at once!" We submitted to his command and retraced our steps. Upon entering the house I [was handed a Koran]. . . . Said Agha entered escorting Ali Pasha Fahmi, the husband of a second cousin, and Saad al-Din Bey, an officer in the Palace Guard, who later married Gazibiyya Hanim. When they came towards me, I hastened to my room thoroughly bewildered, but they followed and I retreated to the window, where I stood with my back to them. To my utter astonishment, Ali Pasha Fahmi announced, "The son of your father's sister wants your hand in marriage and we are here on his behalf."

Only then did I understand the reason for the various preparations underway in the house, as well as a number of other mysteries. With my back to the men, I cried without speaking or moving. I stood sobbing by the window for nearly three hours. Occasionally passers-by glanced up sympathetically. Eventually Ali Pasha Fahmi and Saad al-Din Bey asked, "Whom do you wish to designate as your *wakil* (agent) to sign the marriage contract?" I said nothing, and after a long silence, Said Agha whispered in my ear, "Do you wish to disgrace the name of your father and destroy your poor mother who is weeping in her sickbed and might not survive the shock of your refusal?" Upon hearing these words, which pierced my heart, I replied, "Do whatever you want." . . .

My mother surprised me one day when she came to my room with a document which she asked me to read aloud to her, adding that my future husband had refused to sign it. It stipulated that my cousin, upon his marriage with me, would have no further relations with the mother of his children, nor would he ever take another wife. Until then, always mindful of his wife and children, I was certain that the marriage would not take place, but after reading the document reality struck home and I wept. My mother, thinking I was upset at my cousin's refusal to sign said, "Everything has been done to secure his written consent but all efforts have failed. The preparations for the wedding have been completed and the invitations issued. It would be a disgrace to stop the wedding now. Accept things as they are for the moment, my daughter, and, God willing, in the future he will agree to these conditions. This is your destiny and God is your guide." I didn't utter a word; when my mother pressed me to speak, I said only, "Do as you please," and left in tears.

Reprinted and excerpted, by permission, from Huda Shaarawi, *Harem Years: The Memoirs of an Egyptian Feminist (1879–1924)*, translated, edited, and introduced by Margot Badran (New York: The Feminist Press at The City University of New York, 1987), 52–55. Copyright 1986 by Margot Badran. Note omitted.

At thirteen, Huda found it impossible to refuse the wedding even though Islamic law provides that a woman must agree to her marriage. The marriage began with a separation—a most unusual event in Muslim society. Her husband had freed his slave concubine (who had remained in bondage for fifteen years after slavery was legally outlawed in Egypt) when he committed himself to a monogamous union with Huda. Then Huda and her mother discovered that Ali Shaarawi had returned to his former companion, who was expecting another child. That caused the separation, which lasted seven years before a reconciliation. They later had two children.

In 1908, Huda, then twenty-eight, modestly began the feminist stage of her life by organizing public lectures for women and helping to found a charity clinic for mothers and children. More radical activities followed.

Near the end of World War I, her husband, Ali Shaarawi, and two other men organized the Wafd, a revolutionary nationalist movement for Egyptian independence. In 1882, the British army had occupied Egypt; it did not leave until 1956. British officials ruled Egypt through a protectorate that ended in 1922, but even then, the British government continued to control defense policy and to protect foreigners in Egypt. Egyptian nationalists objected to the British presence. Huda became president of the Wafdist Women's Central Committee in 1920.

Still veiled, she participated in public demonstrations. She recalled one in 1919 involving 150 to 300 upper-class women:

We women held our first demonstration on 16 March to protest the
repressive acts and intimidation practiced by the British authority. In
compliance with the orders of the authority we announced our plans
to demonstrate in advance but were refused permission. We began to
telephone this news to each other, only to read in *al-Muqattam* that
the demonstration had received official sanction. We got on the telephone again, telling as many women as possible that we would proceed according to schedule the following morning. Had we been able
to contact more than a limited number of women, virtually all the
women of Cairo would have taken part in the demonstration. . . .

We assembled according to plan at the Garden City Park, where
we left our carriages. Having agreed upon our route and carefully
instructed the young women assigned to carry the flags and placards
in front, we set out in columns towards the legation of the United
States and intended to proceed from there to the legations of Italy and
France. However, when we reached Qasr al-Aini Street, I observed
that the young women in front were deviating from the original plan
and had begun to head in the Direction of *Bait al-Umma* (The House
of the Nation), as Saad Zaghlul's house was called. I asked my friend
Wagida Khulusi to find out why we were going toward Saad Pasha's
house and she returned saying that the women had decided it was a
better route. . . . Reluctantly I went along with this change. No sooner
were we approaching Zaghlul's house than British troops surrounded
us. They blocked the streets with machine guns, forcing us to stop
along with the students who had formed columns on both sides of us.

I was determined the demonstration should resume. When I advanced, a British soldier stepped toward me pointing his gun, but I
made my way past him. As one of the women tried to pull me back, I
shouted in a loud voice, "Let me die so Egypt shall have an Edith
Cavell" (an English nurse shot and killed by the Germans during the
First World War, who became an instant martyr). Continuing in the
direction of the soldiers, I called upon the women to follow. A pair of
arms grabbed me and the voice of Regina Khayyat rang in my ears.
"This is madness. Do you want to risk the lives of the students? It
will happen if the British raise a hand against you." At the thought of

our unarmed sons doing battle against the weaponry of British troops, and of the Egyptian losses sure to occur, I came to my senses and stopped still. We stood still for three hours while the sun blazed down on us. . . . I did not care if I suffered sunstroke—the blame would fall upon the tyrannical British authority—but we stood up to the heat and suffered no harm.

Reprinted and excerpted, by permission, from Huda Shaarawi, *Harem Years: The Memoirs of an Egyptian Feminist (1879–1924),* translated, edited, and introduced by Margot Badran (New York: The Feminist Press at The City University of New York, 1987), 112–14. Copyright 1986 by Margot Badran. Notes omitted.

Ali Shaarawi died in 1922. The following year, Huda founded the Egyptian Feminist Union and headed a delegation to an international women's conference in Rome. On their return to Cairo, Huda and her companions stepped off the train with their veils drawn back from their faces. In 1924, she resigned from the Wafd because, when it gained a majority in the Egyptian legislature, the party reneged on both feminist and nationalist promises. Huda Shaarawi died in 1947, a decade before the first women voted in independent Egyptian elections, which saw two women seated in the legislature.

9.3 Women and the Iranian Revolution of 1978

Women in Turkey discarded their veils, voted, and ran for political office nearly a generation before those in Egypt. Educated feminists, active backers of the nationalist Young Turks who overthrew the Ottoman monarchy, entered professions after 1908. Halide Edip removed her veil in a 1919 nationalist demonstration in Istanbul. In the 1920s, when Mustafa Kemal (Ataturk) denounced women's veiling—as well as men's traditional robes and fez—as "uncivilized," a new woman's identity was put at the forefront of the Turkish Republic's secular politics. Rejecting the *Shar'ia* meant banning polygamy, giving women equal rights to initiate divorce and to custody of their children, and allowing them to inherit equally with men. The Women's League of Turkey envisioned "revolutionary women" being educated, voting, and serving in the army. They won suffrage rights in 1934, and by 1937, the eighteen women elected to the legislature constituted nearly 5 percent of its membership. Tansu Çiller became Turkey's prime minister in 1993 and, after her 1996 defeat, remained at the head of the True Path Party; yet only one other woman sat in the legislature during Çiller's ministry.

In 1990, 40 percent of women over twenty-five remained illiterate, although Turkey's elite women held exceptionally high proportions of university professorships in engineering, science, and mathematics. The military, the dominant force behind the scenes in contemporary Turkish politics, remained exclusively male.

Among Islamic countries, Iran is the foremost example of dramatic reversal since 1979 of women's equalitarian gains. Conservative Iranian religious leaders of the revolution sought to repudiate the rights women had gained over a century. In a country where the state provides modern education and health care, where the economic system requires professional workers, and where women had experienced many rights, the political struggle over whether women would be subjected to male patriarchy in the name of religious fundamentalism has been particularly stark.

Twentieth-century emancipation of women in Iran under the Pahlavi monarchy compared more closely to that of women in the Turkish republic than to the conservative monarchies of Saudi Arabia or Jordan. The first public elementary school for girls opened in 1918, and expanded separate public secondary education for young women opened admission to Teheran University to them in the late 1930s. By then, the marriage age had been raised to fifteen for women and eighteen for men. When Reza Shah abruptly banned the veil in 1936, he ordered police to deal harshly with modest women who insisted on covering their heads and to protect unveiled women from harassment. The political repercussions from both men *and women* who preferred to remain veiled forced the shah to allow the return of the veil in 1941. For Iranians, this struggle identified Westernization and foreign domination with unveiling and greater rights for women.

Nevertheless, the Pahlavi dynasty pursued its policy of secularization and economic development, cooperating with European and United States governments while seizing a larger share of profits from its oil industry. In 1963, women received the vote, and soon afterward divorce laws were reformed. The prosperity from increasing oil revenues opened jobs for women at all levels, including professional. Women's literacy had reached 56 percent in urban areas and 17 percent in rural areas by the mid-1970s. Although feminists publicized these gains and lobbied for more, many women, especially outside the cities, were unaware of most of these changes.*

In 1978, demonstrations and strikes led by the religious leaders supporting Ayatollah Ruholla Khomeni broke out against the shah's government. The revolution reflected the disgust Iranians felt toward the monarchy, its identification with Westernization policies, its corruption, and its brutal suppression of dissent. Women actively participated and suffered imprisonment, torture, and death along with men. The next year, the shah fled, to be replaced with a committee of mullahs (local religious leaders) who proclaimed an Islamic republic. Attempting to restore a non-Western, traditional society meant repressing all opposition and replacing secular legal codes with the *Shar'ia*. Religious conservatives demanded the most ancient punishments, including stoning for prostitution and adultery. The veil became a center of contention. Mary E. Hegland, who was living in a village, recounts an incident that illustrates how revolutionary fervor spread:

In March of 1979, the welder . . . who lived in the village and had taken a village woman as a second wife was visited by his cousin, her fiance, and another young man. The young woman was very properly seated in the back of the car and wore a *chadur* [a black veil covering the entire body except the face, the hands and the feet], while the two young men sat in the front. When the young people got out of the car at the village gate, people stopped them and accused the young woman of being a "madam." The three were able to reach the welder's home, although they were taunted along the way. A group of some thirty men and boys gathered outside of the courtyard, shouting and swearing at the welder's village wife and claiming that she was lying, that the young woman was a prostitute and not the welder's cousin.

Mary E. Hegland, "Alibad Women: Revolution as Religious Activity," in *Women and Revolution in Iran,* edited by Guity Nashat (Boulder, CO: Westview Press, 1983), 188.

---

*Guity Nashat, "Women in Pre-Revolutionary Iran: A Historical Overview," in *Women and Revolution in Iran,* edited by Guity Nashat (Boulder, CO: Westview Press, 1983), 21–31.

The couple had to get the police in a neighboring village to confirm the truth of their statements. Incidents like this brought out large demonstrations of women in response to initial moves of revolutionaries to force them to wear the *chadur*. Mahnaz Afkhami summarizes the effects of the revolution upon women:

Once the Islamic Republic was firmly established, the government began to rewrite the laws and rules relating to women's recently acquired rights. The new regime tried to force women out of the job market in a variety of ways, including early retirement of government women employees, closing of childcare centers, segregating women and enforcing full Islamic cover (*hejab-e islami*) in offices and public places, and closing nearly 140 university fields of study to women. But the problems arising from the enforcement of the veil and other Islamic tenets in the streets and homes showed clearly that there were limits in Iran to what a fundamentalist regime could do. Women fought seriously for their rights, making the strict enforcement of government intent costly. The regime succeeded in putting women back in the veil in public places, but not in resocializing them into fundamentalist norms. As the economy suffered after the revolution, women worked in villages and cities, often harder than men, to make ends meet. As the revolutionary elan subsided, women reasserted themselves in other domains: in the arts, in literature, in education and in politics, creating an atmosphere of tension and contradiction that has propelled the issue of women's status to the center of the debate on the creation of an Islamic society in Iran. Needless to say, loss of government support has cost Iranian women dearly. In addition to the economic, social and cultural problems shared by all, women also lost significant ground in the struggle for gender equality.

Mahnaz Afkhami, "Women in Post-Revolutionary Iran: A Feminist Perspective," in *In the Eye of the Storm: Women in Post-Revolutionary Iran*, edited by Mahnaz Afkhami and Erika Friedl (Syracuse, NY: Syracuse University Press), 12. Originally published by I.B. Tauris & Co. Ltd., London. Reprinted by permission of I.B. Tauris. Notes omitted.

Almost immediately, the social and economic consequences of the disastrous war with Iraq between 1980 and 1988 forced some concessions to women. With a large portion of the adult male population in the armed forces, women had to replace men in the workforce. Moreover, high war casualties created a surplus of women and left numerous young widows with small children—creating a serious obstacle to the mullahs' aim of having every women married and confined to raising children.

In 1980, a new parliament was elected with four women deputies in a membership of 270. A woman deputy's bill to permit women in the civil service and in government-owned companies to work half-time with the permission of their superiors gained the support of the government. Women employees were needed in wartime. Other inducements to mothers' employment included three months of maternity leave, plus further leave to breast-feed infant children. Later, the Ministry of Education introduced a bill to extend maternity leave for teachers to twelve months in order to persuade more women to teach. They were needed because the government was encouraging girls to attend sex-segregated elementary schools, to reduce the still high rate of illiteracy. The female deputies protested that all women should have a year's maternity leave, and the bill failed.[*]

In November 1990, the Iranian president, Hashemi Rafsanjani, publicly recognized that women's sexuality was important, a rare acknowledgment for an Islamic leader. He advocated temporary marriage for war widows. Shiite theologians have long accepted temporary marriages. Shahla Haeri explains the requirements:

In its present form, temporary marriage is a form of contract in which a man (married or unmarried) and an unmarried woman (virgin, divorced, or widowed) agree, often privately and verbally, to marry each other for a limited period of time, varying anywhere from one hour to 99 years. The couple also agree on a specific amount of brideprice, to be given to the woman. Unlike permanent marriage, temporary marriage does not oblige a husband to provide financial support for his temporary wife. A Shii Muslim man is allowed to make several contracts of temporary marriage at the same time.

---

[*]Haleh Esfandiari, "The Majles and Women's Issues in the Islamic Republic of Iran," in *In the Eye of the Storm: Women in Post-Revolutionary Iran,* edited by Mahnaz Afkhami and Erika Friedl (Syracuse, NY: Syracuse University Press, 1994) 70–76. Originally published by I.B. Tauris & Co. Ltd., London. Reprinted by permission of I.B. Tauris.

Women, however, may not marry either temporarily or permanently more than one man at a time.

At the end of the mutually agreed period the couple part company without a divorce ceremony. After the dissolution of the marriage, no matter how short, the temporary wife must observe a period of sexual abstinence in order to prevent problems in identifying a potential child's legitimate father. The children of such unions are accorded full legitimacy, and, theoretically, have equal status to their half-siblings born of a permanent marriage. Although children inherit from their parents, temporary spouses do not inherit from each other. . . .

The Shii ulema [religious leaders] perceive temporary marriage as distinct from prostitution. . . . For them, temporary marriage is legally sanctioned and religiously blessed, while prostitution is legally forbidden . . . and therefore challenges the social order.

Shahla Haeri, "Temporary Marriage: An Islamic Discourse on Female Sexuality in Iran," in *In the Eye of the Storm: Women in Post-Revolutionary Iran,* edited by Mahnaz Afkhami and Erika Friedl (Syracuse, NY: Syracuse University Press, 1994), 105–6. Originally published by I.B. Tauris & Co. Ltd., London. Reprinted by permission of I.B. Tauris. Notes omitted.

President Rafsanjani's speech created a national debate on temporary marriage, female sexuality, marital fidelity, and stability. He also recommended temporary marriage to young people who were sexually mature at fifteen but expected to remain chaste and virginal until they married permanently between the ages of twenty-five and thirty. Men expected virginity in young brides, so that type of temporary marriage seldom occurred. But the situation of divorced women was different, as Shahla Haeri explains:

Women who contract temporary marriages tend to be primarily young divorced women from lower-class backgrounds, but middle-class women occasionally do so as well. Contrary to the popular image of prudish Muslim Iranian women, research reveals that temporarily married women are not only aware of their own needs and their sexual appeal to men (which they enjoy) but that they also often initiate a relationship.

Shahla Haeri, "Temporary Marriage: An Islamic Discourse on Female Sexuality in Iran," in *In the Eye of the Storm: Women in Post-Revolutionary Iran,* edited by

Mahnaz Afkhami and Erika Friedl (Syracuse, NY: Syracuse University Press, 1994), 107. Originally published by I.B. Tauris & Co. Inc. Reprinted by permission of I.B. Tauris. Notes omitted.

Suggested Further Readings

Leonard Helfgott's *Ties That Bind: A Social History of the Iranian Carpet* (Washington, DC: Smithsonian Institution Press, 1994) is unusual in the immense literature on Oriental rugs in discussing the gender of producers. Donald Quataert's "Ottoman Women, Households and Textile Manufacturing, 1800–1914," in *Women in Middle Eastern History: Shifting Boundaries in Sex and Gender,* edited by Nikki R. Keddie and Beth Baron (New Haven, CT: Yale University Press, 1991), 161–76, concentrates on one of the most important industries of the Ottoman Empire.

Opening the Gates: A Century of Arab Feminist Writing (Bloomington: Indiana University Press, 1990), edited by Margot Badran and Miriam Cooke, presents a broad range of Muslim women's feminist writings from 1867 to 1988. Oral histories of contemporary women from Syria, Lebanon, Palestine, and Algeria can be found in Bouthaina Shaaban, ed., *Both Right and Left Handed: Arab Women Talk about Their Lives* (Bloomington: Indiana University Press, 1991). An overview of key issues in the modern period is found in part 3 of Leila Ahmed's *Women and Gender in Islam* (New Haven, CT: Yale University Press, 1992). For this period, Egypt is the country whose women are best documented: Judith E. Tucker, *Women in Nineteenth-Century Egypt* (New York: Cambridge University Press, 1985); Mervat Hatem, "The Politics of Sexuality and Gender in Segregated Patriarchal Systems: The Case of Eighteenth- and Nineteenth-Century Egypt," *Feminist Studies* 12 (1986): 251–74; and Margot Badran, *Feminists, Islam, and Nation: Gender and the Making of Modern Egypt* (Princeton, NJ: Princeton University Press, 1995). Nawal El Saadawi, *The Hidden Face of Eve: Women in the Arab World* (London: Zed Press, 1980), is the memoir of a novelist and crusading doctor who served as Egypt's director of public health. Anthropologist Evelyn A. Early describes her experiences living among the working class in *Baladi Women of Cairo: Playing with an Egg and a Stone* (Boulder, CO: Lynne Reinner, 1993). Arlene Elowe Macleod, *Accommodating Protest: Working Women, the*

New Veiling and Change in Cairo (New York: Columbia University Press, 1991), explains why some women want to veil. Readings in *Women in the Muslim World,* edited by Lois Beck and Nikki Keddi (Cambridge, MA: Harvard University Press, 1978), concern Egyptian women as well as those from other Middle Eastern and North African countries. Fatima Mernissi's *Beyond the Veil: Male–Female Dynamics in Modern Muslim Society,* rev. ed. (Bloomington: Indiana University Press, 1987), is a classic by a Moroccan scholar that has been in print for more than twenty years. How shifting Islamist, Ottomanist, and Turkish nationalist discourses on women became political issues after 1838 is the topic of Deniz Kandiyoti, "From Empire to Nation State: Transformations of the Woman Question in Turkey," in *Retrieving Women's History: Changing Perceptions of the Role of Women in Politics and Society,* edited by S. Jay Kleinberg (New York: Berg Publishers, 1988). Aysegul C. Baykan discusses Nezihe Muhittin's feminist activities in the 1920s and 1930s in the Turkish Republic in *"The Turkish Woman:* An Adventure in Feminist Historiography," *Gender and History* 6 (April 1994), 101–16. Robert A. Fernea and Elizabeth W. Fernea explain "Variations in Religious Observance among Islamic Women" in *Scholars, Saints, and Sufis: Muslim Religious Institutions since 1500,* edited by Nikki R. Keddie (Berkeley: University of California Press, 1972), 385–401.

–10–
INDIA
National Unity,
Gender Divisions

Poster, Maharashtra. Vibhuti Patel. From *The History of Doing: An Illustrated Account of Movements for Women's Rights and Feminism in India, 1800–1990* by Radha Kumar. (New Delhi: Kali for Women and London: Verso, 1993. Reproduced by permission from Kali for Women.)

The power of the Mughal monarchs waned in the eighteenth century. Indian Hindu maharajahs regained control of independent kingdoms in the south, and Europeans vied for dominance of coastal territories ceded as trading stations. One of the prizes Great Britain won from its 1763 victory over France in the Seven Years' War was monopoly of European trade with India. On this foundation, supplemented by the 1805 defeat of the Indian Marathas, the British built their colonial empire, which dominated the subcontinent for nearly 150 years.

Under British governors, English law, language, education, literature, and ideals of womanhood were forcefully projected as the most civilized and most progressive in the world. English trade laws, enacted in London to benefit British businesses, and English officials dramatically reshaped the economy of India. By the late nineteenth century, India was no longer one of the world's preeminent exporters of hand-manufactured products; instead, its economy was geared toward growing and mining raw materials for English factories.

India's women did not rush to adopt English ways—in fact, they were a conservative force preserving traditional Hindu and Muslim gender patterns during most of the nineteenth century. But the long political dominance of both European cultural practices and the economy left a deep impact on India, one that continued after the British left in 1947. Women, influenced by both European feminism and indigenous struggles, emerged from the seclusion of their homes to join nationalist and other reform movements. One outcome of colonialism and the decades of nationalist struggle against the British was heightened tension between Hindus and Muslims, which resulted in the partition in 1947 creating India and Pakistan. Further partition occurred in 1973, when Bengal's secession from Pakistan created Bangladesh. It is notable that women have been elected to lead the governments of each of these nations as well as Sri Lanka. In no other region of the world have women been so prominent as heads of state as in South Asia. A paradox remains that in South Asia's nations, having a woman hold the reins of democratic power has contributed no more to the empowerment of the female populace than did the informal power of Nur Jahan.

Modern India after 1947 provides an example. Its 1950 Constitution proclaimed women's equality and voting rights, as well as abolishing untouchable status among Hindus. Prominent female members of the Indian National Congress received appointments as ambassadors and state governors. In the 1950s and 1960s, more women won seats in state legislatures and the National Parliament of India than were elected in Western countries. However, thirty years later, the proportion of women elected to sit as members of parliament has never exceeded 8 percent. Women from elite families have monopolized access to education and public office. Efforts to implement civil rights for women traditionally called untouchables by Hindus (now called *Dalits*) faced pervasive opposition. Before independence, they had done the dirtiest jobs and were humiliated by some Hindus who considered contact with a *Dalit* so polluting that a purification ceremony had to be performed; after being freed from state-sanctioned segregation, *Dalit* women still suffered unemployment, poverty, and high levels of domestic violence. India's election of one of the world's most famous national leaders, Indira Gandhi, as prime minister from 1966 to 1977 and from 1980 to 1984 did little to improve the condition of women generally or of *Dalit* women in particular. Although she relied upon the votes of women, Indira Gandhi did not consider herself a feminist. In the West, she is best known for her family-planning campaign, 1975–77, to speed economic development by reducing the Indian birthrate.

10.1 Indian Women and the Disaster of British Rule

The British arrived on the west coast of India in 1619 and on the east coast in 1690. In the eighteenth century, after defeating the Mughal Empire, the British focused on expanding trade in the Ganges River region of Bengal, with its growing commercial city of Calcutta. Their overwhelming goal in Bengal (and elsewhere as their influence spread) was to make as much money as possible. Initially, this was done by exporting India's celebrated fabrics to other parts of the world. But as England's own textile industry grew, developing from home-woven woolens to factory-made cotton cloth, British manufacturers demanded that the government end competition from Indian products. The British raised tariffs on Indian textiles imported into England while flooding India with cheap British-made goods—destroying the Indian industry. As industrialization spread in England, control of India's government made it possible to manipulate markets for other products to the advantage of British producers and the disadvantage of Indian ones. Excessive taxation had already forced the agricultural population into poverty. Recurring famines throughout the nineteenth century drove increasing numbers of peasant families off their own land as women and men faced destitution.

Susie Tharu and K. Lalita describe women's plight in Bengal, the first region of India to feel the impact of English rule.

Gradually, from about the middle of the seventeenth century onward, British presence, mercantile, military, and political, established itself. The East India Company ... by the late eighteenth century ... had established its military and administrative authority over large parts of the country. Indian historians and their British counterparts broadly agree that what followed was a period of wholesale plunder. Enormous revenues—principally from land taxes and unequal trade exchanges—were remitted back to England. ... In 1764 and 1765, the last year of Indian administration in Bengal, the land revenue totaled £817,000. Company administration realized £1,470,000 from 1765 to 1766; the Permanent Settlement [for Bengal] was fixed in 1793 at £3,400,000. In many Bengal provinces one-third of the inhabitants died in the terrible famine of 1770. With surplus siphoned off so systematically, the peasant cultivators had no reserves to fall back on when the crops failed. Nevertheless, in 1771 the Company was pleased to report to its shareholders that revenue collection had actually increased. ...

Both agricultural self-sufficiency and what by many accounts was a growing industrial economy were broken down. For the peasant, insecurity, impoverishment, and indebtedness followed. ... In earlier years taxes varied—with drought, or flood, or unforeseen expense, but the new tax structure called for the same amount to be transferred to British coffers come whatever calamity. Half the rapidly increasing number of landless and impoverished peasants, pushed further and further into indebtedness by the burden of the new taxes, and evicted when they were unable to pay, were women.

Many thousands of people were also affected by the deindustrialization, most so, perhaps, by the collapse of the textile industry, but also of iron, glass, paper, pottery, and jewelry. For centuries India had been exporting fine cloth—silks and muslins—to the whole world. In 1813, under pressure from the Lancashire textile industry, the British government imposed a high tariff on the import of Indian textiles. British goods, on the other hand, had virtually free entry into India. The shattering results are well known. Between 1814 and 1835 British cotton goods exported to India rose from one million yards to thirty-one million yards; the value of Indian cotton goods exported in the same seventeen years fell to one-thirteenth its original size. The thriving textile towns—Dacca, Mushirabad, Surat, and Madurai—were laid waste.

The weavers in the cities had generally specialized in creating the fine muslins and brocades in demand among the aristocracy in India and famous the world over. But equally badly hit by the new tariff structure were the weavers in the countryside. During months when there was little to do in the fields, and in years when the rains failed and the harvests were poor, women and men working in their homes spun and wove the coarser cotton cloth into the colors and designs of the saris and dhotis worn in the areas they lived in. The new tariffs and the shifts in textile production left the peasants, now solely dependent on agriculture, even more vulnerable. In Europe the peasants and the handloom weavers who had been displaced found jobs in the new industries, which employed many women. In India even the men had few such alternatives. For the women there were almost no openings.

Both women and men who were forced off the land left to find work in the new plantations. But many more men were able to do so than women. Women stayed back caring for the household, dependent on what little of the men's earnings they were able to send back, and what little they were able to earn. They were always insecure, always anxious. One could reconstruct a parallel narrative for the women who went with their husbands and children to work on the new indigo, rubber, jute, and tea plantations that the British had set up; another for the women who moved to the already overcrowded cities in search of work; and yet another for the women who sometimes with their men, but surprisingly often alone, were taken as "indentured labour" to plantations in other British colonies as far abroad as South Africa and the West Indies. . . .

The peasants and artisans were not the only ones hit by the violent changes that were taking place. As the flourishing textile cities of Dacca, Mushirabad, Surat, and Madurai declined in importance and the old urban aristocracy lost power, a whole community of women court artists, poets, singers, musicians, and dancers was displaced.

Reprinted, by permission, from Susie Tharu and K. Lalita, *Women Writing in India, Volume I, 600 B.C. to the Early Twentieth Century*, edited by Susie Tharu and K. Lalita (New York: The Feminist Press at The City University of New York, 1991): 145–48. Copyright 1991 by Susie Tharu and K. Lalita. Note omitted.

———————————

In the nineteenth century, the British colonial government initiated a series of political reforms, including an educational program to train Indian males to become clerks in the civil service. Other laws prohibited female infanticide and *sati* (widow burning) and permitted widows to remarry. Even before these British reforms, an important Hindu social reform movement had espoused similar causes. Indian and British reformers were met with a rising tide of opposition from Hindu revivalists and Muslim fundamentalists who defended customary social practices as essential to their religious heritages. Women educated by their fathers at home, by women tutors who came to their homes, or in girls' schools joined male reformers after 1850. They called for women's emancipation through education to prepare wives to be literate companions to British-educated husbands. Though these pioneers themselves sometimes taught or practiced medicine, their prescription for Indian women was not careers but home and motherhood. For elite women, though, the ideal home was drawn from British models. It little resembled the joint family in which most Indians still lived even as the nineteenth century ended.

To understand the lives of the majority of Indian women of the rural and urban middle and upper classes, it is necessary to enter their homes. Several generations of a family lived in the same place, eating together twice a day. A part of the family residence was considered public, in that the men of the family met visitors there. The women and small boys of the family were confined to the *antahpur*, a group of rooms, a courtyard, terrace, roof, and kitchen in which women lived and worked. (*Antahpur* is a regional Bengali term for what is generally called a *zenana* in India or a harem in the Middle East.) Only certain male relatives were allowed in the *antahpur*. According to Malavika Karlekar, this domain of female seclusion was:

not only vital to the male world but was organized according to distinct rules and a rigid internal hierarchy. The dominant figure was that of the mother-in-law or another senior woman. . . . Each day was well organized and duties apportioned systematically. In the case of disputes, arbiters were usually the women themselves. . . . A primary role of the *antahpur vis-à-vis* the man's world was one of ensuring ritual purity for the family. It included strict adherence to rules of commensality, [and] provided physical sustenance as well as sexual services. However, in order to make the system work effectively, women, particularly those in large households, had to develop the art of distributing largesse as well as tasks, mediating between rivals, or putting to use tensions of these rivalries judiciously, as well as managing the budget. . . . Despite the fact that in most *bhadralok* [upper middle-class] homes domestic servants were routinely employed, women of the family played a vital role in the planning and preparation of meals, cooking and serving the men. This was in addition to child bearing and rearing as several pregnancies were common. . . .

Life was centred around the courtyard, and it became the focus of varied activities. Some days, it was organized around frying puffed rice, on others, women were involved with husking paddy [unpolished rice]. In winter, jaggery [a molasseslike liquid] was made from date palm, while in the summer, the making of pickles and preserves from mangoes kept everyone busy. All the women of the household were involved in these activities. At one corner of the courtyard was the lying-in room. . . . Clearly, the courtyard was central to many confined to the inner quarters. . . . Within the home, and around the courtyard, older women trained the younger ones, controlled domestic servants and managed the daily budget. In fact, organization of food, clothing, maintenance of household assets and so on took an enormous amount of time and energy. Life was indeed claustrophobic, but 'it was rich in human contact.' There was plenty of opportunity for friendly interaction, squabbles and consolation, 'for comfort was never far away, but neither was condemnation.'

Jnanadanandini [Tagore] recalled how every now and then women in her village home would decide to have a night-long *jagaran* (staying awake) session on a full moon night. After the menfolk had retired to bed women would gather in the chosen courtyard which had been freshly washed and cleaned for the occasion. Then began the gossip-cum-story telling session. Some sang, while others danced in a manner typical of the region. Invariably, this all-women's session used to continue until the early hours of the morning. Its therapeutic value in a secluded society was considerable, providing as it did a legitimate forum for airing one's grievances, expressing hopes and lodging complaints against in-laws. . . .

The importance of *bratas* in socializing girls for correct feminine roles has been described by a number of women. These socio-religious observances had functions as varied as fasting for the long life of one's husband to curing girls of their bad temper. While initiating girls into these ceremonies it was usual for mothers and other female relatives and occasionally the *napitini* or barber's wife to tell the girls why they were expected to perform them. A common theme in many *bratas* was propitiating either the gods or the planetary system so as to ensure a life of relative affluence, a 'good' husband, kind in-laws and so on. . . . They were a highly ingenious way of teaching girls what to expect from life. . . . They instilled a sense of routine, discipline and understanding of nature through the use of flowers, and vegetable dyes for painting *alpana* (complicated patterns) on the floor or earth and moulding of mud figures and so on. . . .

Apart from the daily routine of cooking, cleaning and other household chores, *bhadramahilas* [women of the upper middle-class] spent considerable time and energy in planning, organizing and performing *bratas* and listening to *kathakata,* mythological stories 'in the colloquial language, often in contemporary terms of reference.' In this, upper class *bhadramahilas* shared a common culture with working class women, and often *bratas* involved the participation of women from the service castes. The popular culture consisting of theatrical performances, poems and skits written in a more accessible everyday Bengali was enjoyed by a sizeable female audience; a number of these women lived in *antahpurs.*

Malavika Karlekar, *Voices from Within: Early Personal Narratives of Bengali Women* (Delhi: Oxford University Press, 1991), 61, 66, 69–71. Notes omitted.

Bengali women of the middle and upper classes lived in an isolated world within each family's *antahpur.* Men, even husbands, made little impression on the *antahpur* on a day-to-day basis. The family men were fed, treated as if they were gods, and provided sexual service but seldom intruded into women's society.

The preferred age of marriage for females at this time in Bengal was eight years, although the married child did not normally move to her husband's *antahpur* until puberty or later. Husbands were ten or more years older than their illiterate child brides and lived in the world outside the *antahpur*. Consequently, husband and wife had almost no common experience to provide a basis for friendship. Men expected their wives to bear their children— often numbering the live births in double digits since pregnancies started when the wife was in her early teens. To wives, husbands were distant authority figures. However, if a wife seldom became a companion to her husband, companionship was found in the *antahpur*.

The *antahpur* system could pose serious dangers to women. Without a way to earn income, the women were entirely dependent upon their male relatives, who sometimes lost or squandered the family fortune. Widows had trouble gaining control of their children's inheritance from their husband's estate. Harassment of widows was accepted as normal. The mistreatment of young brides by the senior women was routine.

Child marriage, women's seclusion and illiteracy, and the continuation of *sati* embarrassed educated Indians. Westerners had harped on the "uncivilized" treatment of women to justify their conquests of Asians and Africans. They claimed that the condition of women in a country was a test of the degree of its civilization—measured, of course, against an idealized version of their home countries' practices.

Nationalists responded with a program of liberal reforms for women, including equality in the legal process; suffrage; mass education; the rights to own property, enter a profession, and enter politics; and the end to obvious discriminations. Necessary to the equalitarian feminist vision of the nationalists was a complete change in the lives of Indian wives: end the *antahpur* as a segregated world for women; live in separate nuclear families; and remake wives into intellectual companions of their husbands. As Kumari Jayawardena explains, education became the crucial problem for reformers.

With the growth of local bourgeoisies and the rise of nationalism in non-European countries, women's emancipation and education became primary issues, both for the women of the bourgeoisie and for male reformers, including intellectuals and national leaders. . . .

The first modern girls' school was established in India in 1820, in Sri Lanka in 1824, in China in 1844, in Egypt in 1846. . . . Girls began to move on to higher education. . . . Women graduates appeared in India from the 1880s onwards, and women in all these countries started to enter the professions as teachers, nurses, midwives, lawyers and doctors. Medicine was the first prestigious profession in which women made a breakthrough. The first Indian doctor qualified in 1886. . . .

But what type of education was advocated? To start with, it was class biased, since it was geared to providing good wives and mothers for those men who had risen on the economic and social ladder of colonial society. . . . 'Modernity' meant educated women, but educated to uphold the system of the nuclear patriarchal family. . . . Bourgeois women in Asia began to agitate for further educational opportunities that would give them access to new avenues of income-earning opportunities and, hopefully, greater freedom. . . . The indigenous bourgeoisie, while willing to grant some concessions to women of their own class, had no intention of applying the concepts of natural rights, liberty, equality and self-determination to the masses of women or to the workers of their own countries.

Kumari Jayawardena, *Feminism and Nationalism in the Third World* (London: Zed Books, 1986), 15–17.

Near the end of the nineteenth century, Indian nationalists organized to seek independence from the British. The Indian National Congress, founded in 1885, became the largest and most powerful nationalist organization. In 1905, the British divided the large Bengal state into two, one largely Hindu and the other Muslim. Indian protest of the division, led by the Congress, included a boycott of British goods (*swadeshi*), supported by Bengali women for four years.

The Congress program called for many reforms for women, including ending *sati,* polygamy, child marriage, and seclusion and giving women suffrage, mass education, and the rights to own property and live in nuclear families. These reforms were mainly sought by women of the middle class. Little was proposed to reduce women's subordination to men in society or in the family, and little was proposed to help peasant women. The owners of the land and industry, both Western and indigenous, were happy that women were encouraged out of seclusion, since peasant women were being hailed as the cheapest source of labor for the new plantations, cash-crop agriculture, and industry.

The great twentieth-century Congress leader Mohandas K. Gandhi attracted many women supporters. They were the non-violent soldiers in his army of liberation. To protest imports of British cloth, they made and wore the hand-spun and handwoven cloth that was the uniform of the movement. To protest the tax on salt, they made salt and did not pay the tax. They picketed liquor shops and foreign retailers, and they demonstrated by burning foreign clothes.

In the 1920s, demonstrations were attacked by the police, who beat the nonviolent resisters with special sticks, which could knock a person unconscious. The Congress countered by having women lead the demonstrations, for the police would not hit women. In 1930, the police began hitting women demonstrators, spraying them with fire hoses, arresting them, and eventually shooting and killing two demonstrators. Perhaps twenty thousand women were arrested and imprisoned in 1930–31. Nearly 10 percent of the people jailed in the independence struggle were women, often with babies in their arms.

These public acts of bravery could never have occurred if an earlier generation of Indian women had not faced the frightening experience of leaving the seclusion of their homes.

10.2 Coming out of *Purdah*

Women who lived in seclusion had to come out of their homes to fully participate in public activities of the modern world. How did they feel about the change? Nineteenth-century accounts are rare, but fortunately, some are available for the early twentieth century. Seclusion, called *purdah* by Muslims in India, today is most frequently found in Islamic countries. *Purdah* does not just mean never leaving the women's part of the home. When women in *purdah* have to go out in public, many wear a cloak or veil, usually white or black, a *burqa,* that entirely covers them from their head to their feet. The *burqa* has eyeholes that so limit a woman's vision that she may walk on the streets with someone holding her hand. Older women and young children do not wear the *burqa*, whose purpose is to make female sexual beings invisible.

Hanna Papanek relates the experience of an Indian Muslim friend, Hamida Khala, whose coming out of *purdah* in the early twentieth century was one of the most terrifying experiences of her life. Her father, a highly educated man, had taught her that the Quran required *purdah*. His young daughter, Hamida, longed to put on the *burqa* because that would mean she was grown-up. She was married at thirteen to a much older man. Hamida decided that if he asked her to leave *purdah*, she would return to her family. She did not live with her new husband until she was about fifteen:

His job took them to Calcutta, thousands of miles from her family. . . . The trip to Calcutta, by train, was a nightmare: She heard voices of men all around her and found it hard to walk in her burqa, even though her husband was beside her. She remembered: "I felt helpless, I could do nothing. . . . I wondered will I really have to take off my burqa? He is a man and he will want me to do whatever he wants." . . . Hamida felt increasing pressure to accommodate her husband's wishes and yet remain true to her father's early training.

As a civil servant in colonial India, her husband worked with British, Hindu, and Muslim colleagues. In this sector of colonial society, social life was organized around couples. A married man whose wife could not participate in the tea parties and dinners—because she was in purdah—was at a serious disadvantage because social life and work were closely connected. . . . Hamida's husband was clearly affected by these circumstances. She tried to accommodate him by visiting the wives of friends and going for walks with him in her burqa.

The climax of the young Hamida's struggles over remaining in purdah came unexpectedly, at a dinner party in the home of friends where she had visited before. With great emotion, she recalled this event more than forty years later:

They were trying very hard, my husband's friends . . . that somehow or the other I should come out of purdah. A friend had arranged a dinner. His wife was not in purdah but, because of me, women were arranged to sit separately. The men were always in another room. [On this occasion], the time came when we were supposed to go in to dinner. All the women went into the dining hall. They were told to sit leaving one chair empty in between [them]. I thought they were probably expecting some more women. . . .

Suddenly the men came into the room. They sat in all those empty chairs. What I experienced, I just can't tell you. There was darkness all around me. I couldn't see anything. I had tears in my eyes. I was sitting with my eyes downcast, I couldn't look up. I tried to look once at my husband but he avoided my eyes. . . .

I don't know when the dinner was over. What I ate I don't remember . . . I was on fire. All my attempts, my endeavors to keep my purdah were over. I felt I was without faith, I had sinned. I had gone in front of so many men, all these friends of my husband. They've seen me. My purdah was broken, my purdah that was my faith.

Reprinted and excerpted, by permission, from Hanna Papanek, "Afterword: Caging the Lion: A Fable for Our Time," in *Sultana's Dream and Selections from the Secluded Ones,* edited and translated by Roushan Jahan (New York: The Feminist Press at The City University of New York, 1988), 72–74. Copyright 1988 by Hanna Papanek.

Hamida's husband explained that he had not planned the incident and asked her to forgive and forget. For a long time, she felt she had sinned and wondered how God could forgive her. She wrote to her father for guidance. His reply was that she should leave *purdah* if her marriage was endangered, explaining that the present practice was not Islamic but a Muslim social custom. Eventually, on a trip, her husband threw the *burqa* out of the train.

10.3 *Dalit* Women

Independence freed Indian women from British colonial rule but not from the barriers of social customs. The 1950 Constitution provided for equality between women and men and between peoples of different castes and religions. Implementing the constitutional guarantees created immediate political controversies in the 1950s, some of which are not resolved in the 1990s. Women's rights to vote and hold office were not contested, but enlarging their rights within the family was. Religious authorities prevented adoption of a uniform national civil code. By 1955, a compromise secured Hindu women some reform of marriage and divorce statutes but left the minority of Muslim women subject to the Islamic community's customary family laws.

Constitutional guarantees of equality between castes and religious communities have proved as problematic to enforce as gender equality. The social stigma of "untouchability" (being outside a caste within the Hindu community) was abolished. Laws established special quotas for university scholarships and government jobs for the people who called themselves *Dalits*. Continuing discrimination made it difficult for *Dalits* to escape poverty, while their protective educational and job quotas evoked continuing political controversy. Since the 1950s, class and gender equality issues have persisted in Indian politics.

Legislation was passed to provide for equal pay for equal work in 1976, to punish violence against women (including dowry deaths of brides, infanticide, and rapes of all kinds) in the 1980s, to prevent *sati* in 1987, and to mandate equal education for women in 1995. These new laws helped women, sometimes by eliminating loopholes in earlier laws, but did not entirely prevent the crimes they defined.

Under the influence of a new women's movement in India, emphasis turned from reliance on legal reforms in the 1980s to education of women to make them conscious of their rights and to encourage them to use them. *Dalit* women are among the poorest in India and still have a high rate of illiteracy. They have traditionally suffered from caste-Hindu oppression as well as gender oppression, so improvements in their lives have been very difficult to achieve.

Dalit women also suffer from physical and psychological abuse within their families. In the preface to a book of oral histories, Frances Maria Yasas explains their feelings:

Woman, as daughter-in-law and wife, in these oral histories, experiences relative powerlessness and lots of sufferings, especially at the hands of the mother-in-law, until she conceives and bears a son. Bearing a son is the first definite rise in her status in the family. Later, when she becomes a mother-in-law herself, her power is consolidated at its height. This power she often uses against her daughter-in-law, forgetting how much she suffered as daughter-in-law.

In her specific role as wife, the *Dalit* woman, in these oral histories, feels a complete failure, as its fulfillment requires reciprocity from her husband, which he does not give. He does not see her as a person, but only as a woman in a prescribed role in which she performs certain prescribed duties, largely as an object of sex. Her feelings of humiliation in having to subject her body and mind to her husband leave a permanent scar on her psyche. Most of the *Dalit* women studied here, appear to hate sex. A man's "untamable" sex urge is proof of his manliness and so it does not occur to him to exercise control. Women recognize it and use it as part of the power game; while men use sex as exploitative power, women use it as a manipulative power.

If the *Dalit* women in this study are not completely bitter against men . . . , it is because of the rise in status in the family they begin to gain through the birth of a son, and much later in life, the power they finally consolidate and exercise as mother-in-law, again through the medium of a son. The son thus acts as mediator against the anger and bitterness the woman feels against her husband.

The role of the brother is of special note. A brother is a protector, one in whom a sister can confide, turn to, and who always helps. The intimacy, trust and benevolence shared between a brother and sister in this protected relationship, also compensate to a degree for the lack of personal relationship between husband and wife.

The predominant image of the *Dalit* woman that thus emerges from these oral histories is that of a strong person, capable of many deprivations and sufferings, and still able to rise above them and keep the family together. Conversely, the image of the *Dalit* man that is glimpsed appears to be largely that of the spoiled child, the irresponsible adult and the pitiful old man.

Sumitra Bhave, *Pan on Fire: Eight Dalit Women Tell Their Story*, translated by Gauri Deshpande (New Delhi: Indian Social Institute, 1988), xii–xiii. Typographic errors corrected.

One of the oral histories of *Dalit* women from urban slums was taken from "Rakhma," age thirty-five, who was bigger and taller than most of her neighbors. She lived in a one-room house that was very clean, and her children looked healthy and well cared for. The influence of the consciousness-raising and legal education Rakhma gained at her community center is obvious from the following:

So listen. The river rose very high one year and I wanted to see the water. So I made the breakfast and all, and started out early with my nephew. My husband told me to be back soon, "Don't stand there gawking," he said and I said, "I'll be back right away" and I took the umbrella and we went along to the river bank and started upstream slowly. The *zopadpatti* near it had been flooded and plastic pails, pots and boxes came floating by, then a dead and swollen bullock. We were fascinated. It was quite awful. Look at this! Isn't that terrible, and so we went on.

My husband had said come back in 15 to 20 minutes but we were a little late, say, 15 more minutes. So when we came home he said, "Have you finished seeing the sights then? And when are you going to cook lunch? The children will be home soon." "Yes, so they will! Didn't you also go to see the water? Go on, go see, it's quite something." "I can go any time I want. Your case is different." "Why is it different?" "You have got work at home. I haven't got lunch to cook." And I said, "Yes, I have got all the work, haven't I?"

He lost his temper and gave me a box on the ear! I was taken aback. I said to myself, My! He sure is angry, so I had better keep my cool and so I didn't say anything. Just took the slap and kept quiet. Now, anyone who sees someone keep quiet after being hit, is going to think, I have made my point! So I just kept quiet. He asked me later, where the children were, if they had eaten, but I didn't say a word. I just put away everything in its place and went to sleep on the cot. I was sure he would come along and talk to me. Give the children their lunch, and this and that.

Sure enough he came and said, "Get up, get up!" I just turned on my side. "Get up!" "I'm not going to listen to anything now. I've got an ear-ache. When my mother gave me to you in marriage she didn't sell me to you whole! What if I were to hit you, eh! What then? Let me give you notice!" "So hit me!" So then, I went up to him and pulled both his ears, really hard! So he said, "Is that what they teach you at the centre? Is that what the *bai* teaches you?" I said, "That's not so!" So he told me, he earns for us all and so everything belongs to him. So I said, nothing doing, I have the same rights as he. If things belong to him then they belong to me too! I told him straight out! So he said, "You're becoming smart now getting to know these things, aren't you?" And he laughed—so I said, "Not just these things, all sorts of things." So he laughed some more.

You see, men get annoyed easily. If they are hot we should be quiet; if they are hot, we should be cool. They then cool off too! It's in women's hand to quietly cool them off, see? And if I get angry, then you can be sure, he keeps quiet. I have a temper, I tell you. When he makes a mistake and I point it out, then he doesn't say a word. Not a word. No answer! But I must see to it that I don't make too many mistakes either!

He doesn't mind it if I spend a little more time and am a bit late going home [from the center] because he knows I'm not just wasting my time with some illiterate women, chatting. He knows that I learn things here. Things like—you know, like the time when my daughter couldn't get admitted to school and I found out there was no reason why [she] shouldn't and then Dr. Toradmai gave me a note. Actually, I said to those people that they know all the laws and rules and circumstances, they shouldn't obstruct us, shouldn't make trouble for us. But they wouldn't listen, so I took the note from the Doctor and then they told me everything properly and helped out. I could do all this because I go to the centre, isn't it? Then I learned about our rights and laws and how men can't say "no" to women; they can't force them. If they do then we can complain to the police and the men will be punished, isn't it?

Sumitra Bhave, *Pan on Fire: Eight Dalit Women Tell Their Story*, translated by Gauri Deshpande (New Delhi: Indian Social Institute, 1988), 61–62.

10.4 Women as National Leaders: Prime Minister Indira Gandhi

Clearly, the status of women has been and is an important political issue in modern India. Indira Gandhi, the best-known Indian woman of the twentieth century, was prime minister for fifteen years (1966–77, 1980–84). She might be assumed to have been a feminist who used her power to improve the position of women in India. Instead of helping women, she gave little support to women's issues. In politics, she acted fairly consistently as if she were a male politician, as did Margaret Thatcher, British prime minister from 1979 to 1986. Indeed, Indira Gandhi is regarded as being more confrontational in style and more inclined to rely on military force to resolve disputes than her father and predecessor, Jawaharlal Nehru, who practiced the consensual politics of his mentor, Mohandas K. Gandhi.

Indira Gandhi's actions were not based on party. Unlike the Conservative Party leader Margaret Thatcher, Gandhi led the liberal, socialist Indian Congress Party. Though her party was committed to women's equality, Gandhi paid no more attention to that platform than her male compatriots. She did not practice gender politics because her power was based on being Jawaharlal Nehru's daughter rather than on being a representative of India's women. Benazir Bhutto, also heir to her father in leading Pakistan as prime minister (1988–90 and 1993–96), commented that her social class permitted her to "transcend gender."[*]

The common factor in the rise to national power of a series of women in South and Southeast Asia since 1945 is their membership in elite political families. Several widows followed their husbands into political office. The first was Sirimavo Bandaranaike, prime minister of Sri Lanka from 1960 to 1965, from 1970 to 1977, and from 1994 to the present. In her last term, she succeeded her daughter, Chandrika Bandaranaike Kumaratunga, who was appointed prime minister in August 1994 and elected president in October 1994. Corazón Cojuangco Aquino won election to the presidency of the Philippines following the assassination of her husband while he was a leading candidate for the office. She served from 1986 to 1992. Khaleda Zia entered politics in Bangladesh after the assassination of her husband, who was president in 1981. She was elected president in 1991. Her main opponent is also a woman, Sheikh Hasina Wajed of the Bangladesh Awami League. She and her sister are the only surviving heirs of Sheikh Mujibur Rahman, the assassinated founding president of Bangladesh. Daughters of celebrated nationalist fathers have risen to prominence as leaders of the opposition to military rule in contemporary Burma (Myanmar) and Indonesia

---

[*]Benazir Bhutto, *Daughter of Destiny* (New York: Simon & Schuster, 1989), 169.

as well. Often, these women have been chosen by male party leaders for their presumed docility as much as for their name recognition. Some have disappointed that expectation. It is remarkable that women have been able to forge alliances to emerge as viable leaders in volatile nations that swing between military dictatorship, civil war, and democracy. In patriarchal societies such as Pakistan and Bangladesh where *purdah* still prevails, the presence of a woman as public head of state is a political statement, and one that is much condemned by conservative Islamists.

Feminist politicians outside South Asia often deny feminism in public because that label gives their opponents a weapon. Indira Gandhi also publicly denied sympathy for feminism, identifying it with Western equalitarian demands by women. In a conversation with her friend Pupul Jayakar, she defined her position, which falls easily into the popular Indian tradition of relational feminism. Jayakar reported Gandhi's views after her death:

"You know I am not a feminist in the accepted sense of the word," she said. "Till I was 12 years old I hardly knew the difference between being a boy or a girl. I was brought up amongst boy cousins, climbed trees with them, flew kites and played marbles." But, she said, "That is not the normal experience of girls in our country. Women in India, perhaps in most of the world, are so dominated and discriminated against. There is so much unnecessary cruelty and humiliation. . . ."

She was critical of the West where the emancipation of women was equated with an imitation of men and a fierce determination to acquire their behaviour patterns.

"To be liberated," she said, "a woman should be free to be herself. Rivalry between women and men is unnecessary, in fact is destructive and itself a bondage."

We discussed the freedom struggle and the support the Mahatma[*] and Jawaharlal Nehru gave to women. Their support brought women to the forefront without a major struggle. There were few obstacles in India to a woman reaching the highest position. In villages a woman still lived in an epic flow of time: myth and mystery were re-enacted

---

[*]Mohandas K. Gandhi, the mahatma of the Indian independence struggle, who was not related to Indira Nehru Gandhi's husband.

within her and renewed energy. A peasant woman had little need to be other than what she was—this gave her a rootedness and dignity. . . . We spoke of women amongst the land-owning aristocracy and certain sections of the middle-class where the woman was rudderless, treated as a possession passed from father to husband to son. Her bondage was real, society was relentless and no enactment of laws could ensure her freedom. It was education, the capacity to be economically independent and an energy that could erase her conditioning, that alone could free her from her fears and the bondage of centuries. . . .

"Why is it," she asked "that in seeking to be free there is this demand to deny the essence of being a woman? Why do we compare?" She paused, "My mother was fragile but could stand alone. . . ."

"I have taken my own decisions throughout my life. I can stand alone," she said. "But there is so much possessiveness. One needs space to be alone with oneself. The question really is, can a woman be a wife, share companionship with a husband, be a mother and yet be herself, live a life of the mind or a life of action—political, social, cultural."

"Does our present culture and society permit this?" I asked. "The Indian male is so inordinately spoilt by tradition and society. His ego needs continual attention, nourishment—otherwise he feels neglected and is at times destructive."

She chuckled.

From *Indira Gandhi: A Biography* by Pupul Jayakar (New Delhi: Viking [Penguin Books India (P)], 1992), 265–67. Copyright © 1988, 1992 by Pupul Jayakar. Reprinted by permission of Pantheon Books, a division of Random House, Inc.

Gandhi and Jayakar shared sympathy for the "bondage" of women of the landowning and urban middle classes, but their perspective on the lives of the majority of India's women was mythic and tragic in its lack of comprehension. When this conversation took place in June of 1975, more than 215 million Indian women remained illiterate, and their numbers were increasing. More than 75 percent of women lived in rural villages where they constituted more than 30 percent of the labor force in agriculture, an occupation that still employed 72 percent of India's workers in 1990. Few women were protected by labor unions. A 1974 report of the Commission on the Status of Women concluded that, for rural women, economic development increased the already profound gender inequities of the traditional rural society. Gandhi's failure to understand India's peasantry led in part to her only electoral defeat, in 1977.

The story of that defeat is tied to the actions that followed her declaration of a state of emergency in June 1975. This allowed her to rule dictatorially, by decrees, and with press censorship. She approved lists of leaders to be arrested, including activists in the women's movement, who promptly went underground. Criticism, both internal and external, rose as India seemed to have given up democracy. The one reform that provoked the most internal criticism, and was an important cause for her subsequent electoral defeat, was the sterilization program.

Since 1947, India's government had been committed to achieving economic growth through planned development. By 1975, experts agreed that the country's birthrate was outpacing its annual economic growth rate. And people's incomes could not rise if population growth continued. Years of public financing of birth-control clinics and family-planning education programs were pronounced failures. The government then undertook a massive program to lower the birthrate through compulsory sterilization, relying mainly on male vasectomies. Pupul Jayakar describes the scope of the sterilization campaign:

The concentration was on vasectomy. But the nature of the operation was such as made it inevitable that simple village folk saw in it a threat to their virility and so they came to equate sterilization with impotence. The absence of social service personnel to prepare the ground, to educate people, to alleviate primal fears and heal psychological wounds, was traumatic. . . .

By the middle of 1976, the family planning drive reached a peak; the targets for sterilization were laid down for every state and district. As the figures for sterilization were reviewed they were continually revised upwards and impossible targets set, with little consideration or concern for the facilities and medical personnel available for such an escalation in numbers. . . .

There was constant pressure from the Central Government to improve performance. The state governments were left free to introduce their own incentives and disincentives. Incentives included the preferential allotment of houses, land, educational facilities etc. In certain states, the salaries of teachers were withheld if they could not fulfill the quotas allotted to them for motivating citizens to undergo sterilization. Many of the teachers were widows, who found it impossible to approach men to ask them to undergo sterilization. To refuse salaries to these vulnerable women caused massive resentment.

In Delhi the family planning drive came under the direct supervision of Sanjay Gandhi [Indira Gandhi's son]. Programmes for sterilization were associated in the minds of the people with the massive demolition [of slums] that took place in the city. . . . The people's anger led to violence—*lathi* [baton] charges, arrests and police firings followed. The suddenness and ruthlessness of the operation took the people by surprise; it was as if an earthquake had struck; people cowered in fear.

In Uttar Pradesh, Madhya Pradesh and Haryana as family planning targets were raised and the officers in charge found it impossible to fulfil their quotas, some young men were taken off buses and forcibly sterilized. In other areas opposition to the family planning drive led to rioting, violence, shootings and deaths. . . .

The achievements in family planning during this time were, by any standard, remarkable. From 2,624,755 cases of sterilization reported in 1975–76 for the whole country, the figures rose to 8,132,209 in 1976–77—an increase of over 300 percent. In the two years of the Emergency the number of sterilizations reported was 10,756,964.

From *Indira Gandhi: A Biography* by Pupul Jayakar (New Delhi: Viking [Penguin Books India (P)], 1992), 300–301. Copyright © 1988, 1992 by Pupul Jayakar. Reprinted by permission of Pantheon Books, a division of Random House, Inc.

Gandhi called an election for March 1977 and ended the state of emergency. She had always relied upon the peasant women for their votes, but in her 1977 campaign speeches, she noticed a coolness among the peasants. Pratima Singh, a member of parliament and friend of Prime Minister Gandhi, sought the reason for the unenthusiastic receptions:

[She] travelled from village to village, spoke to women, reminding them of the Prime Minister's concern for women and their welfare. On one occasion a woman spoke up: "That's all right, but sister, what about the *nasbandi* (vasectomy)? Our men have become weak, we women have become weak. . . ."

In Haryana a tough Jat woman, an agriculturist, when approached for her vote, spoke of vasectomy, and commented in a strong earthy idiom, "What is the use of a river without fish?"

From *Indira Gandhi: A Biography* by Pupul Jayakar (New Delhi: Viking [Penguin Books India (P)], 1992), 318. Copyright © 1988, 1992 by Pupul Jayakar. Reprinted by permission of Pantheon Books, a division of Random House, Inc.

The message was clear: the rural voters had lost confidence in Gandhi and her party, the Indian National Congress. They lost the election. The government retreated from population control through forced male sterilization. Sterilization of women remains a principal form of family planning in India.

Suggested Further Readings

The English view of colonial women is discussed in Helen Callaway's "Purity and Exotica in Legitimating the Empire: Cultural Constructions of Gender, Sexuality and Race," in *Legitimacy and the State in Twentieth Century Africa: Essays in Honour of A.H.M. Kirk-Greene,* edited by Terence Ranges and Olufemi Vaughan (London: Macmillan, 1993), 31–61. The Indian view is summarized in the chapter on India in Kumari Jayawardena's *Feminism and Nationalism in the Third World* (London: Zed Books, 1986), 73–108. Women's disappointment in independent India is explained in Partha Chatterjee's "The Nationalist Resolution of the Women's Question," in *Recasting Women: Essays in Indian Colonial History,* edited by Kumkum Sangari and Sudesh Vaid (New Brunswick, NJ: Rutgers University Press, 1990), 233–53. *The History of Doing: An Illustrated Account of Movements for Women's Rights and Feminism in India, 1800–1990,* by Radha Kumar, published by Kali for Women in New Delhi in 1993, is a very readable historical narrative, with biographic sketches and some documents, all from a contemporary feminist perspective. Thematic exploration of the subordination of women in twentieth-century India is found in *Daughters of Independence: Gender, Caste, and Class in India,* by Joanna Liddle and Rama Joshi (London: Zed Books, 1986).

Sati is considered from different perspectives in Anand A. Yang, "Widow-Burning in Early Nineteenth-Century India," in *Expanding the Boundaries of Women's History: Essays on Women in the Third World,* edited by Cheryl Johnson-Odim and Margaret Strobel (Bloomington: Indiana University Press, 1992), 74–98; and in Lata Mani, "Contentious Traditions: The Debate on *Sati* in Colonial India," in *Recasting Women,* 88–126. The complex forms of social isolation for both Muslim and Hindu women encompassed in the term *purdah* are considered in Patricia Jeffrey's classic study *Frogs in a Well: Indian Women in Purdah* (London: Zed Books, 1979). Discussion of recent field studies can be found in three articles in *Separate Worlds: Studies of Purdah in South Asia,* edited by Hanna Papanek and Gail Minault (Delhi: Chanakya Publications, 1982), 3–109. The decline of *purdah* among rural Rajput caste women between 1955 and 1975 is the subject of Leigh Minturn's *Sita's Daughters: Coming out of Purdah* (New York: Oxford University Press, 1993). The drive to provide education for women in Bengal is traced in Manisha Roy's *Bengal's Women* (Chicago: University of Chicago Press, 1992). An excellent collection of articles and essays focused on socioeconomic problems of women in the 1980s is *In Search of Answers: Indian Women's Voices from Manushi,* rev. ed., edited by Madhu Kishwar and Ruth Vanita (New Delhi: Horizon India Books, 1991). Disparities between stereotypes and realities in the lives of minority Muslim women are shown in Shahida Lateef's *Muslim Women in India: Political and Private Realities, 1890s–1980s* (New Delhi: Kali for Women, 1990). The rise of fundamentalist conservativism among both Hindus and Muslims since 1985 is the subject of *Against All Odds: Essays on Women, Religion and Development from India and Pakistan,* edited by Kamla Bhasin, Ritu Menon, and Nighat Said Khan (New Delhi: Kali for Women, 1994).

There are numerous essays and books on Indira Gandhi; among the most informative are chapters 5 and 6 in Rajeswari Sunder Rajan's *Real and Imagined Women: Gender, Culture and Postcolonialism* (New York: Routledge, 1993). Mary C. Carras analyzes gender as a career factor in "Indira Gandhi and Foreign Policy," in *Women in World Politics,* edited by Francine

D'Amato and Peter R. Beckman (Westport, CT: Bergin and Garvey, 1995). Gandhi's own views shortly before her assassination on October 31, 1984, are revealed in *Indira Gandhi on Herself and Her Times,* an interview with Nemai Sadhan Bose (Calcutta: Ananda Publishers, 1987).

–11–
SEEKING LIBERATION IN NEW EAST ASIAN SOCIETIES
China and Japan after 1800

Women of the revolutionary People's Liberation Army playing the PiPa, a traditional Chinese instrument. (People's Republic of China, 1971. Photograph by Audrey Ronning Topping.)

Few modern nations have experienced such rapid, wrenching social changes as those that transformed China and Japan after 1850. Efforts to overthrow China's Qing rulers began with the mid-nineteenth century Taiping Rebellion and ended when the monarchy collapsed in the revolution of 1911. Sun Yat-sen's dream of a democratic China brought reforms to urban areas, but civil war, as well as Japanese aggression, wracked China until the communists seized power in 1949. Then, a second era of revolutionary change on a Marxist model repudiated ancient Confucian beliefs and private property. Reform of the feudal Japanese Tokugawa shogunate began with the Meiji restoration in 1868. Rapid industrialization based on intense nationalism eventually led Japan into World War II. Another restructuring occurred under American auspices following the Japanese surrender in 1945.

Profound changes in women's lives—sometimes explicitly sought, but often unintended consequences of other reforms—accompanied each attempt to transform Chinese and Japanese societies. Women's active participation in revolutionary movements as well as their experiences in factories, on farms, in offices, and in their homes created successive new feminist demands for recognition of past contributions and of continuing gender inequities.

11.1 Women of the Taiping Rebellion, 1850–64

The Taiping Rebellion is a well-documented historical instance of women fighting as soldiers in battle. At this time, when China was ruled by the Manchurian Qing dynasty, Chinese women ordinarily had bound feet, which limited their mobility and kept them inside their homes. Yet the Taiping warrior women were not handicapped by foot bindings. Why did these women soldiers have unbound feet?

The revolt originated in South China about two hundred miles northwest of Canton. Several dissatisfied groups had been attracted to a new religious leader; the largest one, the Hakka, was most important. They had migrated from North China about six centuries earlier and remained enemies of the original inhabitants. They were very poor, with hill farms too small to support their families. Most men had to work in the cities, leaving their families behind. The women farmed without their adult male relatives. Women even drove water buffalo. Given their responsibility to feed their families, the Hakka women couldn't afford the handicap of bound feet. Besides, Chinese mothers bound their daughters' feet to make them more desirable as brides who might marry influential and wealthy men. Hakka couples had so little property that dowries were not important: they married for love, and they often sang about love.

The rebellion leaders' appeal for their followers was conversion to Christianity—a combination of pseudo-Christian and traditional Chinese religious concepts. They emphasized the equality of men and women. Conventional Chinese accepted female inferiority to males; the sale of women as brides, concubines, or maids; and widespread prostitution. Rebellion leaders refused to accept the devaluation of women.

At the beginning of the revolt, whole families joined, having sold their farms and put the money into the rebellion's common treasury. Men and women were assigned to separate dormitories: sex was not allowed, even for married couples. To prevent rapes in battle, the rebellion's soldiers could not enter houses that contained women. Prostitution was forbidden. Illicit sex could be punished by execution. Separation of the sexes and suppression of desire was believed to be necessary to discipline all efforts and focus on defeating the government. However, the rebellion's leaders promised that when they took the important city of Nanking, married couples would live together.

Women fought in battles, too. A government supporter described their behavior:

Among the bandits there are female soldiers. . . . Being of vile minorities . . . , they grew up in caves and run around with bare feet and turbaned heads. They can scale steep cliffs with ease, and their courage surpasses that of men. On the battlefield, they carry weapons and fight at close quarters. Government troops have been defeated by them in battle.

The Taipings were reported to have six thousand women soldiers at their greatest number and several famous women generals. One, Su Sanniang, was the subject of a poem. She and her husband were farmers when robbers killed her husband. Donning mourning clothes, she led several hundred men in a search for the robbers. Soon government troops pursued her. The exploits of her band gave her a Robin Hood reputation. At the outbreak of the rebellion, she and two thousand troops joined the rebels.

Drums and bugles sound clearly atop the city wall.
Soldiers stand at attention, their flags and banners unfurled.
Passersby push and shove each other,
As they rush to catch a glimpse of Su Sanniang.

The daughter from Ling Mountain is extremely skilled.
Ten years with the bandits, she's called a valiant woman.
Dressed in crimson before an audience, she receives an official rank.
Dressed in white mourning clothes for her husband, she beheads her foes.
Her arms have fought more than one hundred battles.
She doesn't lower her spear until she's killed one thousand.

The Qing general, hearing of her fame, summons his forces for war.
Galloping on their horses, shouting loudly, their spirits running high,
Five hundred stalwart youths under her command charge the enemy soldiers,
Who flee like so many thousands of forlorn rats.
Upon his return, the Qing commander washes his knife and curses madly.
He shamefully lies about his losses and is promoted to a high position.

When the Taipings occupied Nanking, female recruits with bound feet sought to join them. Their forces had no place for adults who could not contribute to their maximum potential. So off came the wrapping around the new women's feet before they were assigned tasks that often required walking miles—and must have caused them great pain. The Taiping Rebellion was finally defeated by the government in 1864.

11.2 Women Hold Up Half the Sky: Communist China after 1949

The valor of Hakka women in the Taiping Rebellion had no effect on the vast majority of Chinese women, who continued to live within traditional patriarchal society until the communist victory over the Guomindang (Kuomintang) in 1949. Sheila Rowbotham's summary is harsh but succinct:

In order to understand the significance of changes brought by the revolution [of 1949] the nature and degree of degradation and domination which previously existed have to be remembered. While a small minority of the upper classes lived as aesthetic ornaments, most of the women worked ceaselessly and could be beaten and even killed with no hope of redress. Bride-price and wife-selling were normal; so too were polygamy and concubinage. Girls were sold or kidnapped into prostitution. Child streetwalkers could frequently be seen in the larger towns. Within the family the older women disciplined the younger, the mother-in-law beating the younger wife. The wife had no rights until she had a son. All women were subject to the authority of husbands, brothers, and finally sons. Although this traditional family was related to the agrarian economy, its effects on women were more severe than in western European peasant societies, because in the evolution of Chinese society women could never inherit. There was no possibility of protection coming from her father's family in opposition to the way in which her husband was treating her. . . . True, the wife's family might apply pressure but if they weren't powerful wives could be sold as they had been bought and even rented out.

From *Women, Resistance and Revolution: A History of Women and Revolution in the Modern World* by Sheila Rowbotham (New York: Vintage Books, 1974), 173–74. Copyright © 1972 by Sheila Rowbotham. Reprinted by permission of Pantheon Books, a division of Random House, Inc.

A commitment to women's emancipation was an essential part of the reform program of Chinese intellectuals from their first efforts in the late nineteenth century. Various laws were passed by administrations before 1949, but few had a perceptible effect. Even the Qing Empress Cixi issued a decree in 1902 against footbinding. Many men joined organizations protesting it and signed oaths not to marry anyone with bound feet. Nevertheless, the practice continued, and footbinding was prohibited again by the revolutionary government in 1911. Gradually, the practice became less common in cities, but legal bans were not enforced in rural areas, where the majority of Chinese women lived. Many of the leaders of the successful communist revolution, including Mao Zedong, supported women's issues even before they became communists.

In 1923, the revolutionary nationalist party, the Guomindang (KMT), and the Chinese Communist Party (CCP) formed an alliance. The Guomindang issued major demands in 1924 and 1926 for equality between the sexes, permission for women to inherit property, free marriages and divorces, and labor laws to provide the same pay for the same work by men and women.

Women were significant supporters of these activities: they were killed in demonstrations and fought as soldiers in battles against the warlords. They also organized women's committees in cities and rural areas to educate women. In 1927, the Guomindang viciously attacked the CCP. Sharon Sievers explains what happened to radical women:

In the attacks that drove the CCP from the cities, left KMT [Guomindang] and CCP women were special targets. The White Terror that began in Hankow in 1927 singled out any women with bobbed hair and shot them for their supposed radicalism; in Canton, young women thought to be members of the CCP were wrapped in gasoline-soaked blankets and burned alive; and everywhere the White Terror prevailed women were physically mutilated—often their breasts were hacked off—and raped before they were finally killed by KMT agents and troops.

After 1928, the KMT ... began redefining women's roles. ... KMT philosophers offered a formula of legal reform, Confucian morality blended with Christian individualism, and a return to the virtues of the family. ...

The KMT's most significant effort to legislate equality came in the 1930 Civil Code, a document that gave important legal rights to women in the family, while preserving the patriliny. Women, under the new code, were supposed to be able to choose their own husbands, apply for divorce, and to inherit property; adultery was a punishable offense, not only for women, but for men as well. New factory legislation protected women from work that might be physically harmful and theoretically paved the way for equal pay for equal work. Male educators and members of the KMT now proclaimed Chinese women emancipated.

Sharon L. Sievers, "Women in China, Japan, and Korea," in *Restoring Women to History: Teaching Packets for Integrating Women's History into Courses on Africa, Asia, Latin America, the Caribbean, and the Middle East,* edited by Cheryl Johnson-Odim and Margaret Strobel (Bloomington, IN: Organization of American Historians, 1988), 101–2.

The Guomindang women's policy under the leadership of Soong Mei Ling (Mme. Chiang Kai-shek) emphasized patriarchy and male supremacy and urged women to work in welfare activities, hygiene, child care, and relief efforts. Coeducation in colleges had been attained in the 1920s, and the graduates found job opportunities expanding. Women in urban areas made considerable progress in the 1930s and 1940s. Modern marriages were increasingly contracted among the upper and middle classes. Women, no longer in seclusion, entered the social scene wearing French perfume, permanent waves, high-heeled shoes, silk stockings, and even the one-piece bathing suit.

After the White Terror, those women who sought greater equality and the end of patriarchy often chose to work with the communists. Forced out of the cities, the CCP concentrated on building bases and armies of peasants in rural areas. It promised a thorough reorganization of society, including women's equality, after the triumph of its revolution. Mao Zedong's 1927 statement (the "four thick ropes") summed up party analysis that women, like men, were subject to the three oppressive systems of political authority, clan authority, and religious authority but that women also had one more: domination by men. However, the party did not try to transform patriarchal peasant culture and ordered women members to support the civil war with the Guomindang.

In 1949, the communists won that war. It took almost another decade to regain order and stability. By 1958, the government needed women's labor as it tried to increase production of steel, electricity, and coal significantly in a campaign called the Great Leap Forward. In the same year, collectivization of agriculture put large numbers of workers in unified organizations, the communes; each had on average about twenty-five thousand people, though some were more than twice as large. Both men and women farmers of each commune were mobilized in production brigades and teams. Jan Myrdal interviewed Li Kuei-ying, who was an official in the Liu Ling People's Commune:

In the winter of 1959–60 we had a discussion about our work among the women. I sent a proposal in to the committee of the party association for setting up a special women's committee for our work among the women. I told them that, in my opinion, so far I had been the only one working on the women, and that we could not let so important a matter be dealt with like that. . . . The party association decided to set up a labour group for work with women. Ma Ping and I were elected Liu Ling's representatives in the group. This group now has regular meetings. It has representatives from the various villages [in the commune], and we now plan our work among the women properly.

I was head of the women's organization in Liu Ling from 1955 to 1961. It wasn't a real organization. It automatically comprised all the women in the village. It was one way of activating the women in social work and getting them to develop and accept responsibility and get up at the different meetings and give their opinion. We abolished it in 1961, because . . . we had quite enough women then who realized that women can be in the ordinary organizations and speak at their meetings. Instead, we formed a women's work group. I was chosen leader of this. We work directly in production.

But the party group for women's work still functions. It has five different tasks: (1) To organize women to take an active part in production; (2) To spread literacy among women and get them to study and to take an interest in social questions; (3) To help them do their domestic work effectively and economically, to help them when any economic problem arises in their family; (4) To teach them personal and public hygiene; (5) To give help and advice over marriage or other problems of wedded life. . . .

That was when Tuan Fu-yin's eighteen-year-old daughter, Tuan Ai-chen, fell in love with a boy from Seven-mile Village. But her parents refused to let her marry. They said that the boy was poor and that they wanted her to marry someone better off. One evening Tuan Ai-chen came to me and wept and complained. I went with her to her cave and talked to her parents. I said to them: "You have no right to prevent your daughter from marrying, you know that, don't you? Purchase marriage is not allowed in the new society. It is a crime to sell your daughter these days. Before you could sell your daughter like a cow, but you can't do that any longer." I told them about the things that used to happen in the old days, about girls drowning themselves in wells, of girls hanging themselves and that sort of thing, about all the unhappiness purchase marriage caused. At first, Tuan Fu-yin tried to stand up to me. He said: "I had to pay dearly for my wife. Now I have been giving this girl food and clothes. I have brought her up and she just goes off. It isn't right. I just lose and lose all the time. I must get something back of all the money I have laid out on her. If she can't fall in love with a man who can pay back what she cost, then it isn't right for her to marry."

I talked a long time with them that evening, and in the end I said: "You don't live badly in the new society. If you ever have difficulties, your daughter and son-in-law will help you. They are not rich, but they won't refuse to help you." Then they replied: "We must think about it." The next time I went there, only the girl's mother was at home. She had thought about it and she now told me her own story. . . . She said: "I was sold to Tuan Fu-yin when I was a little girl. I was sold in the same way you sell a goat. But my parents got a lot for me. Tuan's father had to take out a loan. That made them nasty to me. I was forced to work hard so as to make the loan worth while. They were all nagging at me. I can remember how much I used to cry. Now that I think of that, I don't want my daughter to marry someone she can't like." Then she wept. Tuan Fu-yin didn't say anything more.

Jan Myrdal, *Report from a Chinese Village,* translated by Maurice Michael (New York: Signet Books, published by arrangement with Pantheon Books, 1966), 254–56. Copyright © 1965 by William Heinemann.

The Great Leap Forward was an economic disaster, but it did help women. Their labor outside the family was publicly encouraged, including the establishment of communal child care and kitchens to reduce their domestic work. A national public health system that brought medical care to the countryside benefited women. Women began doing men's tasks, although their pay was less. But even as work was redistributed between women and men, gender remained paramount, for tasks were still defined as feminine or masculine.

By the late 1980s, Chinese women had made real advances over their position before 1949. Yet equality still eluded them. Seventy percent of women worked at least part-time, but most jobs were low-paid, without benefits or chances for advancement. Following Mao Zedong's death in 1976, decollectivization in agriculture meant that many decisions passed from commune officials to families, where men retained authority, and income was paid to the senior male. Sidelines such as pig or chicken raising, which women had pursued to increase income, became the prerogative of men once market enterprises were encouraged by the state.

Arranged marriages were seldom found in the cities, but in rural areas, which had 70 percent of the population, they were on the rise. Wedding costs rose also, with the groom's family paying amounts of as much as ten times a person's average annual income. Such investments suggested that a wife was valued, but also too valuable to lose. Divorces initiated by the wife were possible, but the courts made them difficult to obtain.

The state's promotion of economic growth through private initiatives imperiled women in China when, instead of demanding that wives provide productive labor for the nation, it urged wives to reduce male unemployment by returning to their homes and the care of their own families. In 1979, the option of motherhood was sharply restricted, however, by the government's population-control policy, which permitted the birth of only one child to each family.

City dwellers, with crowded homes and hectic lives, accepted their loss of choice in the national interest more willingly than farm women. Resistance in the rural areas led both to female infanticide and to official compromise allowing women a second pregnancy if the first child was a daughter. After forty years of communism, the ancient Confucian joy in the birth of a son and despair at the birth of a daughter had not quite disappeared in the countryside. Though daughters were valued more than sons in the cities by the late 1980s, rural families still wanted a son to support parents in old age, inherit the land, and maintain the family name.

When the communists won the civil war and took over the government, many inside and outside China expected that the liberation of women so long promised would occur. While China remained closed to the West in the 1950s and 1960s, it seemed as though women might "Hold Up Half the Sky." By the late 1970s, feminist scholarship of anthropologists and sociologists provided disappointing evidence of partial accomplishments and of failures. In China, as in other Marxist revolutions after World War II—including Cuba, Vietnam, Nicaragua, Yugoslavia, and Mozambique—true emancipation and social equality remained elusive. Scholars disagree on whether the cause of the unfulfilled socialist promises was the insincerity of men who dominated revolutionary leadership or the pervasive resistance of conservative rural populations.

11.3 Women's Contribution to Japan's Industrialization

The leaders of the nineteenth-century Meiji restoration transformed Japan from an agricultural country into an industrial one. The process of rapid industrialization was based on silk and cotton textile exports. Sales of cloth in foreign markets earned the currency needed to finance imports of machinery and raw materials for the steel and armaments industries. The government, starting with one silk-reeling factory in 1872, its famous Tomioka mill, had by 1914 become the world's dominant producer of both silk and cotton fabrics. Often overlooked by historians is the fact that Japan's industrialization was the result of the labor of Japanese women.

The first workers in the government's Tomioka mill were women from poor samurai families. When private mills were built, the owners began recruiting daughters from poor farm families. Their fathers signed their labor contracts, and the daughters moved into a dormitory within the mill compound. Sharon Sievers explains why they wanted to work:

The dramatic story, now well known in Japan, of young women textile workers who year after year braved the winter snows of

Nomugi Pass to work in the mills of neighboring Nagano prefecture illustrates both the courage and the desperation that characterized their lives. Wearing only straw sandals, or walking barefoot through the snow and ice, long processions of factory workers made their way across the mountains, leaving a trail tinged reddish-pink from the cuts on their feet and the dye of their red underskirts. They clung to each other in the blowing snow, and when someone fell, tied their obi [sashes] together and tried to pull her back up to the path.

At the end of what was for some a 100-mile journey was the mill and the knowledge that, if they could survive the work and its hardships, they could go home again at the end of summer. For some who crossed over in the early days, bringing home a small wage was a luxury; the real point of a year's work in the mill was to be fed by someone else. Shimokawa Aki, who was eleven when she traveled over the pass in 1884, remembered: "In those days, because we went to reduce the number of mouths to feed, money was not the issue. It was better than being at home, because we could eat rice." Later, when wages were paid, they were not for the young women themselves, but for parents, whose gratitude could sometimes erase the memory of intolerable working conditions.

> I don't know how many times I thought I would rather jump into Lake Suwa and drown. Even so, when I went home with a year's earnings and handed the money to my mother, she clasped it in her hands and said, "With this, we can manage through the end of the year." And my father, who was ill, sat up in his bed and bowed to me over and over. "Sue," he said, "it must have been difficult. Thank you. Thank you."
>
> Then we put the money in a wooden box, and put the box up on the altar and prayed. . . . Whenever I thought of my mother's face then, I could endure any hardship.

These "excess" daughters of Japan's countryside, born in a predominantly patrilineal, patrilocal society, where their value was always tempered by the expectation that they would eventually marry and become workers in someone else's household, soon became the backbone of the country's economy. Though a daughter's potential value as a bride required careful family management, daughters were, in the best to the worst case, commodities to be managed, and if necessary sold, to keep the family going. Their domination of the Meiji work force, where they constituted an average of 60 percent of Japan's industrial labor from 1894 to 1912, probably did not come as much of a surprise to a government that had encouraged young women to join the labor force in the 1870s "for the good of the country." Working in a textile mill was patriotic. . . .

Reports from government officials and visits by observers to spinning mills in England reinforced what the government already knew: that spinning and weaving industries, with little or no government encouragement, might become competitive in world markets by using at least one resource the country already had in abundance. Japan, like Europe and the United States, had a reserve labor force of young women who were used to hard work and whose low wages were easily justified.

In fact, this "resource" came to dominate factory labor in Japan down to 1930, not just in sheer numbers, but in the value of exports produced. Silk was one of the nation's few exportable commodities in 1868, accounting for nearly two-thirds of all export volume in that year; by the end of the Meiji period (1912), Japanese women had made their country the world's leading exporter of silk. The growth of cotton spinning and weaving . . . came into its own after 1900. By 1914 Japan was dominating world cotton manufacturing. . . . What these exports meant to the country's ability to build both heavy industry and military strength without extensive borrowing is clear enough. Without the work of Japan's women, the apparent miracle of Japan's economic growth might not have been possible.

11.4 Japanese Women in World War II

Japanese women experienced significant social changes in the period beginning with World War II. Before that, they had lived a subordinate, submissive, domestic life within a type of extended family. Afterward came suffrage, the nuclear family, and almost sole responsibility for nurturing family members. The magnitude of change must be measured against women's situation during the eighty years before 1945.

Reorganization of Japanese society began after the Meiji restoration in 1868. The new national leaders had industrialization as one of their goals. Other reforms included abolition of feudal privileges and universal compulsory education. The family was to be one of the building blocks of the new society, with the wife's role defined in the slogan "Good Wife, Wise Mother." Womanhood was partly identified with motherhood, with responsibility for raising new members of the state who knew their duty and performed it. Mothers were excluded from politics, did not work, and remained at home. In general, women were subordinate to husbands, who had to consent to any contract into which their wives entered. Husbands got the children of divorce, and adultery was a ground for divorce of a woman but not of a man. New wives were treated as maids by their mothers-in-law.

The war began for Japan with its 1937 invasion of China. Wartime shortages and extraordinary situations forced intimacy among neighbors, regardless of class and status restrictions; gender conventions might even be breached. Sumie Seo Mishima wrote about her war experiences in Tokyo. Born in Japan, she had attended Wellesley College in Massachusetts in the 1920s, then returned to Japan to marry a college professor. She noticed how personal behavior changed on the home front:

About a year before Pearl Harbor, the controlled national economy, necessitated by war, worked out a drastic leveling down of our social structure. For the rationing of daily necessities as well as for the general regimentation of the people's lives, the neighborhood cooperative system, which had once flourished under the Tokugawa Shogunate regime, was revived, although in a greatly modified form. The government ordered the people throughout the country to group themselves into units called "neighborhood societies," each unit to be formed by some dozen families grouped together solely on the basis of "residential adjacency." . . .

The neighborhood society to which my family belonged consisted of eleven families headed by two peers [aristocrats]. Then came a war millionaire, a government official, a beautiful widow, a steward and a chauffeur—both in service to a rich baron—a semi-government official, a gardener, a factory worker, and a school teacher—my husband. . . .

These member families took semi-yearly turns in officiating as society president and air-defence captain. . . . With the aggravation of the war situation, food and fuel questions became acute, and air-raid drills and defense installations more and more urgent. The member families had to work in compact cooperation. Moreover, the increasing difficulty in traffic and communication made it impossible for any family to depend, in an emergency, on the cooperation of its scattered relatives. A next-door neighbor became much more reliable than a brother only a mile away. And thus the traditional Japanese family sentiment for turning to relatives in case of need was superseded by a democratic way of not feeling ashamed to disclose one's plight to non-relatives, and to ask for help.

So the people, particularly the housewives in my neighborhood society, became very intimate with each other, and many times a day they stepped through their broken garden fences and called at each other's unrepaired kitchen doors to pass on the ward-office's circulars, or to borrow a spoonful of sugar, a pint of soy-bean sauce or an ounce of dried bonito chips.

As a whole, we got along very congenially because we had so much in common to complain about, all practically being servantless and occupied equally with patching clothes, cooking meals and chopping firewood. . . .

Food shortages became keenly felt by our family from the second year of the Pacific War. A family like ours, whose economic foundation consisted solely of the meager teaching salaries of my husband, and the small fees for my sporadic writing and translating work . . . suffered severely from food and clothing shortages. As for clothes, we could go about in multi-patched, nondescript garments, although it was never a pleasant sensation to wonder whether your clothes would properly stay on your back. But food was imperative. Practically all my time now was spent running from one food rationing office to another, going out into the country for fresh vegetables, and then cooking these costly foodstuffs with meagerly rationed fuel. . . .

The government-rationed food was not enough to keep one alive and going, and more and more, sweet and Irish potatoes, often mildewed, and flour—frequently of a strange taste—came to be substituted for our rice and barley. . . . Soon it became absolutely necessary for me to obtain some unrationed food supplies directly from farmers.

I went on a buying-out trip nearly once a week. Each week I had to travel farther from the city, because the distance and the price varied inversely for this rural traffic. Moreover, my visits to country farms had to be financed by gifts in kind—cotton goods and soap, in particular. Farmers, more than anyone else, scorned money. But I had none of these attractive gifts to court farmers' favors with, so I usually cooperated with a neighboring housewife, who had stores of cotton pieces and sewing thread. . . . Out of the material offered by her I made shirts and trousers on my sewing machine . . . and she and I usually went to the country together. Sometimes I took sewing orders directly from the farmers, to whom I was known as "the tailor-woman." . . .

[Sumie experienced directly the American bombing raids on Japanese cities.] Night-raids, which generally aimed at burning residential houses and in which we could not well observe the behavior of the attacking planes, filled us with much more fear and sense of uncertainty. Daytime raids were somewhat different. . . . [She describes one daylight raid during a country buying trip.] It was a bright, clear day and from the morning I was filled with misgivings, for usually the Bees [B-29 bombers] came on such a day. But rain, fire, bombs or whatever else might be falling, I had to travel into the country to get food supplies. I went out with my usual companion, Mrs. T.

When the train pulled into the station on the other side of the river that marked the northwestern border of the city, we heard a long-drawn out whooping of sirens. "It's only the preliminary alerting," we said self-comforting. "We can't tell yet which of the hundred cities of Japan is going to be hit." The train stood still and presently sharp peals sounded. All the passengers got off and ran to the shelters in the station compound, taking with them only those of their possessions that they could carry in their hands and still run. But these public shelters were too few. Many ran out of the station into the town street. The sirens had finished their ten weird diminuendos, and in the dead silence that now reigned over heaven and earth came a distant boom.

"Run quick into our shelter!" a man's voice shouted. Mrs. T. and I gratefully accepted the invitation.

In the eastern sky loomed a flight, another flight and yet another of B-29's. Keeping a 10,000 meter height and trailing white streamers of exhaust gas, they sailed in perfect formation through the blue-gold sky. . . .

Suddenly came z-z-z-z-z-z, a sound like that of ocean billows breaking on a sandy beach. The people, who had been enticed to the mouths of their dugouts by the sheer beauty of the high-flying planes, simultaneously pulled in their heads. Then came heavy rolling sounds like thunderclaps, mingled with ponderous thuds vibrating into the earth. Now sharp volleys of anti-aircraft guns joined in from the ground. . . . [The raid ended.]

"We have wasted four hours here, thanks to the wicked Bees," grumbled Mrs. T. and I, thinking of the tedious trip still ahead and fearing that we could not possibly get home before dark.

"You are buying-outers, aren't you?" A farmer suddenly spoke to us and offered to sell us some flour and vegetables, if we walked with him to his farm. We were astonished because we had never been very hospitably received by a farmer in any of our previous food-traffic adventures. . . .

The kind host, after treating two tired and hungry women with a cup of tea and a plateful of steamed toro roots, took out two big basketfuls of good Irish and sweet potatoes, measured some rice and flour, . . . and gave us some burdock roots and onions in addition. His charge was surprisingly low even taking into consideration the cotton shirt we had presented to him.

With a hearty smile we each shouldered a load of 50 pounds, grasped an additional big bundle, and triumphantly began to walk back. . . .

The train was crowded as usual and there was no way of getting on it through any of the overflowing decks with such heavy loads on our backs. Following my companion's and many other people's examples, I pushed in my big bundles through one of the train windows and jumped on the window myself, feeling most grateful for my tight *mompé* trousers. During my desperate struggle to climb in, I felt a strong hand supporting and pushing up my feet. . . .

It was not the first time I had received a helping hand from an unknown man. Under the stress of war, some Japanese men had cast away their peculiar show of indifference toward women and had become quite chivalrous.

Excerpts from *The Broader Way: A Woman's Life in the New Japan* by Sumie Seo Mishima (Westport, CT: Greenwood Press, 1971), 10–11, 18–21, 30–32, 35–36. Copyright 1953 by the John Day Company. Reprinted by permission of HarperCollins Publishers, Inc.

Sumie did not have a full-time paid job during the war. If she had lived in Great Britain, where women were conscripted, or the United States, where even married women were recruited for war work, she probably would have had a job.

11.5 The Promotion Track versus the "Mommy" Track in Postwar Japan

Following Japan's unconditional surrender to the Allies in 1945, its government, economy, and society were consciously re-shaped by the American occupying officials, who sought to impose democracy, competitive capitalism, and the nuclear family on their defeated rivals. Women made gains that seemed momentous to Sumie Mishima in 1953 at the end of the occupation.

The greatest democratic change that has come to postwar Japan, as far as I can see, is the liberation of women. The national bankruptcy and the subsequent social and economic chaos called forth women's cooperation for the rehabilitation efforts. Men, in their desperate need, did not even mind if women led them. . . .

The new National Constitution gave women equal rights with men in all fields of our national life. The new Civil Code freed them to a large extent from family feudal laws. The enormous number of women employed in the offices of the General Occupation Head-quarters and other Occupation offices were, by the Basic Labor Law, paid on an absolutely equal basis with men, which was an unheard-of thing in prewar Japan, and which made these women workers a big power in our postwar economy. Both government and private offices have followed the Occupation examples in the treatment of their women employees.

Japanese women of all classes, whether married or unmarried, have to work now, and women have jobs in more varied fields than men and find it far pleasanter to work with men now than in the old days. . . . Some commercial firms show off their charming women presidents and directors. An attractive woman with some ability to speak English often may command a top-ranking salary.

The abnormal boom of entertainment industries, in the midst of the general business depression, is even turning the tables completely. Night clubs, dance halls, tea-rooms and restaurants demand endless numbers of women workers, with the result that many totally or partially unemployed husbands cook and wash and take care of the children at home while their gayly dressed wives go out to earn money. . . .

Beyond doubt Japanese women have gained much freedom from the war and the Occupation. Freedom, however, is a thing not to be given but to be earned. And in the case of our women, the price has been dear. The sudden loss of all material resources and the consequent shattering of all social and family formalities has meant the total removal of both protection and fetters for them. It is like being thrown overboard. You are perfectly free to struggle for your life, or sink underwater. Heroic efforts are made everywhere, but unfortunately prostitution has been resorted to frequently. It must be noted, however, that even prostitution is freely chosen now, unlike the prewar days when girls were commonly sold into this profession by their hard-pressed parents.

Excerpts from *The Broader Way: A Woman's Life in the New Japan* by Sumie Seo Mishima (Westport, CT: Greenwood Press, 1971), 165–67, 173. Copyright 1953 by the John Day Company. Reprinted by permission of HarperCollins Publishers, Inc.

———

Women's liberation seemed more ambiguous a generation later. By the 1980s, the limits of the equal legal rights Japanese women obtained under the 1947 Constitution were evident, as were the profound changes in family structures. Sharon Sievers explains some details:

Shortly after the new constitution took effect in 1947, the Japanese parliament approved abortion in cases of economic necessity, believing that population control was crucial to Japan's economic development. In practice, however, birth control was not widely available to Japanese women, and access to safe abortions was limited to married women who could justify it on the basis of economic need. As a result, Japan's population has grown very slowly in the postwar period, but Japanese women have continued to be controlled by fairly rigid social norms in matters of sexuality.

The revised constitution has been most beneficial to working women, primarily those with union backing, who have been able to litigate inequities in the courts. Japanese justice has moved very slowly in this area, but an impressive number of court victories have been won by women over such issues as differentials in age of retirement mandated by large companies. Hiring practices have been more difficult to reach, because, on the surface, equality seems to prevail. Japanese women and men tend to be hired at the same entry level, but through a number of devices large companies, favoring seniority as a means of measuring value and loyalty, encourage Japanese women to drop out of the work force, to marry and raise children, then return. In effect this deprives women of most of the accrued privileges of the Japanese system. Only in recent years [mid-1980s] have major Japanese companies blatantly announced that they will not interview young women with four-year-degrees, sending a message to ambitious young women that they need not apply. Most of these companies, of course, will not interview men from two-year colleges; for valued employees, only four years of college is acceptable as a starting point. . . .

[The women's movement began a second wave in the 1960s, growing out of women's experiences in the anti–Vietnam War movement.]

Still, the most dramatic change in women's lives in postwar Japan came, not from the actions of any group, but from an economy that, in its rapid growth, changed fundamentally the nature and structure of the Japanese family in both city and countryside. The current generation of young families in Japan's major cities are not productive units; for the first time in Japan's history, the typical pattern is the nuclear family in which the husband goes off to work, and the wife stays home to care for the children.

What was especially liberating for women, of course, was that mothers-in-law no longer lived with them; eventually they came to realize a power in their households few women in recent memory had enjoyed in their own right: they became the primary agents in the education of their children, and they were responsible for managing family finances. Only recently, in the past decade, have women in increasing numbers come to realize that the price for this change, in the absence of other developments, has been very high. Mothers-in-law are not always available to provide child care, and children in urban nuclear families are no longer socialized by several adults and siblings—which was the pattern in the extended family. Generally, Japanese society does not provide adequate child care, but there is a real social expectation that women raise well-behaved, successful children. In the family itself, there is the general expectation that wives will manage the budget efficiently; in practice that often means she will supplement her husband's income with part-time work if necessary. She will take part-time work because she has an obligation to her children, especially to their ability to pass crucial examinations that are necessary to their success as students, and ultimately, as members of Japan's economic and political world. She must, in other words, take only the kind of work that will allow her to perform all of her routine duties as wife and mother. . . .

It is clear that the Japanese family system is in transition, and that many of its former tasks—care for aging parents, for example—have not been assumed by any other agency. . . . "Education mothers" it is said, are producing neurotic children; "working mothers" are abandoning their primary social responsibilities. . . . A catalogue of the most dramatic problems attributed to the failure of the family system . . . includes child suicide, family violence that spills over into the school system, and unwillingness or inability to care for aging parents.

The difficulty is, of course, that young wives and mothers are made the primary culprits in this scenario; mention is rarely made of the structural change in the Japanese family or of the fact that Japanese business practices assure the continuance of what is, in practice, a single-parent family in contemporary Japan. Salary men in Japan work, on the average, a six-day week; they leave early and return home very late. They typically spend, at most, part of one day a week with their children. Grandparents, on the other hand, though they occasionally want to locate close to their children, tend to be angry because they are the first generation of Japanese parents whose children are not duty-bound to take care of them in old age. . . .

Japan is a post-industrial society; it has a powerful economy, but women—necessary as they clearly are [to] Japan's success—continue to find it as difficult as ever to find any kind of economic security in their own right.

At the same time, Japanese women are enrolling in larger numbers in four-year academic institutions. They are, often independent of major corporations, making their own economic success; and they are a very effective force in local and regional politics, where they are most active. But it seems their history in postwar Japan has just begun, and they still face enormous barriers.

Sharon L. Sievers, "Women in China, Japan, and Korea," in *Restoring Women to History: Teaching Packets for Integrating Women's History into Courses on Africa, Asia, Latin America, the Caribbean, and the Middle East,* edited by Cheryl Johnson-Odim and Margaret Strobel (Bloomington, IN: Organization of American Historians, 1988), 108–10. Notes omitted.

In response to passage in 1986 of the Equal Employment Opportunity Law, Japanese employers have avoided more than nominal compliance by instituting a two-track system in which women were forced to choose either a promotion track geared for managerial responsibility or a general, or "mommy," track that accommodated family responsibilities. Men were not required to make such choices. Since then, as increasing numbers of Japanese women college graduates choose the career promotion track, the average number of births to each woman has declined to 1.5 in 1992, less than the number required to sustain the current population.

Suggested Further Readings

Very useful summaries of Chinese and Japanese women's political history to the end of World War II can be found in Kumari Jayawardena, *Feminism and Nationalism in the Third World* (London: Zed Books, 1986). Emily Honig's analysis of *Sisters and Strangers: Women in the Shanghai Cotton Mills, 1919–1949* (Stanford, CA: Stanford University Press, 1986) is definitive. A generation after the communist revolution of 1949, American feminists have judged the policies that were intended to implement gender equality to be a failure. Judith Stacey's *Patriarchy and Socialist Revolution in China* (Berkeley: University of California Press, 1983) argues that communist male leaders made a fundamental commitment to peasant patriarchy in the 1930s that consistently undermined attempts to foster feminist reforms. Other critics of revolutionary praxis are Phyllis Andors, *The Unfinished Revolution of Chinese Women* (Bloomington: Indiana University Press, 1983), and Kay Ann Johnson, *Women, the Family, and Peasant Revolution in China* (Chicago: University of Chicago Press, 1983). Margery Wolf, in *Revolution Postponed: Women in Contemporary China* (Stanford, CA: Stanford University Press, 1985), sees the revolutionaries hampered by unconscious patriarchal culture as they hoped to achieve both social and economic change; she judges women's status as still unequal to men's but much improved. Another extensive literature explores China's family-limitation policies, a topic reviewed by Susan Greenhalgh and Jiali Li, "Engendering Reproductive Policy and Practice in Peasant China: For a Feminist Demography of Reproduction," *Signs* 20 (spring 1995): 601–41.

Although extensive modern women's history has been written in Japanese, little has been translated. The essential role of women in Japanese industrialization is documented in E. Patricia Tsurumi, *Factory Girls: Women in the Thread Mills of Meiji Japan* (Princeton, NJ: Princeton University Press, 1990). Louise Allison Cort demonstrates the persistence of household cloth production in "The Changing Fortunes of Three Archaic Japanese Textiles," in *Cloth and Human Experience,* edited by Annette B. Weiner and Jane Schneider (Washington, DC: Smithsonian Institution Press, 1989). Sharon L. Sievers, *Flowers in Salt: The Beginnings of Feminist Consciousness in Modern Japan* (Stanford, CA: Stanford University Press, 1983), provides the best narrative of Japanese women's history in the nineteenth and twentieth centuries. For a brief review, see Noriyo Hayakawa, "Feminism and Nationalism in Japan, 1868–1945," *Journal of Women's History* 7 (winter 1995): 108–19. The postwar period is the focus of *The Hidden Sun: Women of Modern Japan* (Boulder, CO: Westview Press, 1983), by Dorothy Robins-Mowry, who was a USIA officer in Tokyo, 1963–71. Essays on women's issues of the last twenty years, as well as an excellent bibliography of studies published in English since 1980 can be found in *Japanese Women: New Feminist Perspectives on the Past, Present, and Future,* edited by Kumiko Fujimura-Fanselow and Atsuko Kameda (New York: The Feminist Press at The City University of New York, 1995). A study with both historical and comparative perspectives is Barbara Molony, "Japan's 1986 Equal Employment Opportunity Law and the Changing Discourse on Gender," *Signs* 20 (winter 1995): 268–302.

–12–
THE AMERICAS
The Personal Is Political

Barbara Kruger. *Untitled* (Your body is a battleground). (112 x 112", photographic silkscreen/vinyl, 1989. Collection: Eli Broad Family Foundation, Santa Monica. Courtesy: Mary Boone Gallery.)

In the 1970s, the women's movement in the United States coined the phrase "The personal is political/The political is personal" to describe its program. In retrospect, this can be seen as a comment on and disavowal of the division of society into private female spheres and public male spaces. In 1800, throughout the Americas, most aspects of a woman's life were private. She had no public voice, no vote, could hold no public offices. She was expected to limit her activities to home and church. In most of the United States and Canada, following English common law, she had no control of her property or her wages. In every sense, she was a dependent of her husband or father. If a woman had a problem, she could not act for herself; men would act for her. It was assumed that every woman should marry to gain male protection and pursue the only career open to her: motherhood. Women might exercise personal authority within the domestic realm, but only as long as they had tacit male approval. Men controlled the public worlds of politics, religion, and economics.

Women ventured into male public spaces of society in every country of the Americas during the nineteenth and twentieth centuries. By the 1970s, feminists could demand the end of gender divisions by proclaiming that there were no personal acts that did not have political implications as significant for society as those "male" issues of war and foreign policy. Furthermore, no one's private life was free of regulation by state and society. Implicit in the phrase "The personal is political" was women's right to participate in both spheres. Women could by then participate in public life because they had achieved significant, if not complete, legal equality. Free of male legal and economic control, women in the late twentieth century had unprecedented opportunities for education; personal choice in marriage, motherhood, and career; and full rights as citizens. New questions had arisen, though, about what social or psychological inhibitions kept women from actualizing their personal and political powers.

In the United States, during the first half of the nineteenth century, women began moving into the public world. Private high schools graduated women teachers who were hired by expanding public school systems. Women worked for wages in the new textile mills. Middle-class women formed voluntary associations devoted to various social welfare tasks, including aid for orphans and the indigent. Their most memorable work was within the antislavery movement, where incidentally they broke the tradition prohibiting women's participating in public political meetings. Finally, at Seneca Falls, New York, in 1848, women demanded civil rights equal to men's.

In Latin America, women had fewer opportunities to penetrate male public spaces. Iberian traditions of female seclusion remained after Spanish and Portuguese colonies won independence. Complex stratification by class and color enclosed women in a web of respectability, leaving the unfortunate ones outside its bounds, prey to every man. The dominance of the Roman Catholic Church in both religion and education meant that teaching careers were limited to women who took religious vows. Schooling was gender-segregated, so girls were bound to their own curriculum longer than in the coeducational classes that sprang up in the United States. Though Spanish law protected women's right to inheritance, Latin American culture protected male dominance. *Machismo* permitted no public female challenges to male power.

As late as 1925, it was necessary to have separate male and female self-help associations in Argentine unions. However, by then, middle-class feminists had already begun campaigns for social welfare measures and woman suffrage. Latin American women willing to risk their reputations drew upon subversive traditions of Indian and mestizo resistance to Spanish domination. In the Mexican Revolution, *soldaderas* fought beside and cooked for men in their brigades. Everywhere by the early twentieth century, the pace of economic development—of mines, of plantations, of factories, of railroads, and of cities—affected women's lives. Families were disrupted by male migration in search of work. Women left behind challenged village customs and necessarily controlled their children and homes. If their husbands returned, wives proved less docile; if abandoned, women found work as maids, in mines, and on plantations to support their children.

Trends apparent among working-class women of Latin America were exaggerated in the Caribbean. There, the plantation owners had often been absentees. As slaves were emancipated in the nineteenth century, the islands developed unique societies where most women worked for wages and exercised a degree of personal independence within their families uncommon in either Latin America or the United States.

Women's drive for empowerment culminated first in the United States. It occurred in two waves of feminism. During the first wave, from the 1840s to 1920, women contested many issues, including civil rights and access to both profitable employment and education. The public school movement in the United States allowed girls to attain more years of schooling in each decade. Proliferation of women's colleges offered ambitious women a higher education. By the 1880s, it was not unusual for a determined few to choose a career over marriage. New vocations opened to women: nurses, telephone operators, librarians, stenographers, waitresses, and retail clerks. After failing to gain the right to vote following the Civil War, women waged political campaigns for another half century before winning the suffrage struggle in the United States in 1920.

The second wave of feminism, beginning in the 1960s in the United States, opened for women further opportunities in the public world that were once reserved by custom for men only. Quotas that limited women's access to education were discarded. This was most significant in Latin America, where women's illiteracy dropped sharply and the numbers graduating from universities rose after 1970. Practically all professions, including the military, have women practitioners. Rather than choosing between marriage and career, women may choose which career and whether to marry. An option in some countries of the Americas is a woman-identified lesbian life. Improved birth-control technology and access to abortion make it possible to choose or reject motherhood. Domestic violence has emerged from being a dark secret of the private home to being a criminal act deserving public prosecution. Even in most Catholic nations, divorce is legal, and women's increasing economic independence makes it a practical alternative.

Women of the Americas have a comparatively poor record in using their votes to elect women, except in the small Caribbean nations. Institutional and political support does not exist for electing women to head governments in most nations of the Americas, including the United States, where mobilization of women's political power was pioneered. Nevertheless, women's political potential has sparked movements to restrict and criminalize abortions as well as to limit divorce.

12.1 The 1837 Anti-Slavery Convention of American Women

The first public political meeting of women in the United States proved to be an early challenge to men's control of the public sphere. Dorothy Sterling describes what happened:

On May 9, 1837, they came together "in fear and trembling"—some two hundred women from nine northern states, to constitute the first Anti-Slavery Convention of American Women. In an age when True Women (always capitalized) were required, on Biblical authority, to be silent and submissive, they met for three days in New York's Third Free Church . . . to speak and act independently for the abolition of slavery. . . . It was also the first interracial gathering of any consequence. . . .

Before the convention adjourned, the delegates had organized a campaign to collect a million signatures on petitions to Congress asking for abolition of slavery in the District of Columbia and the Florida Territory. They had also prepared six pamphlets and "open letters" for publication. . . .

In addition to working for freedom for slaves, the women at the convention took a big first step toward freeing themselves by resolving that "the time had come" for women "as moral and responsible beings" to break the silence imposed upon them and "plead the cause of the oppressed." . . .

No men were permitted to attend this historic meeting. When a prominent abolitionist, Theodore Weld, . . . offered his help, he was firmly told that the women had "found that they had *minds* of their own and could transact their business *without* his direction." Barred at the door, frustrated reporters tried to peer through the windows to observe, "the Amazonian farce" inside. Poking fun at "our female brethren . . . the misguided ladies" and their "very silly convention," the *New York Commercial Advertiser* described the "oratoresses" who had put aside their frying pans to debate weighty matters of state.

Reprinted, by permission, from "Turning the World Upside Down: The Anti-Slavery Convention of American Women, Held in New York City May 9–12, 1837," edited with an introduction by Dorothy Sterling (New York: The Feminist Press at The City University of New York, 1987), 3–4. Copyright © 1987 by The Feminist Press at The City University of New York.

The American abolitionist movement developed in the northern states, which had abolished slavery in the decades following the American Revolution. Although the most prominent antislavery leaders on the national scene were men, women joined the movement in larger numbers each decade after the 1830s. Abolitionist actions, such as boycotting slave-grown sugar and cotton, often fell within the feminine domain. Two public campaigns were particularly effective. Abolitionists sent pamphlets in the mail to the South to be circulated locally. And they sent numerous signed petitions to end slavery in the District of Columbia to Congress, where friendly representatives read them on the floor. Southern congressmen were so annoyed that they succeeded in preventing the reading of antislavery petitions in the House of Representatives and forced the United States Post Office to censor all mail sent to the South.

This had not yet happened in 1837, when the Anti-Slavery Convention of American Women voted to organize a petition drive for 1 million signatures to abolish slavery in the District of Columbia and in the Florida Territory and to publish six pamphlets. In one of the pamphlets, the group publicized the treatment of enslaved women and children in the South and argued that such treatment shamed all women and the nation. In answer to male attacks on women's right to political activity, they claimed sisterhood with southern slave women:

. . . where women are degraded and brutalized, and where their exposed persons bleed under the lash—torn from their husbands and forcibly plundered of their virtue, and their offspring, surely in *such* a country it is very natural that women should wish to know "the reason why.". . .

The great mass of female slaves in the southern states. . . . are our countrywomen—they are our sisters, and to us, as women, they have a right to look for sympathy with their sorrows, and effort and prayer for their rescue.

Women, too, are constituted by nature the peculiar guardians of children, and children are the victims of this horrible system. Helpless infancy is robbed of the tender care of the mother, and the protection of the father. There are in this Christian land thousands of little children who have been made orphans by the "domestic institution" of the South.

From "Turning the World Upside Down: The Anti-Slavery Convention of American Women, Held in New York City May 9–12, 1837," edited with an introduction by Dorothy Sterling (New York: The Feminist Press at The City University of New York, 1987), 27–28.

From a historical perspective, the New York convention was a precedent for the Women's Rights Convention at Seneca Falls, New York, eleven years later. The Seneca Falls convention, better known and more significant, was the first public demand in the United States for equal rights for women. Its Declaration of Sentiments paraphrased the Declaration of Independence in calling for women's rights as citizens of a democracy. Though profoundly radical and shocking in 1848, the demands of The Declaration of Sentiments seem mild today: "that all men and women are created equal"; that male authority over women's personal life and property was not legitimate; that women had inalienable natural rights to citizenship, including voting and holding office; that discrimination against women in education, jobs, and property ownership, which demeaned their self-respect, should end. At Seneca Falls, the decades of organized struggle to achieve equal rights began.

12.2 Feminism and Class in Argentina and Chile, 1900–25

By 1900, middle-class feminists in Latin American countries had raised demands similar to those made fifty years before at Seneca Falls. But in the intervening period, in both North and South America, economic development, based on global industrialization and trade, changed the lives of millions of women. Increasingly, the lives of urban middle-class and working-class women diverged. However, the very fact of women's working beside men in factories forced rethinking of old ideologies of women's subordination in private domesticity.

As Latin American women in the rapidly growing cities took jobs in export industries and retail and other services, feminists and labor organizers sought solutions to their problems. In Argentina, the largest labor organization was a union that was partnered with a socialist political party. In Chile, organizers were mostly anarchists, who could not form a national party.

Discussions of the problems of women in both countries were

normally framed within relational ideology, with emphasis on the family and on protecting women as reproducers of the nation's future generations and as teachers of children. The concepts of the family as a necessary peaceful retreat from society and of women as followers of men's leadership were accepted by almost all adults. Because a large degree of gender segregation still prevailed, and was considered essential to protecting women's respectability, labor unions created parallel women's organizations separate from the men's. A union would establish separate societies, for example, to help unemployed members or to pay for funerals. Asunción Lavrin explains why this elaborate organizational strategy was necessary:

Such a model was built upon the unquestioned acceptance of the physical weakness of the female sex, an ideology which had first served as the basis for questioning the female presence in the work place and for urging the restriction of certain occupations to the male. Women needed male protection at the personal level as much as they needed labor associations to defend them against the oppressive social institutions and the economic interests of capitalism. . . . Women were more often than not depicted as men's companions—if not followers—and providers of solace and tenderness to the head of the house. Woman's role was to sweeten the "bitter hours of he who sustains, guides and pilots the ship of his home." In exchange, men's duty was to love and protect women, and be truly responsible for the welfare of their families. . . .

One factor that added considerable fuel to the discussion of the nature of female work and to an eventual change of attitudes about it was the emergence of feminism in both countries. First discussed by an Argentinean professional woman in 1901, the shaping of feminism and its intellectual acceptance took place in the first decade of the century. . . . Feminism and women's liberation were terms interchangeably used by women and men of several social strata and ideological orientation who . . . shared a belief in the intellectual equality of men and women and the right of women to a more active and influential participation in the body politic. The professional middle-class women who developed in Argentina before 1910 focused at first on the civil rights and educational aspects of feminism. . . .

An increasing political sensitivity and concern for the complex

social problems bred by urbanization, lack of labor regulation, housing, and public health problems developed in both countries in the
early years of the second decade of [the twentieth] century. This
trend, and the changing role forced on women as a result of World
War I and suffrage campaigns in both Europe and the United States,
gave South American feminists . . . a better sense of direction by the
mid-1910s. After 1918, feminism, far from an embarrassing proposi-
tion, became the basis for advocating reforms in the Civil Code and
social welfare legislation, and for discussing the possible involvement of women in the political process.

The question remained, however, whether feminism would furnish
an agenda for individual liberation or buttress the recognition of a
special sphere of action for women to which they would bring a
distinctive "female" touch. That sphere would be that of family,
motherhood, education, and social service. The prevailing attitudes
toward gender relations in what were culturally patriarchal societies
led Argentinean and Chilean feminists to the acceptance of feminism
as a form of asserting women's equality within a feminine—that is
separate sphere—context.

Asunción Lavrin, "Women, Labor, and the Left: Argentina and Chile, 1890–1925,"
Journal of Women's History 1:2 (1989): 104, 96–97. Note omitted.

Between 1932 and 1953, most Latin American women won the
right to vote and run for office. In Argentina, immediately after
women won the franchise in 1944, Eva Perón, first wife of General Juan Perón, created the Partido Peronista Femenino (Feminist
Peronist Party) to incorporate women into national political life.
General Perón's second wife, Isabel, elected vice president in
1973, succeeded her husband on his death in 1974 and served
two years before a military coup removed her. The state terrorism
of the years 1976–83, during which between twenty thousand
and thirty thousand individuals were murdered, led to the Ma-
dres (Mothers) de Plaza de Mayo mobilizing to protest the vicious dictatorship. Relying upon the high value of motherhood,
these relational feminists (though themselves jailed) played a critical role in bringing down the military regime.

Since Isabel Perón's 1974 presidency, three women have held
interim posts as prime minister or president in Bolivia, Canada,

and Haiti. Three other women have been elected to regular terms of office: M. Eugenia Charles, prime minister of Dominica (1980–); Maria Liberia-Peters, prime minister of the Netherlands Antilles (1984–85; 1988–); and Violeta Barrios Chamorro, president of Nicaragua (1990–96).

12.3 Village Women in Mexican Migrant Culture

The large migrations of women from farms to cities occurred not only in Argentina and Chile but also throughout most of the Americas. Mexicans migrated from villages and ranches to the cities, especially Mexico City. A different migration pattern took Mexicans north to the farms of the United States. Men made this temporary trek to work for a few months, mainly harvesting. Conceived in 1917 as a temporary immigration program for the duration of World War I, workers continued to be recruited under government auspices periodically thereafter. When the United States entered World War II in 1941, the Mexican program was expanded in part because of a labor shortage as U.S. workers flocked to defense industries. It was renamed the *bracero* program. Although this program began in 1942, its recruiters did not reach the village of Teotitlán (twenty miles from Oaxaca) until 1944, probably because Tijuana, the entry point into the United States, was more than thirteen hundred miles to the north. Lynn Stephen reports on the impact of this migration in Teotitlán:

That year [1944] fifteen to twenty Teotitecos signed up for eight-week contracts for the months of May, June, and July . . . Former *braceros* recalled that many men . . . did not go in 1944 because of rumors that they were not going to work on farms, but would be sent off to fight the North Americans' war. But in July 1944, the first Teotitecos to go to the United States returned safely with shoes, blue jeans, other items of clothing, and, most importantly, cash. In 1945 . . . between 150 and 300 men left the community to be *braceros*. As one man recalled . . . "I got paid $0.20 per box for my work picking tomatoes in the United States. I could pick thirty to thirty-five boxes per day and earn up to $8.00 per day. At that time in Mexico . . . I could earn about the equivalent of $0.25. You couldn't compare it. . . ."

Women in Teotitlán recall the *braceria* of the 1940s and the continued absence of men in the 1950s as a time of great hardship. They

had no sources of income while men were gone and they were sad-
dled with additional chores. Many women reported that their husbands sent them little or nothing, leaving them as the sole income
earners for their families. While some men later returned with savings, others did not. Some women wove [traditionally, only men
wove] during this time, but also had to maintain their food processing, child care, and animal care in addition to taking care of agricultural work [traditionally men's work]. Many tried to earn extra cash
by selling the yarn they spun, not having time to weave it themselves
or not knowing how.

From *Zapotec Women* by Lynn Stephen (Austin: University of Texas Press, 1991),
112–13. Copyright © 1991. By permission of the author and the University of
Texas Press. Notes omitted.

The village men were small farmers growing grains and weaving
blankets and serapes for sale in neighboring markets. Women
raised turkeys, chickens, and hogs for the family protein and sale.
In the late 1950s, tourist demand for handwoven cloth in traditional patterns began to pick up. The woven textiles were sold
first to local merchants, then later to merchants from Mexico City
and the United States who began appearing in Teotitlán. Lynn
Stephen explains how the migration permanently changed the
lives of the families of the participants:

When the men returned, their small savings were quickly spent or
invested, primarily in oxen [for plowing], looms, or raw wool. During the late 1950s, several men who are now the largest merchants in
Teotitlán began investing savings earned in the United States in wool
for yarn. . . .

The following narrative [by Josefina] captures the experiences of
many women who married at the ages of fourteen and fifteen, had
never been alone, and then suddenly, when their husbands migrated,
found themselves in charge of running a small farming and weaving
enterprise as well as having to feed and clothe their children. . . .

I first got to be independent when my husband went to work in
the United States in 1952. I had to be. He was gone most of the
time from 1952 until 1964, from two to twelve months per year.

The whole time he was away he only sent money twice—about $20. I didn't spend this money, I saved it until he returned. I had six children born during that period. When he left the first time, I already had two little ones.

When he was gone I carded the spun wool so that my father would make my serapes. He used to come to my house and work here. I couldn't weave because I had to take care of my children and my animals. I also used to make yarn to sell while the men were gone. This gave me money so that I could go to the market and buy things. I would also sell the blankets my father made. My children were too little to weave.

You know this whole time I worked like a mule. . . . It was a hard life.

Josefina later recalled that while her husband was gone he sent money to another woman he was involved with, but not to her. The fact that men were sometimes involved in multiple relationships with children in other households could further reduce the financial resources sent to their wives. In the end, most women stated that they learned how to survive. They also noted that, after their husbands returned, they no longer accepted their dominance in decision making. As one aptly states, "If I could get along all of those years and raise eight children, why should I suddenly stop being able to decide what is best for them?"

From *Zapotec Women* by Lynn Stephen (Austin: University of Texas Press, 1991), 114–15. Copyright © 1991. By permission of the author and the University of Texas Press. Notes omitted.

The *bracero* program ended in 1964, although Teotitecos continued to migrate to the United States as undocumented workers. Women began weaving in the 1970s to supply the growing demand for handwoven textiles. Young women began migrating with the men in the 1970s to urban centers in Mexico. In the 1980s, they crossed the Río Grande to the United States.

12.4 Second-Wave Feminism in the United States in the Sixties

The first wave of feminism in the United States began in the 1840s and continued until women won the right to vote in

1920. During the first era of feminism in the United States, women mobilized to achieve their goals through government action. Besides organizing to gain the franchise, women organized to ban manufacture and sale of alcohol, to extend public schools to rural areas, and to develop public health and visiting nurses programs. Progressive women reformers sought laws providing minimum wages and maximum hours for working women, kindergartens in public schools, and inspections to insure the purity of foods.

In the 1920s, women lobbied for an amendment prohibiting child labor and for federal funding of pediatric and maternal clinics. These agendas, with their focus on community and family, suggest the power of relational feminism in the United States. At the same time, the media publicized the "New Woman." She was young, educated, independent, and career-oriented, although she might marry and have children later in her twenties. The image of this New Woman was projected to the world in glossy American magazines and Hollywood films. More women joined the workforce each year, but it was still assumed that, after a fling of independence, most of them would accept male authority in marriage.

World War II brought change to American women in Nebraska and California as well as in Teotitlán. Women responded to the call to serve their country by working in defense industries and enlisting in the armed forces. When peace came in 1945, women were told to return to their homes. A concerted publicity campaign told women that by going to work during the war, they had denied their basic need for domesticity and motherhood. Their absence from the home led to delinquency among their children and to alcoholism and impotency for their husbands. Furthermore, experts charged that working women were inevitably neurotic. The prevalent American ideal of the 1950s was familial, and working wives continued to be disparaged. Women's paid employment continued to rise, however, as educated women found frustration as often as fulfillment in motherhood. In the 1960s, reports from federal and state commissions on the status of women documented limited job opportunities, pervasive discrimination against women, and pay inequities.

One response to these reports was to seek redress from the government. But the more significant response was to change people's minds rather than laws. Men were directly confronted as the cause of women's subordination, and changes in their personal and collective behavior were demanded. Women also explored their own consciousness—as shaped by family, education, and the media—to discover ways in which they were complicit by believing in their own inferiority. This was the second wave of feminism in the United States.

The young women who dominated the second wave gained their organizing skills and their distaste for government in the civil rights movements of the South, in organizing the poor in northern ghettos, and in the antiwar movement protesting American intervention in Vietnam. They formed autonomous local groups, condemned leadership, and stressed consensus and equality. They issued manifestos, published their own newspapers, and conducted demonstrations.

In its early years this women's liberation movement developed a radical analysis of women's oppression drawn from a revision of Marxian theory of class conflict. The following manifesto, from the New York Redstockings, was issued in July 1969:

Women are an oppressed class. Our oppression is total, affecting every facet of our lives. We are exploited as sex objects, breeders, domestic servants, and cheap labor. We are considered inferior beings, whose only purpose is to enhance men's lives. . . .

Because we live so intimately with our oppressors, in isolation from each other, we have been kept from seeing our personal suffering as a political condition. . . . We identify the agents of our oppression as men. Male supremacy is the oldest, most basic form of domination. All other forms of exploitation and oppression (racism, capitalism, imperialism, etc.) are extensions of male supremacy: men dominate women, a few men dominate the rest. . . .

Attempts have been made to shift the burden of responsibility from men to institutions or to women themselves. We condemn these arguments as evasions. Institutions alone do not oppress; they are merely tools of the oppressor. To blame institutions implies that men and women are equally victimized, obscures the fact that men benefit from the subordination of women, and gives men the excuse that they are forced to be the oppressors. On the contrary, any man is free to renounce his superior position provided that he is willing to be treated like a woman by other men.

Sisterhood Is Powerful: An Anthology of Writings from the Women's Liberation Movement, edited by Robin Morgan (New York: Vintage Books, A Division of Random House, 1970), 533–34.

The mass media's emphasis on beauty was an early target of second-wave authors. Dana Densmore's "On the Temptation to Be a Beautiful Object" was published in a pamphlet that circulated widely on North American college campuses in the early 1970s.

We are constantly bombarded in this society by the images of feminine beauty. . . . It is used extensively in advertising, particularly in advertising directed at women: be like this, they are saying, use our products. . . . And oh! those beauty products. Shimmering, magical, just waiting to turn the plainest girl into a heartbreakingly beautiful, transfixing graven image. Or so they claim and imply, over and over, with extravagant hypnotizing advertising copy and photograph after photograph of dewy-fresh perfect faces. . . .

We may be sophisticated enough (or bitter enough) to reject specific advertising claims, but we cannot purge the image from us: if only we *could* get that look with a few sweeps of lambsdown buffer dusting on translucent powder making our faces glow like satin, accented with shimmery slicked-on lip glow, a brush of glittery transparent blusher, eyes soft-fringed and luminous, lash-shaded and mysteriously shadowed . . . suppose we *could* get the look they promise. . . . Ah! how few could resist.

Many of us are scarred by attempts as teenagers to win the promised glamor from cosmetics. Somehow it always just looked painted, harsh, worse than ever, and yet real life fell so far short of the ideals already burned into our consciousness that the defeat was bitter too and neither the plain nor the painted solution was satisfactory. . . .

When we do succeed we make ourselves objects, outside ourselves, something we expect others to admire because we admire, and which we admire through others' admiration. But it's not us really. Narcissism is not really love of the self, because self is the soul, the personality, and that is always something quite different, something complex and complicated, something strange and human and very familiar and of this earth.

That beautiful object we stand in awe before has nothing to do with the person we know so well, it is altogether outside, separate, object, a beautiful image, not a person at all. A feast for the eyes. . . . That beautiful object is just an object, a work of art, to look at, not to know, total appearance, bearing no personality or will. . . . One perceives object not person. . . .

It is unthinkable that this work of art has a will, especially one which is not as totally soft and agreeable as the face it presents. You cannot be taken seriously, people will not even hear what you say. (If they did they would be shocked and displeased—but since they do not take it seriously they say "You are too pretty to be smart"—by which they mean, you are an object, do not presume to complicate the image with intellect, for intellect is complex and not always pleasing and beautiful. . . .)

How can anyone take a manikin seriously?. . . . This only goes for women, of course; men's character and personality and will always shine through their appearance, both men and women look at them that way. But one is taught in society by the emphasis on the images of female beauty to view women differently. The important thing is not the mind, the will, but the appearance. You ARE your appearance. . . .

If we are ugly and plain men demand angrily (at least in their own minds) why we don't DO something with ourselves; surely a more becoming hairdo, better make-up, or even (if the situation is bad enough) a new nose.

Women react the same way to women. All are victimized by the image of woman as object, appearance. "Why doesn't she DO something with herself?"

Dana Densmore, "Sex Roles and Female Oppression." (Boston: New England Free Press, n.d.), 12–15.

These arguments had an impact: in the universities, most women changed their appearance. They stopped using makeup; hair was natural; bras, girdles, and stockings were abandoned; and jeans replaced skirts in classrooms. Outward appearances marked inward changes as women pursued degrees in law and medicine in record numbers, as well as boldly entering masculine blue-collar jobs. Factory women demanded equal opportunities to work at higher-paying jobs. Hitherto unknown figures appeared: female carpenters, truck drivers, soldiers, and television broadcasters.

Changes initiated by the second wave of feminism were institutionalized in changes in civil rights laws and court decisions and publicized in the failed campaign for passage of the Equal Rights Amendment. In 1973, the Supreme Court affirmed in *Roe* versus *Wade* that state laws forbidding abortion were unconstitutional. This decision dramatically underlined the politics of the personal. For women who valued personal autonomy within or outside marriage, abortion became the litmus test of choice. But other women disagreed. For many, who invested their lives in marriage and family, the obligations of motherhood outweighed individual desires.

The volatile politics of abortion obscured other changes. Feminists insisted that sexuality could and should be discussed. The sense of shame that had long limited public discourse was brushed aside as women talked about orgasm, breast cancer, rape, and wife battering. Women were elected to public office, especially on state levels. In 1969, there were only 301 women state legislators; in 1981, there were 908; and by 1991, one of every five state legislators was female. Representation in the United States Congress still lags far behind equaling the 50 percent of the population that is female. Two female justices sit on the Supreme Court in 1996; one woman has been nominated for vice president by a major political party.

The second wave of feminism spread rapidly beyond the borders of the United States in the 1970s. This influence, coinciding with the beginning of the United Nations Decade for Women in 1976, transformed women's activities in Canada, the Caribbean, and Latin America. Seizing upon relevant aspects of feminist theory new groups of women attacked the theory of *machismo,* explored suppression of their sexuality in motherhood, and established programs to combat rape and domestic violence.

12.5 Different Voices

Leaders of the second wave of feminism in the United States made overtures to minority women inviting their cooperation in women's activities. Once their analysis revealed the obvious double oppression by race and gender of minority women, feminists dreamed of the potential power of a multicultural sister-hood. These white middle-class women wondered why their gestures were not returned. They saw themselves as nonracist and considerate of minorities. When they were not only rebuffed but also met with hatred, white feminists were shocked. Barbara Cameron, a Lakota who grew up on a reservation, is both frank about her early hatred of white women and ambivalent about her later feelings toward those who became her friends:

One of the very first words I learned in my Lakota language was *wasicu* which designates white people. At that early age, my comprehension of wasicu was gained from observing and listening to my family discussing the wasicu. My grandmother always referred to white people as the "wasicu sica" with emphasis on the *sica,* our word for terrible or bad. By the age of five I had seen one Indian man gunned down in the back by the police and was a silent witness to a gang of white teenage boys beating up an elderly old man. I'd hear stories of Indian ranch hands being "accidentally" shot by white ranchers. I quickly began to understand the wasicu menace my family spoke of.

My hatred of the wasicu was solidly implanted by the time I entered first grade. Unfortunately in the first grade I became teacher's pet so my teacher had a fondness for hugging me which always repulsed me. I couldn't stand the idea of a white person touching me. Eventually I realized that it wasn't the white skin that I hated, but it was their culture of deceit, greed, racism, and violence.

During my first memorable visit to a white town, I was appalled that they thought of themselves as superior to my people. Their manner of living appeared devoid of life and bordered on hostility even for one another. . . . The white people always seemed so loud, obnoxious, and vulgar. And the white parents were either screaming at their kids, threatening them with some form of punishment or hitting them. After spending a day around white people, I was always happy to go back to the reservation where people followed a relaxed yet respectful code of relating with each other. The easy teasing and joking that were inherent with the Lakota were a welcome relief after a day with the plastic faces. . . .

I spent a part of my childhood feeling great sadness and helplessness about how it seemed that Indians were open game for the white people, to kill, maim, beat up, insult, rape, cheat, and whatever atrocity the white people wanted to play with. There was also a rage and frustration that has not died. . . .

Because of experiencing racial hatred, I sometimes panic when I'm the only non-white in a roomful of whites, even if they are my closest friends; I wonder if I'll leave the room alive. The seemingly copacetic gay world of San Francisco becomes a mere dream after the panic leaves. I think to myself that it's truly insane for me to feel the panic. I want to scream out my anger and disgust with myself for feeling distrustful of my white friends and I want to banish the society that has fostered those feelings of alienation. I wonder at the amount of assimilation which has affected me and how long my "Indianness" will allow me to remain in a city that is far removed from the lives of many Native Americans.

Barbara Cameron, "Gee You Don't Seem Like an Indian from the Reservation," in *This Bridge Called My Back: Writings by Radical Women of Color,* edited by Cherrie Moraga and Gloria Anzaldua (New York: Kitchen Table: Women of Color Press, 1983), 46–48. Originally published by Persephone Press, 1981.

The barriers to universal sisterhood that arose from differential experiences of race, class, language, nationality, and religion were slowly perceived by women throughout the Americas in the 1980s and 1990s. Personal stories like Barbara Cameron's helped shape feminist theories of differences among women. These theories corrected Western writings that, assuming as normative the experience of white middle-class women, had defined gender as the primary obstacle to liberation.

Suggested Further Readings

Carole Shammas, in "Re-Assessing the Married Women's Property Acts," *Journal of Women's History* 6 (spring 1994): 9–30, evaluates the importance of one of the main feminist reforms in the nineteenth-century United States. Other legal issues are explored in Joan Hoff, *Law, Gender and Injustice: A Legal History of U.S. Women* (New York: New York University Press, 1991). Working-class history is the subject of Joan M. Jensen and Sue Davidson, eds., *A Needle, a Bobbin, a Strike: Women Needle-*

workers in America (Philadelphia: Temple University Press, 1984), and of Sarah Deutsch, *No Separate Refuge: Culture, Class, and Gender on an Anglo-Hispanic Frontier in the American Southwest, 1880–1940* (New York: Oxford University Press, 1987). Also see Claudia Goldin, *Understanding the Gender Gap: An Economic History of American Women* (New York: Oxford University Press, 1990).

Both political and social issues are raised in Noralee Frankel and Nancy S. Dye, eds., *Gender, Class, Race and Reform in the Progressive Era* (Lexington: University Press of Kentucky, 1991), and in Rickie Solinger, *Wake Up Little Susie: Single Pregnancy and Race before Roe v. Wade* (New York: Routledge, 1992). *Women, Politics, and Change,* edited by Louise A. Tilly and Patricia Gurin (New York: Russell Sage Foundation, 1990), explores the informal and formal political activities of a variety of U.S. women from 1880 to the present. First American women of the United States and Canada are considered from historical and anthropological viewpoints in *Women and Power in Native North America,* edited by Laura F. Klein and Lillian A. Ackerman (Norman: University of Oklahoma Press, 1995).

Two books on Brazilian women are June E. Hahner, *Emancipating the Female Sex: The Struggle for Women's Rights in Brazil, 1850–1940* (Durham, NC: Duke University Press, 1990), and Nancy Scheper-Hughes, *Death Without Weeping: The Violence of Everyday Life in Brazil* (Berkeley: University of California Press, 1992). Margaret Randall, in *Sandino's Daughters: Testimonies of Nicaraguan Women in Struggle* (Vancouver, BC: New Star Books, 1981), offers a sympathetic perspective on a revolution that later failed. An autobiography, *I, Rigoberta Menchu* (London: Verso, 1984), personalizes the struggle of Guatemalan women against military dictatorship. In a countrywide survey of *The Women's Movement in Latin America: Feminism and the Transition to Democracy,* edited by Jane S. Jaquette (Boston: Unwin Hyman, 1989), authors explore both the nature of gender-based movements in the resistance to military dictatorships and why so few permanent gains resulted for women. Jill Ker Conway and Susan C. Bourque, eds., *The Politics of Women's Education: Perspectives from Asia, Africa, and Latin America* (Ann Arbor: University of Michigan Press, 1995), discuss schooling in a comparative perspective. Domestic labor in other people's homes, historically one of the largest fields of women's work and still employing about 20 percent of Latin American women, is the subject of *Muchachas No More: Household Workers in Latin America and the Caribbean,* edited by Elsa M. Chaney and Mary García Castro (Philadelphia: Temple University Press, 1989). Bettina Bradbury presents working-class women of English-speaking Canada in *Working Families: Age, Gender and Daily Survival in Industrializing Montreal* (Toronto: University of Toronto, 1993).

GLOSSARY

Androcentric   Centered upon men; catering to men's desires or interests.

Agnate   A person related by patrilineal descent.

Bilateral kinship   Relatives traced through both father and mother.

Bride-price   See **Bridewealth.**

Bridewealth   Marriage payments from the groom and/or his family to the bride's family or to the bride.

Commensal unit, commensality   The only group of people who may eat together according to traditional rules.

Conjugal   Pertaining to the marital relationship.

Consanguineal   A relative by birth in contrast to one related by marriage.

Courtesan   A prostitute or woman paid to entertain men of high rank and/or wealth.

Dowry   Property sent with the bride at her marriage, either as payment to the husband's kin or as the wife's share of her parent's estate.

Endogamy   A practice of marrying only within a specified group, such as an extended family, clan, village, caste, or class.

Exogamy   A practice in which marriage partners are sought outside a specified group, such as an extended family, clan, village, or class.

Extended family   A family unit making up one household, or related cooperating households, consisting of parents, grown siblings, their spouses and children, or other close relatives.

Gentry   Members of established rural families whose social status ranks below the nobility.

Levirate marriage   Practice requiring a dead man's brother (or other close male relative) to marry his widow.

Matriarchy   Literally power exercised by mothers; also refers to female social dominance.

Matrilocal   Residence of a married couple with the wife's kin.

Matrilineal   Principle of descent from parent to child traced through the female line, with links to the mother conferring kin membership.

Misogyny   Male hatred or fear of women.

Monogamy   Marriage of one man and one woman only.

Natal   Relating to the family or place of one's birth.

Nuclear family   A family unit consisting of parents and their dependent children.

Patriarchy   Literally, power exercised by fathers; also refers to male social power or dominance.

Patrilocal   Residence of a married couple with the husband's kin.

Patrilineal   Principle of descent through the male line, with links to the father conferring kin membership.

Pawns   Those, especially women or children, whose individual lives are sacrificed to serve other's interests: a ruler's daughters married for purposes of state or family alliance; dependents sold into temporary slavery as collateral on a family debt; dependents given to a ruler as a sign of fealty.

Polyandry   Marriage of a woman to two or more husbands contemporaneously.

Polygyny/polygamy   Marriage of a man to two or more wives contemporaneously.

Uxorilocal   See **matrilocal.**

Virilocal   See **patrilocal.**

1547